LAW, VULNERABILITY, AND THE RESPONSIVE STATE

This book considers how vulnerability theory provides the basis for a reconceptualization of the liberal ideas of autonomy, equality, and freedom.

Vulnerability theory argues a "vulnerable legal subject" should displace the "liberal legal subject" that currently dominates law and policy. The theory is based on the fundamental empirical realities of the material body and offers an alternative to a social contract or rights-based notion of state responsibility, both of which tend to privilege abstractions such as rationality or dignity. A vulnerability analysis poses law and policy questions based on the "vulnerable legal subject" and requires new thinking about state or governmental responsibility. To achieve a truly comprehensive and inclusive notion of what constitutes social justice or a universal or common good, vulnerability theory mandates a reassessment of both equality and freedom as these concepts are currently conceived. Presenting the work of scholars from a wide range of doctrinal areas, it is this task that the book takes up. In particular, in recognizing that many social or institutional relationships entail uneven positions of dependence and reliance, it maintains that individualized notions of equality or freedom are inadequate and must be reformulated to include a sense of collective or social justice, incorporating asymmetric or unequal allocations of responsibility, and requiring appropriate limitations on the individual.

This book's reorientation of the subject, as well as the central objectives of law and policy, will appeal to scholars and students in law, vulnerability studies, gender studies, critical legal and political theory, politics, philosophy, and sociology.

Martha Albertson Fineman is Robert W. Woodruff Professor of Law and the Founding Director of The Vulnerability and Human Condition Initiative at Emory University, Georgia, USA.

Laura Spitz is Vice Provost for Global Engagement and Professor of Law at Seattle University, Washington, USA.

Gender in Law, Culture, and Society

Series Editor

Martha Albertson Fineman

Emory University School of Law, USA

Gender in Law, Culture, and Society will address key issues and theoretical debates related to gender, culture, and the law. Its titles will advance understanding of the ways in which a society's cultural and legal approaches to gender intersect, clash, and are reconciled or remain in tension. The series will further examine connections between gender and economic and political systems, as well as various other cultural and societal influences on gender construction and presentation, including social and legal consequences that men and women uniquely or differently encounter. Intended for a scholarly readership as well as for courses, its titles will be a mix of single-authored volumes and collections of original essays that will be both pragmatic and theoretical. It will draw from the perspectives of critical and feminist legal theory, as well as other schools of jurisprudence. Interdisciplinary, and international in scope, the series will offer a range of voices speaking to significant questions arising from the study of law in relation to gender, including the very nature of law itself.

Other titles in the series

Gender, Vulnerability Theory and Public Procurement
Perspectives on Global Reform
Edited by S.N. Nyeck
ISBN 978-1-032-44281-5 (hbk)

Law, Vulnerability, and the Responsive State
Beyond Equality and Liberty
Edited by Martha Albertson Fineman and Laura Spitz
ISBN 978-1-032-34665-6 (hbk)
ISBN 978-1-032-34663-2 (pbk)

For more information about this series, please visit: www.routledge.com/Routledge-Handbooks-in-Religion/book-series

LAW, VULNERABILITY, AND THE RESPONSIVE STATE

Beyond Equality and Liberty

Edited by Martha Albertson Fineman and Laura Spitz

Routledge
Taylor & Francis Group
a GlassHouse Book

Cover image: © Getty Images

First published 2024
by Routledge
4 Park Square, Milton Park, Abingdon, Oxon OX14 4RN

and by Routledge
605 Third Avenue, New York, NY 10158

Routledge is an imprint of the Taylor & Francis Group, an informa business

a GlassHouse book

British Library Cataloguing-in-Publication Data
A catalogue record for this book is available from the British Library

ISBN: 978-1-032-34665-6 (hbk)
ISBN: 978-1-032-34663-2 (pbk)
ISBN: 978-1-003-32324-2 (ebk)

DOI: 10.4324/9781003323242

Typeset in Sabon
by Apex CoVantage, LLC

For the future, and for our students—like our dedicated research assistants who worked with us on this volume, Namrata Jacob and Logan Stokes—who are interested in critical theory and rethinking what a just society might be.

CONTENTS

CONTRIBUTORS

Kathryn Abrams is the Herma Hill Kay Distinguished Professor of Law at UC Berkeley Law, scholar of feminist legal theory, social movements, and the relation(s) between law and emotions, and author of *Open Hand, Closed Fist: Practices of Undocumented Organizing* (2022).

Naomi Cahn is the Justice Anthony M. Kennedy Distinguished Professor of Law, Research Professor in Democracy and Equity, and Co-Director of the Family Law Center at the University of Virginia School of Law. She is the co-author of the forthcoming *Fair Shake: The Fate of Women in a Winner-Take-All World.*

June Carbone is the Robina Chair in Law, Science, and Technology at the University of Minnesota Law School. She is an expert in family law, assisted reproduction, property law, and the law of medicine and bioethics, and co-author of the forthcoming *Fair Shake: The Fate of Women in a Winner-Take-All World.*

Ronit Donyets-Kedar is a senior lecturer at the College of Law and Business, and the co-founder of the Corporate Social Responsibility Institute, Israel. Her research focuses on the areas of legal and moral philosophy, political philosophy, corporate social responsibility, and private power.

Martha Albertson Fineman is Robert W. Woodruff Professor and founding Director of the Vulnerability and the Human Condition Initiative at Emory University School of Law. She is an internationally recognized, leading authority on critical legal theory and feminist jurisprudence whose scholarship developed the legal framework of vulnerability theory.

Xiaoqian Hu is Associate Professor of Law at the University of Arizona. She is a scholar of property and social justice issues in the United States and China. Her work examines how property law shapes unequal racial and class dynamics and socioeconomic transformation, and legal strategies for structural change.

Hila Keren is the Associate Dean for Research and Paul E. Treusch Professor of Law at Southwestern Law School in Los Angeles, formerly practicing human rights and antidiscrimination law in Israel for ten years. Her scholarship surrounds contract and business law, feminist and critical race theory, and law and emotions.

Matthew B. Lawrence is Associate Professor of Law at Emory University School of Law and former federal attorney of health care regulatory issues, and a special legal advisor to the US House of Representatives Budget Committee (Majority). He researches and publishes on health care finance, administrative law, and addictions.

Risa L. Lieberwitz is the Professor of Labor and Employment Law in the Cornell University School of Industrial and Labor Relations, and Academic Director of The Worker Institute at Cornell. Her research addresses academic freedom in higher education, labor and employment discrimination law, and workplace freedom of speech and due process.

Martha T. McCluskey is Professor Emerita at the University at Buffalo Law School, State University of New York, a Member Scholar at the Center for Progressive Reform, and serves on the Board of Directors of ClassCrits, Inc. and the Association for Promotion of Political Economy and Law.

Nazune Menka is a Lecturer at UC Berkeley School of Law School. She is Koyukon Athabaskan and Lumbee and serves as a Board Member for the California Indian Law Association. Her areas of expertise are Indigenous human rights, Tribal sovereignty, and environmental policy and management.

Andrew Pilliar is Associate Professor of Law at Thompson Rivers University in British Columbia, Canada, located on the unceded and traditional territory of the Secwepemc People. His research focuses on developing a conception of what access to justice means in the context of Canadian society and contemporary legal institutions.

Marc L. Roark is Professor of Law and Associate Dean of Faculty Development at the University of Tulsa, Affiliated Research Associate at the University of Pretoria, S.A., and co-author of *Squatters and the State: Resilient Property Theory in an Age of Crisis*.

Ani B. Satz is a Professor of Law at Emory University and Public Health and Senior Faculty Fellow of the Emory University Center for Ethics. She is an expert in health and disability law, policy, and ethics; her work addresses access to health care, medical privacy, patient choice, and disability accommodation.

Laura Spitz is the Vice Provost for Global Engagement and Professor of Law at Seattle University. Her current research focuses on the boundaries and construction of legal personhood, including the line between subjects and objects in the common law system. She also writes about the difficulty of translating these categories into concepts cognizable in Indigenous legal systems.

Jessica Dixon Weaver is the Associate Dean for Research and Professor of Law at Southern Methodist University, Dedman School of Law. She is an expert on family law regulation and its intersections with race and gender, focusing on slavery laws' impact on Antebellum-era marriage and divorce, and intergenerational caregiving.

Lua Kamál Yuille is Professor of Law and Business at Northeastern University School of Law and the D'Amore-McKim School of Business. Her research draws into conversation property law, heterodox economics, business law, critical pedagogy, and group identity.

INTRODUCTION

Understanding Vulnerability

Martha Albertson Fineman

"Vulnerability" is a term that is used colloquially in everyday discussions, as well as professionally in scholarly and professional articles. In both types of conversations, the term typically is used to designate an individual or group as "disadvantaged," "discriminated against," "subordinated," or weak. The implication is that a person or group is therefore deserving of some exceptional remedy or in need of special protection. A different understanding of "vulnerability" provides the conceptual framework for this volume.

In the chapters that follow, vulnerability is used as a "term of art," referencing the inevitable, dynamic, and comprehensive nature of the universal human condition. Recognized as a universal description of the human condition, vulnerability clearly has significant implications for assessing the ways in which law and policy currently arrange the organization and operation of society's essential institutions, as well as relevance in assessing the justness and possibilities for reform of those arrangements. Vulnerability theory and the idea of a universal vulnerable subject provides a critique of existing social and legal institutions and relationships, as well as providing the foundational principles for building a comprehensive and inclusive sense of state responsibility.

I. The Fallacy and Foibles of Vulnerability as Particular

The use of the concept of vulnerability as particularized has reinforced or enhanced advocacy of positive legal measures propounding values of equality and principles of antidiscrimination. Such measures were historically vital in expanding the notion of who was entitled to equal treatment and protection of the law. Equality and antidiscrimination remain essential components of

DOI: 10.4324/9781003323242-1

the struggle to prevent and redress contemporary instances of impermissible exclusion and vestiges of bias in social institutions. However, the post-formal equality use of vulnerability as particular and limited (as well as the concept of "vulnerable populations") as a proxy for situations of group exclusion or marginalization may do little to practically improve the structural position of those within the excluded group and may actually impede more inclusive and systematic progressive reforms to social institutions and relationships that would have generalized benefits across groups.

Of course, this argument about the theoretical potential of vulnerability does not mean that an antidiscrimination analysis is never appropriate. It is merely an argument that in situations addressing what after the equality reforms of the 20th century are asserted to be formally "neutral" legal and social institutions and relationships (such as the current design of the family or workplace, as well as the financial, healthcare, and educational systems), the initial critical focus should be those institutions and their function and design, not only on specific excluded or marginalized individuals organized by selected demographic categories.

Initially framing an institutional problem as discrimination necessarily means beginning with attention to the situation of only some. This has implications for the questions raised and the solutions suggested. With inappropriate targeted exclusion defined as the main legal problem, the resolution that would seem to naturally follow is to ensure the inclusion of the excluded individual or group. The ways in which the nature and functioning of the social institution may be failing everyone that must function within them may not be raised or otherwise included in arguments aimed at institutional reform. In a basic discrimination charge, aside from the exclusion of some, the underlying institutional arrangements are either ignored or assumed adequate, even beneficial. The issue is that a particular group does not have equal access or opportunity within them.

Vulnerability theory argues that by treating vulnerability as focused, individual, and variable, we create a conceptual dichotomy with all the practical and theoretical problems that entails. On the one hand, we have a vulnerable being, inadequate or deficient, in need of protection or assistance; on the other hand, stands an assumed independent, self-sufficient individual who, escaping the stigmatized designation of "vulnerable," can avoid paternalistic mechanisms of state intrusion and control.

Importantly, what distinguishes one individual from another in this rendering is not only the claimed differences in their position as vulnerable or invulnerable. There is also a significant difference in the way these individuals are viewed in relation to others: one is dependent on others for protection or provision, the other is not. The need for assistance or protection is deemed exceptional, warranted by the status of vulnerability. This dichotomy is not only inappropriate, but also ultimately works to narrow and confine our vision for social justice and our aspirations for a more inclusive society. The idea that some of us are not vulnerable (or that some of us are uniquely so) operates on the individual level to disadvantage both those deemed vulnerable and those excluded from that category, and it also works on the societal level to ultimately diminish the well-being of the collective community and a more foundational consideration of governmental responsibility for the whole of society.

II. Vulnerability Theory

Vulnerability theory begins by asking us to consider two related questions that are designed to take us back to "first principles" in assessing the human condition and its institutional implications:

FIRST: What does it mean to be human? This is an empirical or descriptive foundational question exploring what constitutes the essence of the human condition.

In answering this question, we will be defining the primary subject of theory, the focus of the legal, political, economic, and philosophic principles we expound. This subject becomes the imagined or assumed ordinary being around which our theories are built.

SECOND: What does our answer to the question "what does it mean to be human" suggest for the way we should organize a just society? This question addresses the normative issues inherent in making choices in designing the social institutions and relationships through which society can successfully and justly reproduce itself.

This second question is intensely related to the first, basically asking us in determining what is "just" or necessary (or even possible) to fully consider how our understanding of the essential human condition should inform both theory and, ultimately, social policy and law.

A. Reasoning From the Body

In considering the question of what it means to be human, vulnerability theory begins with the physical and developmental realities of the body. This is a foundational, essential, and theoretically vital starting point for the analysis. The universal human condition is shaped and should be defined in the first instance by our "embodiment." We are fundamentally corporeal beings. The body referred to here is universal—an anthropological or ontological concept—essentially finite, fragile, mutable, and inevitably physically and socially dependent.

The ontological body is also dynamic—it changes over time physically, as well as in capacity, ability, and need for specific forms of social support and subsidy. Change is sometimes the result of inevitable developmental changes, evolving over time. It also can occur in response to specific individual experiences, like accidents or illness. This inevitable susceptibility to change is intrinsic to the corporeal body, actually defining an essential aspect of the human condition.

Developmental or biological change in the corporeal body can be either "positive" or "negative." Some positive changes are developmental in nature, involving growing capacities as we mature and gain intellectual and emotional skills and experiences. Negative changes in the body can result from illness and are often perceived to be the result of certain incapacities and, perhaps, aging.

There are also circumstantial or environmental situations that can provoke positive or negative changes in the corporeal body. External natural or contrived events, such as disasters, accidents, famine, war, and so on can negatively impact the body. On the other hand, the provision of opportunities for the individual, such as those provided by education, culture, and other forms of social subsidy and support may not only compensate but confer benefits that positively enhance an individual's wellbeing and position in times of inevitable change.

Significantly, from the perspective of crafting governmental policy, positive changes can be encouraged, and negative changes deterred or mitigated. Some specific changes may be predictable, such as those often associated with aging, which also provides the occasion (responsibility) for strategy and programmatic development. While some changes may be difficult to foresee and external to individual control, they can still be anticipated and addressed with forecasting and an informed approach.

B. Embedded—The Necessity of Social (and Legal) Arrangements

In understanding vulnerability theory, recognizing the inevitability of change over the life course also reveals the reality of social dependency. Developmental and circumstantial changes often necessitate alterations or adjustments in the social institutions and relationships in which an individual is located at any particular time in the life course. In other words, because we are "*embodied*," we also are inevitably "*embedded*" beings—dependent on institutions and social structures. This connection between embodiment and embeddedness is at the core of vulnerability theory. The realities of our ontological bodies necessitate we live in social relations throughout life—they provide us with the resources or assets that collectively constitute the resilience necessary to not only survive but thrive in the face of our vulnerability and the inevitability of change.

Dependency on institutions persists throughout life as our developmental and situational circumstances evolve. The nature and form of our dependence may alter and our need for any particular institutional structure may wax and wane, but reliance on some sets of institutional arrangements remains constant. For example, biological dependency on care from others is most apparent in infancy and often emerges in old age. This dependency on care is typically met in the first instance by the family. But instances of our social dependency extend well beyond that particular need or set of social arrangements.

In fact, in vulnerability theory, the ontological body provides the theoretical basis for both the origin of and the justification for society and its variety of institutional structures, not merely the family. Throughout the life course, our bodies require shelter, food, material resources, and the provision of other essential social goods and services. We are consistently reliant upon some set of social structures and practices and various institutions and arrangements, such as those comprising the educational, financial, health, employment, and social welfare systems are designed around these individual needs.

Significantly: the social institutions and relationships human beings are dependent upon, although they are essential, are not universal or constant in form. They vary across governing systems, as well as over time. They are created through governing mechanisms using laws and policies, and, as such, they are influenced by history, culture, as well as power relations and politics. These social institutions and relationships are creatures of the state, which profoundly affect the ways in which individuals experience universal vulnerability.

As creatures of law and policy, social institutions and relationships should be measured by their success or failure in responding to human vulnerability. However, the universal ontological body and its implications are typically undertheorized or ignored in social policy and law. What we see in political and legal theory is an idealized notion of the individual, fashioned as independent, autonomous, and liberty-seeking and leaving the body behind. This inaccurate and incomplete model is centered as the theoretical subject of both legal and political theory. It is a subject inappropriately taken out of social contexts—standing outside of the institutions and relationships that are the structures both in which we inevitably experience vulnerability and upon which we depend for the resources to ameliorate it. This notion of the theoretical subject is a radically individualized entity, imagined as capable of surviving and thriving in many regards independent of the state. Such a subject is easily abandoned to legal tools and devices such as consent, contract, independence, self-sufficiency, self-reliance, and rights, which ultimately are woefully inadequate to address the inescapable and lifelong dependence on society and its institutions that our vulnerability produces.

III. Theoretical Implications of "Reasoning From the Body"

Beginning with the ontological body raises different issues, questions, and concerns than traditional theories. Importantly it shifts the focus of analysis away from an assessment of the position of some categories of individuals to the institutional settings in which all of us live our day-to-day lives. This plane is the primary domain of law, politics, and policy. Viewing law as central to the reproduction of society, vulnerability theory concedes the inevitability of law, as well as some form of governing authority, while also appreciating the potential of the state as a unique mechanism for the construction of a just society. The argument is not that the state always or currently operates consistently in a just manner: it is merely that in contrast to alternatives, such as the market, religion, multinational corporations, and so on, the state imagines and values a democratic and egalitarian framework for doing so.

The theory also recognizes the ways in which the state is currently (and always) acting in the creation and maintenance of the social institutions and relationships in which we live our lives. In addition to defining the relationship between citizen and state through constitutional and other grand administrative governing laws, "mundane" areas of law dictate the rules that govern our day-to-day relationships with each other. These rules are memorialized in tort, contract, family, and employment law doctrine, for example, forming the "infrastructure for our everyday life."

These institutions and relationships are also crucial mechanisms of distribution of social, economic, and political benefits to individuals and significant for the very reproduction of society. On an individual level, everyday social institutions and relationships are not experienced as isolated or independent, nor are their effects. These institutional arrangements act in concert with each other—have a socially symbiotic relationship. The web of distribution they form includes not only the institutions of market, finance, and politics, but also those of the health, family, educational, and social welfare systems, which in concert form the background conditions essential to the success or failure not only of the individual, but also of society. Social institutions allocate privilege and power; distribute risk and reward, as well as subsidy and investment. They confer recognition and structure accommodation, supplying the often-essential arrangements for future generations, as well as those already in existence.

A vulnerability analysis looks at this process of distribution on two dimensions. First, responsibility for distributing essential social goods and services is spread across social institutions (such as those that form family, market, health care, employment, and educational systems). This is accomplished in a variety of ways, including through regulations and administrative practices, as well as constitutional jurisprudence. A preliminary significant allocation of responsibility for social reproduction is accomplished through drawing a distinction and designating some institutions as "public," while others are deemed "private" (for example, the institution of the private family is the way we privatize dependency thus alleviating the state and market from any primary responsibility).

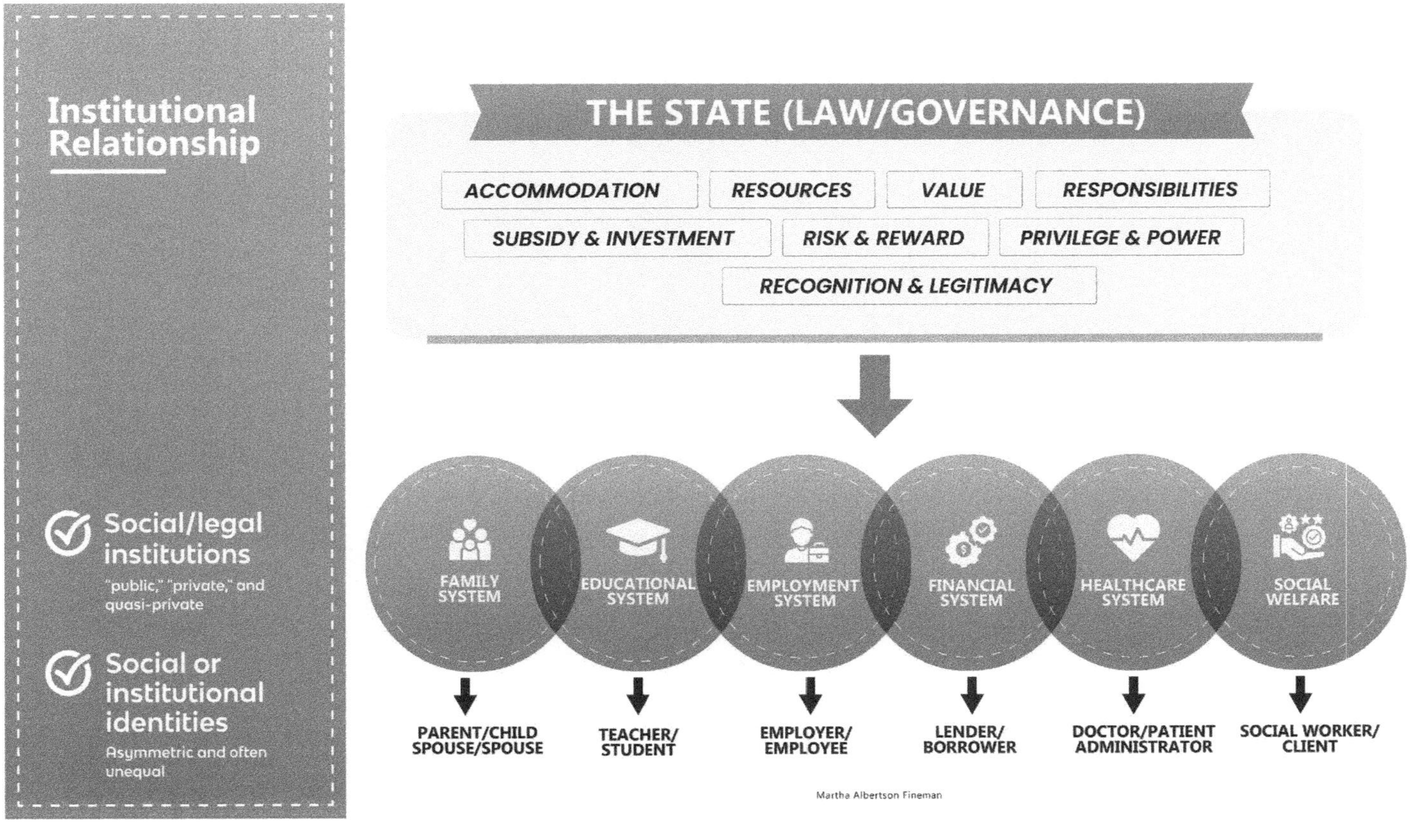

FIGURE 0.1 Visualization of institutional arrangements

Second, within these constructed social institutions, individual identities based on social functions are fashioned and enforced. These social identities are paired, complementary often of necessity unequal relationships—parent/child; employer/employee; shareholder/consumer; doctor/patient, lender/borrower, etc. Through these identities, the social benefits and burdens of the reproduction of society are distributed to individuals using the "everyday" law of contract, corporation, employment, family, criminal, tort law, and so on. Since they allocate benefits and burdens, such laws will ultimately impact everyone in society, even if it is possible in some situations for an individual to choose not to directly participate in an institution (such as the family). These institutional arrangements can be visualized thusly:

Vulnerability theory explores the justice of these primary relationships of distribution, placing the vulnerable subject at the center of law, displacing the autonomous, independent liberal subject that now dominates theory.

IV. Conclusion

While it is a critical theory, the recognition of the necessity for and inevitability of governance and law, and the positive potential this represents, distinguishes vulnerability theory from other "progressive" approaches that seem unable to move far beyond a focus on an oversimplistic notion of an abusive, or punitive state. By contrast, vulnerability theory posits that given the innate human condition of vulnerability and dependency not only is there ample justification for the state (or system of governance), but a vigorous and responsive state is essential to individual and collective wellbeing.

The universal vulnerable subject is also conceptually distinct from the political/legal subject underlying dominant legal/political models: rights-based and social contract paradigms. Vulnerability theory does not begin by identifying and privileging some abstract principles or capabilities, such as autonomy, dignity, or rationality that define the circumstances, as well as the theoretical place and significance, of the individual (and thus also influences or actually determines the inferior position given the state).

Beginning with the ontological body also means vulnerability theory should be classified as a "pre-identity" theory—based on a universal, not fragmented concept of the individual. Referencing an empirical, material, and perpetual reality, the vulnerable human condition manifested by embodiment should be understood separate from and prior to the political development of contemporary identity categories.

The "vulnerable subject" of the theory therefore stands on contrast to the fragmented conceptual figure that underlies most contemporary modes of critique. Therefore, vulnerability theory argues for the universal concept of the embodied vulnerable subject to replace the contingent rational man of economics, the reasonable man of law, the contracting man of political theory, as well as the exploited, subordinated, or oppressed man (or woman) of contemporary critical theory.

This volume presents chapters from eminent scholars using vulnerability theory to frame their inquiry into specific institutional arrangements. The first section addresses legal structures, the second considers the place of social movements or collective organizations generally in vulnerability theory. Subsequent sections consider the institutional systems of family, health care, as well as economic institutions such as employment and the corporation. The collection ends with a consideration of sovereignty and the issue of overlapping and contested organization of governance. The chapters are examples of how vulnerability theory can prove productive in bringing new issues and questions to the fore and how it might offer an inclusive, systemic critical lens with which to consider the just allocation of privilege and responsibility across society and its institutions.

PART I

Legal Structures

The Constitution and the Mechanisms of Justice

1

RESTRUCTURING THE CONSTITUTION FOR HUMAN RESILIENCE

Martha T. McCluskey

Introduction

Constitutional law is fundamentally about structural questions: constituting institutions and allocating authority among them. Individual rights get popular attention, but these can only be realized through institutions. The liberal ideal of a restrained government comprised of autonomous subjects provides a shaky foundation for a polity of embedded, embodied human beings (Fineman 2022:1145).

Capitalizing on liberalism's weaknesses, neoliberalism uses the myth of autonomy to further institutionalize democratic government's incapacity for human well-being. That incapacity in turn invites an illiberal constitutional politics promising strength over human dependency through expanded institutional authority for violence, deception, dominance, and exclusion.

Vulnerability theory offers an alternative constitutional vision for structuring institutionalized power. Today's crises especially require large scale, comprehensive collective action. The ideal of autonomy fuels a politics of despair and division as individual choices become increasingly risky and confusing for many in the face of environmental disaster, disease, inequality, instability, mass surveillance, and rampant disinformation and deception.

The vulnerable subject shifts this frame in two ways. First, it directs institutional accountability from the formal individual to the embodied, embedded human being (Fineman 2015:614). Second, it repositions the state as a provider of human resilience, rather than facilitator of individual autonomy (Fineman 2010:269). These two shifts challenge the structural "common sense" of U.S. liberal political and legal theory, providing firmer ground for a constitutional politics resisting both neoliberalism and illiberalism.

DOI: 10.4324/9781003323242-3

This chapter will begin by summarizing the structural approach and its centrality to constitutional law. I will explain some of the structural ideas behind the recent decades' rise of neoliberal and illiberal constitutional revisions, showing how these amplify liberal ideas of autonomy and legitimate authority. I next outline how vulnerability provides a more robust direction for structural analysis and for an affirmative constitutional politics of democracy and social justice. As an example, I explore how the vulnerability lens can strengthen the structural vision of the federal administrative state, a prime target of right-wing constitutionalism that especially capitalizes on the liberal ideal of autonomy.

I. Structural Principles for Constitutional Power

The structural approach to constitutional analysis focuses on the division of authority between each branch of the federal government, between the federal and state or local governments, and between public and private institutions. The U.S. Constitution stands as the supreme law of the land while remaining supremely ambiguous, vague, and subject to conflicting interpretations and applications. Its text is designed for brevity, generality, and enduring authority, as a collective product shaped by long-ago intentions that can neither be clearly discerned nor objectively applied to contemporary problems (Chemerinsky 2022).

Given the inherent uncertainties of text and historical purpose, U.S. constitutional rulings are especially guided by ideas about the overall functions of government, identified as the structural method of constitutional interpretation. In his classic article about constitutional interpretation, constitutional scholar Philip Bobbitt explained that structural principles are deduced from a holistic view of the Constitutional text and purpose combined with "common sense" ideas about power and human nature (1980:721–2).

The general liberal "common sense" that has guided constitutional analysis anchors legitimate power in a polity of formally equal, independent subjects rationally asserting control over an external social and natural world. With that premise, the liberal constitution is charged with impartially upholding individualized dominion while mediating its conflicts. In the conventional view, the U.S. Constitution divides government authority into separate institutions, each with specialized roles designed to facilitate individual autonomy. In this theory, for example, the federal executive branch, headed by an elected president, defends against foreign domination, and enforces internal law and order; an elected federal legislature (Congress) represents and balances the substantive interests of autonomous citizens; decentralized states can be more responsive to local policy choices; courts hold institutions and individuals to formally neutral principles and procedures that order a society of self-determining citizens.

This liberal structural theory obscures a more complex and contradictory history. In many ways, state, local, and national government have affirmatively directed the substance of business and social relationships in the U.S. based on particular visions of the public welfare (Novak 1996, 2022). American government also has a long history of active support for military conquest of Indigenous and foreign peoples as well as for various forms of subordination directed at groups construed as distinctly or dangerously dependent due to race, class, or gender identity. After the Civil War, the U.S. Constitution's Reconstruction Amendments granted expansive authority to each branch of the federal government to provide broad substantive protections against unjust public and private power, in response to the systemic race-based enslavement enabled by the original Constitution's structure. In the early 20th century Lochner Era, however, courts turned this federal power toward protecting business corporations from accountability for human needs; for example, by suppressing labor organizing and invalidating social welfare legislation.

Political and social resistance to Lochner era rulings led to a mid-century New Deal with a revised constitutional structure. In the newly prevailing theory, "political branches" deserve primary authority over substantive public policy on economic and social matters because these are subject to electoral processes that (in theory) allow citizens to freely and rationally negotiate their interests. Judges should use their power to provide formally neutral procedures in politics, market, and law, supplemented with a limited list of substantive constitutional rights protecting personal freedoms. This constitutional theory also supported extensive policy-making powers for the federal administrative state structured by Congress in the bipartisan Administrative Procedures Act of 1946 (Emerson 2022:116–18).

By the second half of the 20th century, this revised constitutional structure supported new social welfare and regulatory programs mitigating a variety of particular substantive risks and inequalities pressed by social and political movements. During the 1960s and early 1970s, for example, federal legislation established new government administrative agencies and federal spending initiatives providing substantive support for consumers, workplace health and safety, environment, infrastructure, health, education, and for reducing discrimination. Courts were democratized as well, and with new civil and criminal procedural protections, expanded the civil justice system's power to redress personal injuries and increased public investments in legal services and legal professionalism.

This expansion of overt public power for substantive human provisioning and protection risked unsettling the liberal narrative that law functions to facilitate the private values, property, and decisions of autonomous formal subjects. To some extent, this constitutional restructuring limited businesses' discretion over their property and restricted economic power to gain by shifting costs to others and to the environment. Building on liberalism's tensions, a multilayered political movement of business leaders and wealthy investors worked with sympathetic intellectuals to develop a structural constitutional theory challenging this liberal postwar order.

Throughout the second half of the 20th century, this movement promoted a neoliberal ideal centered on the private market as the standard for justice. In this general logic, formally neutral private law institutions such as property and contract, primarily governed by judges, generally work best to guide autonomous rational individuals toward substantive goals of societal welfare. Over several decades into the 21st century, various prongs of this market-centered movement worked to weaken the power of the New Deal vision and Civil War Amendments with a constitutional mythology of an original condition of private freedom and security, threatened by the growth of the welfare state, administrative state, and the general democratization of law's power and protection. Shortly before his nomination to the Supreme Court, Justice Lewis Powell advanced this cause with a famous memorandum to the US Chamber of Commerce, calling for a movement of businesses that would use the judiciary, and especially the Supreme Court, as perhaps "the most important instrument for social, economic, and political change" (Powell 1971). In the Reagan Administration, Attorney General Edwin Meese picked up this call by directing a plan for major constitutional change by the year 2000 (U.S. Dept. of Justice, Office of Legal Policy 1988; Johnson 2007:243–5).

II. Contemporary Right-Wing Constitutional Restructuring

A newly energized right-wing U.S. Supreme Court now stands ready and able to undo the core structures of the imperfect liberal constitutional order (Greenhouse 2021; Cohen 2020). Its rulings use structural arguments to threaten substantive human rights (like abortion and marriage equality), democratic political processes (like voting equality), and federal legislative and regulatory initiatives protecting against a broad range of injuries and inequalities to human well-being (Klarman 2020; Millhiser 2021). By focusing analysis on which institution should decide, rather than on the substantive impact of a specific decision, the Court can deflect responsibility for the political stakes of the ruling. At the same time, by redistributing access to collective power, the Court's structural logic systematically entrenches political barriers to democracy and socioeconomic justice (McCluskey 2016:276–7).

This emerging constitutional order reflects the Federalist Society's decades-long efforts to remake the federal judiciary and foster credibility for dramatic legal change (Montgomery 2019; Hollis-Brusky 2015). Since its first event in 1982, the Federalist Society worked to undermine constitutional support for civil rights, social welfare programs, and regulatory state policies. By

2021, six of the nine Supreme Court Justices were current or former members (Feldman and Kott 2021).

A Federalist Society primer for law students tells a constitutional story centered on a pre-political human condition of autonomy (Sutton and Wurman n.d.). It quotes *Federalist Paper No. 2*: "nothing is more certain than the indispensable necessity of government, and it is equally undeniable, that whenever and however it is instituted, the people must cede to it some of their natural rights in order to vest it with requisite powers." This premise constructs government as a consensual transaction substituting political and legal power for a presumptively more legitimate power marked as naturalized and private.

From this foundation, the Federalist Society primer puts the "structural constitution" at the center of its vision of justice. It explains structural analysis is necessary because legal rules will inevitably depend on imperfect human interpretation (Lawson n.d.). Instead of spelling out substantive rights or policy priorities in detail, therefore, the U.S. Constitution focuses on institutional design. The primer explains that the core of this design is a "divide and conquer" strategy setting up each branch of government to prevent the others from exercising power (Lawson n.d.).

The Federalist Society's structural constitution builds on a market-centered constitutional theory articulated by economists James Buchanan and Gordon Tullock (1962). Taking individual autonomy as the essential human condition, this theory applies an amplified orthodox economic idea of market exchange to politics, analyzing government institutions as the product of rational choice by self-interested individuals (Buchanan 1991:3–18). Somewhat paradoxically, institutions are a central focus of this theory, because individualized rational choice depends on systems of rules and procedures to order competing interests. For this reason, Buchanan's theory prioritized *constitutional* politics focused on institutional structure, not merely specific substantive political goals, as the key to changing society (Berggren 2014:376).

To guide institutional structure, they propose replacing notions of the public interest with an efficiency-based model of private unanimous consent, asking whether pre-political individuals would agree that a particular collective action or institutional rule would generally advance their self-determined private interests over time. (Buchanan and Tullock 1962:14, 63–84, 253–62; Berggren 2014:376–7). Applying this model, Buchanan advocated sharply limiting majoritarian policy-making, strengthening private property rights, and governing through generalized formal rules (McLean 2017:79–80). Buchanan worked with leading U.S. right-wing funders to build a political and legal movement to limit "parasitic" voters dependent on government support (MacLean 2017:117–22). He also advised Chile's brutal Pinochet government on a new constitution requiring supermajorities for substantive change along with strong limits on public spending (MacLean 2017:154–60).

Echoing Buchanan's theory, the Federalist Society primer compares the central structural principle of limited government to a conservative investment strategy: a decision to favor low risks over the possibility for high gains, given the essential dangers of public power (Lawson n.d.). This constitutional metaphor, and its assumption of an ungoverned and self-made individual investor, obscures the inevitable fact that any private investments and individual power to choose would not exist without substantial collective support and public governance, thereby constructing privatized power as natural and presumptively benign. "A structural constitution represents a risk aversion. You worry about what happens when the sorts of people who you know are out there in the world and the sorts of people who you know are going to be attracted to an institution of government actually get in control" (Lawson n.d.).

With this structural vision, the Federalist Society's constitutionalism melds economic libertarian ideas with moral conservativism to bridge key divisions within the political right (McCluskey 2021). Both "free market" and moralistic strands of conservative political theory ground personal freedom and political legitimacy in active government protection for an essential sphere of privatized, inherently beneficial authority over dependent "others." Both use the ideal of autonomy to justify increased government protection of privatized institutions (such as the market, patriarchal family, or church) or branches of government (police, prisons, and military) deemed to provide the discipline needed to control human weakness.

Tightening its embrace of the Federalist Society's blended economic and social vision over the last several decades, the Supreme Court has used structural reasoning to justify new doctrines for invalidating state and federal institutional support for shared human vulnerability. This emerging structural vision does not show consistent or clear principles for allocating power between branches of government, or between private individuals and public institutions. Instead, it appears to draw its logic from an underlying myth of autonomy threatened by suspect human dependency.

For example, in striking down *Roe v. Wade*'s protection for abortion, the 2022 Court majority criticized the longstanding precedent as an exercise of "raw judicial power" interfering with state legislatures' freedom (*Dobbs v. Jackson Women's Health Organization* 2022:2241). By freedom, the Court meant government authority to control and penalize female bodies to make capacity for pregnancy more personally risky. Countering this seeming emphasis on state sovereignty, the Court increased federal judicial powers over states with a new "takings" doctrine expanding private property owners' rights (*Cedar Point Nursery v. Hassid* 2021:2063). Linking a property owner's right to exclude with the fundamental personal freedom to shape one's own destiny, the ruling allowed two large agricultural corporations to refuse to comply with state labor law giving farmworkers' limited access to union organizers at corporate-owned work sites (*Cedar Point Nursery* 2021:2072). Presenting the union organizers as invaders of a corporate person's space, the Court did not consider that the state law was enacted in response to the agricultural industry's dependence on stable labor relationships, in a context of the industry's dependence on extensive state privileges and protections.

Federal courts have also expanded federal preemption doctrine to limit state power to hold private business organizations accountable for harms to human and environmental well-being. For example, an opinion by Justice Antonin Scalia overruled a California unconscionability doctrine prohibiting waivers of class action rights in consumer arbitration contracts. Scalia cited the benefits of encouraging informality and individuality in dispute resolution without noting that the corporate defendants depend on public courts to enforce their formal, collective power to make contracts costly and confusing for unorganized human consumers to understand and enforce (*AT & T Mobility v Concepcion* 2011:344–5).

This neoliberal structural reasoning has produced new constitutional doctrines limiting the power of the federal democratic process to provide collective protection of personal health, safety, dignity, voting, and equitable participation in social and economic institutions (McCluskey 2016). For example, using structural arguments, the Supreme Court has narrowed Congress' commerce and Civil Rights Amendment enforcement powers, invalidating legislative protections against gun violence, gender-motivated violence and discrimination (Law 2002). It has narrowed federal spending power doctrine to limit Congress's power to expand public support for health care. It has created new constitutional exemptions from federal legislative requirements and enforcement powers, for example by expanding the Eleventh Amendment sovereign immunity doctrine to preclude private individuals from seeking legal relief for state violations of their federal rights (*Alden v. Maine* 1999). New First Amendment doctrines have exempted corporate and human persons from laws protecting workers and equal access to private health care and business services (Purdy 2018).

Reflecting on Supreme Court rulings, constitutional law scholar Robin West critically analyzes an emerging paradigm centered on a fundamental individual "right to exit" collective accountability and commitment (2014). She explains that this constitutional paradigm supplants an earlier civil rights vision centered on rights to enter and exercise voice in collective power (p. 897). Defending and expanding this ideal of individualized exit, Federalist Society scholar Ilya Somin argues that individual liberty would be better protected by replacing ballot-box voting with "foot voting" so that geographically mobile, sufficiently unencumbered individuals can "shop" for laws by choosing among jurisdictions offering competing packages of policies designed to attract or induce individual productivity (2020, 2014).

By identifying fundamental freedom with unequal private power to exit, exclude, or extract resources from shared human well-being, this new constitutional paradigm cuts across specific issue areas to direct populist distrust and insecurity toward public institutions and those who most visibly depend on public support. At the same time, by justifying doctrinal changes with formally neutral and technical structural reasoning, this emerging constitutionalism can appear intellectually credible and sophisticated, despite its substantive implications.

III. Vulnerability Theory's Constitutional Reframing

Vulnerability theory zeros in on the foundational idea of autonomy animating this right-wing constitutional order. Rather than deviating from natural forms of power, governments are one manifestation of constant, universal human dependence on social institutions (Fineman 2022:112). Aligned with critical legal theories, the vulnerability lens recognizes that institutions deemed private or formally neutral pervasively depend on active government support for selective substantive privileges and penalties. However, going beyond critique, the vulnerable subject provides empirical ground for an affirmative theory of legitimate government power (Fineman 2022:112).

First, government institutions should be structured for embodied humans, not autonomous formal individuals. That means constitutional authority should primarily be accountable for the well-being of subjects universally existing in non-fungible, temporary, and irreplaceable bodies dependent on social systems and the natural environment. With this premise, fundamental rights to privacy, speech, due process, and equal protection should apply first and foremost to embodied human subjects rather than to corporations or other formal entities. Going beyond expanding individual rights, however, vulnerability theory centers human well-being on institutions (Fineman 2019, 2022).

As right-wing structural theories recognize, collective organizations are fundamental to human existence. Political or legal institutions, communities, and cultures all share qualities of vulnerability to varying degrees while providing resources vital for managing inherent human dependency. The business corporation is one example of how the collective form itself provides distinct potential power for endurance, adaptability, and both destruction and production of human value. Vulnerability theory's institutional focus, however, reverses the frame of both communitarian and authoritarian political theories that emphasize individual responsibility as the key to preserving collective virtue and value.

Instead, with its second conceptual move, vulnerability theory holds *institutions* responsible, and directs this responsibility toward human resilience, not individual autonomy. The condition of inevitable dependency gives humans potentially abundant capacity to organize collectively to foster material well-being, meaning, and power for diversely situated human subjects. The term resilience captures this positive aspect of vulnerability: the capacity to adapt and even thrive through change, to mitigate inevitable risks and loss, and to recover from harms and misfortunes (Fineman 2017:146–8). Resilience requires access to a range of institutional resources and legal privileges, so that differences in individual resilience primarily stem from the qualities and inequalities of the social order, not from personal character.

With these two shifts, vulnerability theory challenges neoliberal and illiberal ideas of freedom as the right to gain by undermining institutional resources for shared human resilience. These vulnerability premises also clarify democracy by grounding legitimacy of political processes on resilience for the embodied human rather than autonomy for the formal subject. For example, recent constitutional election law rulings invalidate protections for human voting and electoral fairness by privileging the constitutional protection for the autonomy of private wealth or state sovereignty (Klarman 2020:178–230).

Going beyond constitutional limits on political discrimination and domination, the vulnerable subject draws attention to the developmental and social nature of human capacities for resilience (Fineman 2019:362–3). From that perspective, democracy requires ongoing, affirmative institutional resources to enable diversely situated people to obtain, understand, and evaluate information in response to changing conditions. Replacing an impoverished idea of liberty as individualized choice or rights, the concept of resilience instead focuses on the societal conditions that provide better options from which to choose (McCluskey 2021). Meaningful power and purpose are undermined when the choices available are confusing or costly to oneself or others on whom we depend.

Democracy also requires institutions that actively promote fairness, integrity, truth, and inclusion. Given the social formation of human subjects and their personal judgments, democracy requires institutional processes that function to broaden ideas of the public interest and to cultivate collective knowledge, solidarity, and trust, rather than to primarily reflect an electoral majority's individualized preferences. If those on the losing side of a particular institutional decision do not believe their interests will be fairly and reasonably considered in future government decisions, they may reject democratic in favor of autocratic strongmen or well-armed self-protection geared toward identity-based division, domination, and exclusion.

It follows that the goal of resilience for subjects who are mutually dependent and non-fungible challenges a standard of overall welfare that legitimates irreparable damage to some particular environments and human lives with formal calculations of offsetting benefits to others. Although vulnerability theory does not readily resolve specific problems of conflicting interests, its focus on resilience directs institutional authority toward system changes aimed at minimizing disparate or devastating human harms and reducing conflict and division over the long run. Further, oriented toward resilience, institutional legitimacy should depend on ongoing attention to the substantive outcomes of formally neutral rules or processes, especially considering actual effects on human and environmental health and the quality and equity of social provisioning.

Applied to constitutional structure, government powers should be allocated to support inclusive mutual resilience, not to divide and conquer institutional capacity to protect an illusion of private autonomy. The separation of government powers responds to the problem that human institutions are inevitably vulnerable to failures of will, principle, and knowledge. Given that no human or human institution can wield independent and omniscient power (Fineman 2008:12–13), resilience for government or citizens requires access to a range of collective avenues of support, each of which can respond to particular and changing substantive needs with specialized expertise, knowledge, and methods of decision-making.

Informed by vulnerability theory, however, structural protection against the risks of institutional power would not primarily focus on policing each institution's sovereignty against encroachment by others, nor would it rely solely on ostensibly formal, value-free principles. Instead, it would turn structural analysis toward coordinated support for other institutions' structural vulnerabilities so that each serves to support, monitor, and reinforce the others in furthering a shared normative goal of resilience for human subjects. Rather than debating which institutional form is the most dangerous or legitimate, constitutional law and politics should push each institution to improve its distinct practices, rules, and substantive decisions to better advance a democracy of universally vulnerable human subjects. Although this foundational shift will not fully resolve conflicts between institutions or between competing views of democratic qualities, it can reframe the debate and clarify the analysis.

IV. Affirming the Administrative State for Human Resilience

Turning to current constitutional politics, vulnerability theory provides firmer ground for a strong administrative state. Because administrative powers are especially designed to make substantive policy insulated from electoral processes, they sit uneasily in the liberal post-Lochner framework. By the late twentieth century, well-funded neoliberal think tanks and business organizations had worked to significantly undermine administrative state protections (McGarity 2013:67–83, 217–27). Using structural reasoning to develop several new doctrines in the 21st century, the Roberts Court has overturned federal agency rules addressing a wide range of subject areas, with major impact on protections for workers, consumers, environment, economic integrity, and civil rights. (Metzger 2017:17–31).

A recent Supreme Court ruling against the administrative state shows how a vulnerability lens might challenge neoliberal structural analysis. In 2021, the Court blocked enforcement of a Center for Disease Control (CDC) moratorium on evictions in counties experiencing an upsurge in COVID-19 transmission from a new virus variant spreading nationwide (*Alabama Association of Realtors v. Dept. of HHS* [hereinafter *AAR v HHS*] 2021). Following Congress's limited eviction moratorium during the initial months of the pandemic in 2020, the CDC issued a more comprehensive moratorium, supported by an executive order of President Trump, which was extended into 2021 by Congress and then again by the CDC through summer 2021 (*AAR v. HHS* 2021:2492); Carpenter 2021). After protests by members of Congress prompted the Biden administration to act (Fandos 2021), the CDC issued a modified moratorium for several additional months.

In an emergency proceeding vacating a stay of a lower court ruling, the majority's *per curiam* opinion stated that the CDC's moratorium was "virtually certain" to exceed its constitutional powers under its authorizing 1944 public health statute (*AAR v. HHS* 2021:2486)). Reinforcing a newly developing "major questions" doctrine (Driesen 2022), the Court reasoned that agencies cannot take action that has "vast" economic and political significance without satisfying a high standard of specific Congressional authorization (*AAR v. HHS* 2021:2489).

This reasoning suggests a structural vision of a hierarchy of sovereign powers threatened by unruly dependents, who must be disciplined by a superior independent authority. Similar to a principal-agent contractual relationship, in this view, agencies must carry out Congressional orders while constraining their own judgment to avoid endangering Congressional sovereignty (Jackson 2022:811). The statute explicitly authorizes the CDC to use its own judgment to issue regulations necessary to prevent the spread of disease (*AAR v. HHS* 2021). Nonetheless, the Court ruled that the "sheer scope" of the CDC's action meant the statute must be narrowly interpreted based on its listed examples of possible public health measures.

The Court's analysis assumes, first, that Congress intends to err on the side of restraining agency action, even when, as in this case, statutory language explicitly grants the agency sweeping powers to use its own judgment and when Congress and both Presidents Trump and Biden had specifically authorized a CDC moratorium in response to COVID-19 (Carpenter 2021; Clark 2020; Federal Register 2020). Second, it assumes that Congress is particularly dependent on the judgment of federal courts to interpret and protect Congressional will. Third, it assumes that the Constitution authorizes federal courts to restrict both federal executive and legislative branches from using agencies to improve each branch's capacity for substantive responses to major social and economic problems.

This logic reflects an "anti-administrativist" constitutional politics (Metzger 2017:4) that positions federal agencies as servants under Congress's direction, with Congress in turn serving as an agent of sovereign citizens whose collective will is represented in the democratic electoral process (Jackson 2022:781–2, 811). Legal scholar Kate Jackson insightfully challenges this analysis by arguing that the administrative state instead enhances "democratic autonomy" by providing processes and resources that help constitute citizens as participants in inclusive and fair collective decision-making (Jackson 2022:809–12, 819–20). For example, rulemaking procedures subject proposed regulations to direct public comments from diverse voices, including those disadvantaged in majoritarian politics, and provide specialized institutional expertise and attention to shape policy judgments on particular subjects like environmental protection and consumer finance (Jackson 2022:812–15).

A vulnerability lens could further advance this structural defense of a strong administrative state by instead understanding agencies' distinct institutional qualities as resources for "democratic resilience." Like individuals, institutions (such as Congress) do not exist in a pre-political condition of sovereignty that must be carefully defended against less deserving dependents. The substantive "will" of Congress or its voting constituents, like the will of other institutions or individuals, is inevitably formed by the collective resources, conditions, and processes in which it is embedded. To effectively advance their interests and goals, both individuals and institutions depend on others' specialized judgment beyond their direct control.

As earlier generations of reformers recognized, the federal administrative state has potential to be a distinctly effective resource for collective human resilience against large-scale privately administered collective power. Faced with a newly complex and integrated national economy and polity in the late 19th century, Congress and the president, with support from courts, began to build a federal administrative state that could inform, lead, and enforce public responses to the growing, diverse risks from powerful national private corporations (Novak 2022).

William Novak (2022) grounds this change in a new ideal of democracy, charging government with going beyond formal rules and processes to affirmatively develop substantive outcomes responsive to the well-being of each and every person (p. 20). Novak explains that federal and state governments used the concept of "public utility" to replace the previous era of extensive local and common law regulation of business with pro-active public involvement and substantive oversight of systems for supplying and distributing energy, transportation, financing, water, communications, agricultural products, interstate travel facilities, physical infrastructure, and other services deemed to affect the public interest (p. 123–45).

In contrast to vulnerability theory's understanding of universal human vulnerability, however, this earlier vision of state responsibility for social change often focused the administrative state on policing or purging particular human persons, bodies, and identities as the source of dangerous social defects (Novak 2022:161–79; Sitaraman 2022). Correcting that understanding, vulnerability theory views institutional or individual failures as problems of unjust and inadequate collective provision of resources for resilience for the universal human condition of situated dependency. The universally vulnerable subject lends support to the goal of turning executive might from policing and punishing human persons with few resources to instead govern private firms to support inclusive human resilience.

In the current political economy, access to many resources for human resilience depends on discretionary judgments made by nationally or globally organized, dehumanized collective entities singularly designed to focus on securing short-term and self-serving financial gain. Contemporary law designs the corporate form to insulate private wealth holders from substantial responsibility for damaging human bodies, communities, and natural environments (Pistor 2020). These losses resulting from private institutional decision-making cannot effectively compensated or corrected ex post through enforcement of specific individually rights or through targeted redistribution (Berger and Richard 2021). The developmental, fragile, and time-bound condition of human embodiment means that many injuries to bodies, minds, and social relationships are cumulative and irreversible. For example, the long-term costs of decisions to invest in oil and gas infrastructure, toxic chemicals, or racially segregated housing may impede the resilience of communities and individuals over generations. These deficits in resources for resilience can make individuals and communities more dependent on other risky sources of support (like unsafe jobs or predatory lenders) likely to extract further resources from individual and social resilience.

Legal scholar Katharina Pistor (2019) explains that so-called private law formal institutions of corporate law, trust, property, collateral, contract, and bankruptcy provide "the mother of all subsidies" to wealthy capital holders (p. 222). These legal institutions combine to form a "code" that specialists can use to flexibly create, secure, administer, convert, coordinate, and invest capital over time, space, and political boundaries without public accountability for major substantive social effects. This coded subsidy gives wealthy capital holders extraordinary resilience, enabling them to recover or even increase assets through misjudgment, misfortune, or even reckless or unlawful risk-taking (as in the case of financial firms in the 2008 global financial crisis).

As Pistor analyzes, the malleable, general nature of these legal forms operate cumulatively and creatively to generate vast private power to change the substantive rules of law, government, and economy over time (p. 205–34). Wealthy individuals and firms routinely delegate substantial power to legal professionals to configure private law rules to gain long term advantages (p. 158–82). Frequently construed by courts and other authorities as negative and neutral rights fundamental to autonomy, capital holders use these private law institutions to trump affirmative public protections or supports for democracy and for social and environmental goals (p. 229).

Without similarly expansive institutional capacities to proactively and flexibly govern the substance of production and distribution under changing conditions, even seemingly sovereign and democratic governments will lose practical power to meaningfully respond to the needs and goals of their human constituents. As institutions dependent on political and judicial support, U.S. regulatory agencies cannot on their own change the rules of the market to reduce human and environmental harm. They have potential, however, to provide forward looking research, rules and enforcement that make life less risky and unfair for more embodied subjects on a fragile planet.

Returning to the 2021 eviction opinion, the Court weighed the equities of allowing the moratorium to continue pending an appeal on the merits of the constitutional question of CDC's powers. The Court determined that the risk of irreparable harm would be greater for landlords temporarily unable to evict than for tenants losing their homes during a pandemic surge (*ARR v. HHS* 2021:2489–90). To support its judgment, the Court reasoned that a property owner's right to exclude is fundamental, unlike the CDC's policy choice to limit evictions as a response to the pandemic (p. 2489). Exemplifying the problem that Pistor critiques, this reasoning establishes a legal hierarchy where a formal idea of property as protection for a private sovereign's discretion trumps the federal administrative agency's discretion to provide specific substantive legal protection against the distinct dependencies of embodied, embedded subjects. By limiting government's options for helping tenants secure housing and health to protect real estate investors' options for financial gain in a pandemic, the Court shifts public resources from embodied human resilience to resilience for the autonomy of formal asset-owning subjects.

The Court describes the moratorium as the CDC's decision to impose the costs of the pandemic on private landlords rather than using other public health strategies (such as vaccines or rental assistance) (p. 2489). This characterization sidesteps the fact that the moratorium delayed rather than relieved tenants of their obligation to pay, and that Congress appropriated substantial funding to support payment of back rent (p. 2492). The opinion emphasizes that landlords of modest means depend on rent payments, and its general use of the humanized term "landlords" deflects attention from the leading plaintiffs' corporate identities as trade associations or property management firms and their owners (p. 2489).

Since the 2008 financial crisis in particular, a large and increasing share of rental properties are under institutional ownership and control (Lee 2017). Institutional landlords are particularly likely to have access to credit to sustain their assets over at least short periods of interruptions in rental income. Large institutional investors have disproportionately used eviction and eviction threats during the pandemic, and corporate landlords have a history of using corporate shells and other legal devices to evade contractual responsibilities to individual tenants (House Select Subcommittee on the Coronavirus Crisis 2022; Ferrer 2021; Raymond et al. 2016).

More generally, if residential property landlords are presumed to be rational, self-reliant market actors, they have chosen to invest in a heavily regulated industry serving a clientele likely to be financially precarious. Accordingly, they could reasonably be expected to have adjusted their rental prices or diversified their assets to cover the risks of unexpected gaps in rental income. Further, in pandemic conditions of widespread disruption of businesses and loss of work income due to family health or childcare problems, a moratorium on evictions plausibly could help protect some small landlords from the risk that a sudden increase in households unable to afford their rent will lead to high vacancy rates and reduced rental prices in local markets.

As the dissent notes, the CDC moratorium at issue targeted only those tenants with no other housing options in communities experiencing high levels of COVID-19 transmission (*AAR v. HHS* 2021:2491). The CDC determined that tenants evicted without stable housing alternatives would be likely to contribute to the interstate spread of contagious variant by moving to congregant facilities, public streets, or crowded housing, placing increased burdens on hospitals and risking general economic disruption (p. 2493). In a New York Times commentary after the ruling, sociologist Matthew Desmond cited empirical evidence that the moratorium had reduced the U.S. pandemic death rate by 11% and that longer state moratoria on pandemic evictions were correlated with lower mortality rates (Desmond 2021; Jowers et al. 2021; Leifheit et al. 2021). Princeton Eviction Lab researchers found that the CDC moratorium dramatically reduced evictions in 2020–2021 (Desmond 2021; Hepburn et al. 2023).

Desmond's extensive research on eviction highlights the risks of devastating harm from eviction faced by human persons and families in rental markets structured to support financial gain for autonomous formal subjects (2016). Unlike transferable and compensable financial assets, the embodied, embedded condition means that loss of some resources for even a short period can set in motion a chain of interdependent harms. For example, access to jobs, health care, schools, transportation, safe streets, nontoxic environments, and specialized support from family and community institutions are likely to depend on stable housing situated in a particular location. Even before the pandemic, one in four households paid more than half their monthly income on rent, a condition correlated with lower overall health and longevity (Body et al. 2021:5).

During the pandemic, research showed that large percentages of renters cut back their spending on education, utilities, food, and medical care, and many households turned to subprime, predatory, or informal debt, putting them at risk of future insecurity and exclusion from economic opportunities (Body et al. 2021:5, 6). Especially in a pandemic, when personal or family illness interrupts work income needed for rent, the difficulties of recovering health and economic stability are likely to be compounded by the physical and mental stress of seeking new housing and interrelated resources or risking homelessness. Contrasting the evidence of harm to rental property owners, Desmond (2021) cited evidence confirming that even small landlords were unlikely to face risks of losing their own homes without temporary access to evictions due to extensive government financial assistance, special pandemic protections against foreclosure for property owners, and the availability of other options for maintaining property owners' financial security.

Taken in context of other constitutional rulings, the Court majority's disregard of the human harms of eviction reflects its constitutional politics aimed at restricting administrative agencies' capacity to protect human resilience against unequal and concentrated private economic power. To gain credible constitutional authority for that anti-democratic goal, rulings like the eviction decision rely on structural arguments to pit administrative agencies against a hollow vision of democracy. The Court majority's focus on the moratorium's "substantial" economic and political impact provides an elusive, highly subjective standard for determining the constitutional limits of agency powers, especially given thin evidence of Congressional intent to preclude that specific public health strategy. The clearest effect of this emerging "major questions" doctrine is to give federal judges broad discretion to disrupt and override agency policy-making (Driesen 2022), especially to protect the interests of private capital.

To affirm the democratic potential of the administrative state, constitutional politics must address the structural arguments that empower the Court's to discount distinctly human vulnerabilities along with meaningful democracy. The inherently imperfect and diverse nature of human knowledge, need, and capacity means that no text, institutional design, formal principles, or decision-making method can independently provide an impartial and fair guide to collective power. By providing overlapping layers of different government branches, with different procedures for substantive decision-making the Constitution offers diverse institutional resources for individuals or groups to press the government to respond to their particular human needs.

Despite agencies' insulation from direct electoral accountability, Congress and the president (and the Courts) govern the procedures and substantive ends that shape their agency rules. By sharing substantive power with administrative agencies, Congress can gain capacity for responding to human harms not well recognized in majoritarian politics (Jackson 2022:815–20). Agencies' specialized attention to specific subject areas can strengthen electoral politics and legislative processes by informing and spurring new political constituencies and coalitions (Jackson 2022:817). This capacity to zero in on specific collective solutions to problems with tangible impact on ordinary citizens, like the permissible level of a particular toxin in drinking water, can help cultivate popular participation and identity as part of a *demos* acting collectively for mutual benefit (Jackson 2022:814–15).

With potential power for substantive change, agencies also can deepen democracy by providing opportunities for members of Congress to proactively build community power and challenge political narratives that serve to discourage, divide, or demonize. Shortly after being elected as the youngest member of the House of Representatives, Maxwell Frost explained that he models his Congressional role on the leadership of Representative Cori Bush, who slept on the Capitol steps and spoke out about her personal experiences with eviction to spur the summer 2021 executive action extending the moratorium (Peterous 2022).

In addition, as one longstanding method for allocating government powers, courts have considered which party is better positioned to secure their interests against improper government authority without direct judicial protection. This principle stems from the liberal concern that federal judges risk becoming super-legislators if they engage in substantive judgments, so that instead they review other branches mainly to correct shortcomings in political process (Regan 1985).

Vulnerability theory can improve on this liberal principle for judicial review by considering that the substantive distribution of collective power shapes the function and outcome of political processes (McCluskey 2016, 2020). To decide whether Congress must directly authorize any restrictions on eviction powers to protect the public health, for example, a vulnerability lens can highlight the parties' differences in institutional resources for human resilience against the risks of unfavorable government power.

With the Supreme Court's ruling, tenants at risk of eviction due to lack of substantial financial reserves in theory could have turned to Congress for legislative action to address their immediate risks. Similarly, if the Court had instead continued the stay, or if future rulings decided against the CDC on the merits, the property owners could nonetheless similarly seek prompt Congressional or Presidential intervention to restrict the CDC's public health powers. Considering the tenants' option to seek Congressional action, the acute and distinctly human conditions of insecurity and distress the moratorium addressed are similarly likely to impede tenants' collective power to push for Congressional extension of the moratorium.

Congress is currently designed to deal with multiple complex issues under procedures that deter quick action on behalf of non-majoritarian groups lacking extraordinary wealth, organizational support, and public visibility. Constitutional experts have long argued that people in poverty are systematically disadvantaged in the U.S. political process (Nice 2008), and those disadvantages have likely worsened with the recently increased constitutionally protections for large-scale organized wealth in politics (Klarman 2020; Gilman 2014). Women (especially single mothers) and people of color faced disproportionate risks of eviction (Hepburn, Lewis, and Desmond 2020; Vagianos 2020), compounding the difficulties of gaining majority support and sympathy for their interests. Insolvent tenants facing risks of illness, job loss, and homelessness are particularly unlikely to be involved in organizations with funding, capacity, and specialized knowledge for mobilizing Congress.

In contrast, the collective interests of residential property investors are especially likely to be well-represented in Congress. Real estate companies and their lobbyists and owners have donated heavily to Congressional campaign funds for both major political parties (Shaw 2019; Open Secrets 2019). For example, shortly before the earlier moratorium expired a real estate billionaire donated $1 million to a political action committee for Democratic members of the House, adding to other large donations from organizations representing billionaires (Perez and Warner 2021). Although smaller landlords may have little national political power on their own, their interests are regularly foregrounded by large real estate firms seeking to rationalize and humanize their political power.

Unlike the generally unorganized tenants at risk of losing health and home, the residential property investors' financial stakes create a likely source of collective funding to support litigation and lobbying likely to pay off with future monetized gains, thereby adding to resources for resilience. Real estate investors are also well positioned to form political alliances with other well-funded business organizations whose constituents stand to gain financially by reducing administrative agency powers. Regardless of real estate investors' actions, Congress also could have protected its powers without judicial action by legislating to restrict the CDC's authority or by pressuring the president to change the policy.

By narrowing administrative powers, the Court majority in theory might restrain Congress from relying on expansive agency powers to evade political accountability for substantive change. Congressional inaction in the face of widespread, severe socioeconomic harms to human well-being does suggest a serious failure of both political process and substance deserving constitutional scrutiny. In the current context, however, that Congressional power has been substantially weakened by judicial structural rulings narrowing

Congress's legislative powers and making electoral processes less democratic and responsive to diverse human constituents.

Similarly, administrative agencies are vulnerable to industry group capture, biased or complacent expertise, and insufficient Congressional funding for meaningful action (Steinzor 2015). But the Court's new structural doctrines exacerbate those problems by giving well-resourced private business interests new opportunities to demand deference from agencies and political leaders. The Federalist Society and other institutions litigating and legitimating this structural constitutional politics are insulated from broad public accountability and oversight, with ample funding and specialized expertise for changing the substance of politics and economy. To resist this power, agency vulnerabilities could be addressed by measures like the proposed Stop Corporate Capture Act, which would institutionalize limits on conflicts of interest in agency rulemaking (2022). Other reforms could increase agency accountability to community organizations and other forms of public participation focused on human effects of organized business (Rahman and Gilman 2019; Sassman 2021).

V. Conclusion

The idea that private autonomy is the fundamental purpose of government can be appealing in a time when many people struggle with systemic disruptions and risks in nature, society, and economy that elude individual understanding or control. Yet that mythical idea discredits the inclusive collective action needed for a democracy responsive to the diverse injuries and insecurities of human subjects. If government is primarily accountable to autonomous formally equal individuals abstracted from specific bodies, relationships, and environments, then formal corporate "persons" that disregard human risks will deserve the greatest public protection. Building on the liberal autonomy myth, neoliberal constitutional politics steers government protection toward unequal and unaccountable collective power to drain others' resources for resilience, to draw on Hila Keren and Ronit Donyets-Kedar's concept in this volume.

Vulnerability theory's emphasis on the universality of human dependency links particular substantive problems to the institutional structures that mask particularly unequal or destructive forms of public protection. Its concept of resilience directs attention to the ways institutions distribute resources for resisting or recovering from losses.

The Constitution's power to structure government institutions provides a key resource for (or against) democratic resilience, as neoliberal activist James Buchanan recognized. By deciding the terms by which government institutions can or cannot respond to particular harms and persons, the Court's structural analysis distributes the power to govern social and economic change over time. By changing the subject of this institutional logic, vulnerability theory clears a path for a multi-issue democratic politics to advance an alternative constitutional vision oriented toward mutual human well-being.

Reference List

Alabama Association of Realtors v. Dept. of Health & Human Services, 141 S.Ct. 2485 (2021).

Alden v. Maine, 527 US 706 (1999).

AT & T Mobility LLC v. Concepcion, 563 U.S. 333 (2011).

Berger, Sebastian and Jacques Richard. 2021. "Alternative National Accounting: From Monetary to Social Cost Accounting." *UWE Bristol Research Repository*, September 15 (https://uwe-repository.worktrikbe.com/output/7338217).

Berggren, Niclas. 2014. "The Calculus of Consent 'at Fifty': Insights for Liberalism." *The Independent Review* 18(3) (Winter):373–89.

Bobbitt, Philip. 1980. "Constitutional Fate." *Texas Law Review* 58(4) (April):695–775.

Body, Dyvonne, et al. 2021. "Current Responses to Housing Insecurity: A Focus on Vulnerable Residential Renters." *Federal Reserve Bank of New York* (White Paper) (file:///C:/Users/mcclu/Downloads/housing-insecurity-1.pdf).

Buchanan, James M. 1991. *The Economics and Ethics of the Constitutional Order*. Ann Arbor: University of Michigan.

Buchanan, James M. and Gordon Tullock. [1962] 1969. *The Calculus of Consent: Logical Foundations of Constitutional Democracy*. Ann Arbor: University of Michigan.

Carpenter, David H. 2021. "Litigation of the CDC's Eviction Moratorium." *Congressional Research Service*, August 2.

Cedar Point Nursery v. Hassid, 141 S.Ct. 2063 (2021).

Chemerinsky, Erwin. 2022. *Worse Than Nothing: The Dangerous Fallacy of Originalism*. New Haven: Yale University Press.

Clark, Dartunorro. 2020. "Trump Gives CDC Broad Authority to Stop Evictions During Pandemic." *NBC News*, September 1 (www.nbcnews.com/politics/white-house/trump-gives-cdc-authority-stop-evictions-during-pandemic-n1239038).

Cohen, Adam. 2020. *Supreme Inequality: The Supreme Court's Fifty-Year Battle for a More Unjust America*. New York: Penguin Press.

Desmond, Matthew. 2016. *Evicted: Poverty and Profit in the American City*. New York: Crown Publishing Group.

———. 2021. "The Eviction Moratorium Saved Lives." *New York Times*, October 3 (Opinion) Section SR, Page 8.

Dobbs v. Jackson Women's Health Organization, 142 S.Ct. 2228 (2022).

Driesen, David M. 2022. "The Political Economy of the Major Questions Doctrine." *SSRN*, August 4. http://dx.doi.org/10.2139/ssrn.4181917.

Emerson, Blake. 2022. "Policy in the Administrative Procedure Act: Implications for Delegation, Deference, and Democracy." *Chicago-Kent Law Review* 97:113–59.

Fandos, Nicholas. 2021. "With Sit-In, a Lawmaker Gets Renters the Help She Never Had." *New York Times*, A10, August 4.

Federal Register. 2020. "Temporary Halt in Residential Evictions to Prevent the Further Spread of Covid-19." *Federal Register* 85(173) (September 4):55292.

Feldman, Noah and Lidia Jean Kott. 2021. *Takeover: How a Conservative Student Club Captured the Supreme Court*. New York: Pushkin Industries. Audiobook.

Ferrer, Alexander. 2021. "The Real Problem with Corporate Landlords." *The Atlantic*, June 21.

Fineman, Martha Albertson. 2008. "The Vulnerable Subject: Anchoring Equality in the Human Condition." *Yale Journal of Law and Feminism* 20(1):1–24.

———. 2010. "The Vulnerable Subject and the Responsive State." *Emory Law Journal* 60(2):251–76 (The 2010 Randolph W. Thrower Symposium: The New New Deal: From De-Regulation to Re-Regulation).

———. 2015. "Equality and Difference—The Restrained State." *Alabama Law Review* 66:609–26.

———. 2017. "Vulnerability and Inevitable Inequality." *Oslo Law Review* 4(4):133–49.

———. 2019. "Vulnerability and Social Justice." *Valparaiso University Law Review* 53(2):341–70.

———. 2022. "Rights, Resilience, and Responsibility." *Emory Law Journal* 71(7):1435–56.

Gilman, Michele E. 2014. "A Court for the One Percent: How the Supreme Court Contributes to Economic Inequality." *Utah Law Review* 2014:389–463.

Greenhouse, Linda. 2021. *Justice on the Brink: A Requiem for the Supreme Court*. New York: Random House.

Hepburn, Peter, et al. 2023. "Protecting the Most Vulnerable: Policy Response and Eviction Filing Patterns During the Covid-19 Pandemic." *RSF: Russell Sage Foundation Journal of the Social Sciences* 9(3):186–207. https://doi.org/10.7758/RSF.2023.9.3.08.

Hepburn, Peter, Renee Lewis, and Matthew Desmond. 2020. "Racial and Gender Disparities Among Evicted Americans." *Sociological Science* 7 (December 16):649–62.

Hollis-Brusky, Amanda. 2015. *Ideas with Consequences: The Federalist Society and the Conservative Counterrevolution*. New York: Oxford University Press.

House Select Subcommittee on the Coronavirus Crisis. 2022. *Examining Pandemic Evictions: A Report on Abuses by Four Corporate Landlords During the Coronavirus Crisis*. Washington, DC: U.S. House of Representatives.

Jackson, Kate. 2022. "All the Sovereign's Agents: The Constitutional Credentials of Administration." *William & Mary Bill of Rights Journal* 30:77–824.

Johnson, Dawn E. 2007. "Lessons from the Right: Progressive Constitutionalism for the Twenty-First Century." *Harvard Law & Policy Review* 1:239–58.

Jowers, Kay, et al. 2021. "Housing Precarity & the COVID-19 Pandemic: Impacts of Utility Disconnection and Eviction Moratoria on Infections and Deaths Across US Counties." NBER Working Paper Series, No. 28394. National Bureau of Economic Research, Cambridge, MA, January (www.nber.org/papers/w28394.pdf).

Klarman, Michael J. 2020. "The Supreme Court, 2019 Term—Foreword: The Degradation of American Democracy-And the Court." *Harvard Law Review* 134(1):1–264.

Law, Sylvia A. 2002. "In the Name of the New Federalism: The Supreme Court's Assault on Democracy and Civil Rights." *University of Cincinnati Law Review* 70 (Winter):367–472.

Lawson, Gary S. n.d. "The Structure of the Constitution: Why Do We Need a Structural Constitution?" *Federalist Society* 86 (website course video series) (11 of 27). Retrieved December 4, 2022 (https://fedsoc.org/no86/module/the-structure-of-the-constitution/video/11#video-anchor).

Lee, Hyojung. 2017. "Who Owns Rental Properties, and is it Changing?" *Harvard Joint Center for Housing Studies*, August 18 (www.jchs.harvard.edu/blog/who-owns-rental-properties-and-is-it-changing).

Leifheit, Kathryn M., et al. 2021. "Expiring Eviction Moratoriums and COVID-19 Incidence and Mortality." *American Journal of Epidemiology* 190(12):2503–10. doi:10.1093/aje/kwab196.

MacLean, Nancy. 2017. *The Deep History of the Radical Rights' Stealth Plan for America*. New York: Viking.

McCluskey, Martha T. 2016. "Constitutional Economic Justice: Structural Power for 'We the People.'" *Yale Law & Policy Review* 35(1) (Fall).

———. 2020. "Countering the Neoliberal Structural Constitution." In *Socialist Constitutionalism Symposium*, September 15. Law and Political Economy (LPE) Project (https://lpeproject.org/blog/countering-the-neoliberal-structural-constitution/).

———. 2021. "Countering Neoliberal Logic with the Vulnerable Subject." In *Tranforming the Political Economy Symposium*, September 8. Law and Political Economy (LPE) Project (https://lpeproject.org/blog/countering-neoliberal-logic-with-the-vulnerable-human-subject/).

McGarity, Thomas O. 2013. *Freedom to Harm: The Lasting Legacy of the Laissez Faire Revival*. New Haven: Yale University Press.

Metzger, Gillian E. 2017. "1930s Redux: The Administrative State Under Siege." *Harvard Law Review* 131(1):1–95.

Millhiser, Ian. 2021. *The Agenda: How a Republican Supreme Court is Reshaping America*. New York: Columbia Global Reports.

Montgomery, David. 2019. "Conquerors of the Courts." *Washington Post Magazine*, January 2 (www.washingtonpost.com/news/magazine/wp/2019/01/02/feature/conquerors-of-the-courts/).

Nice, Julie A. 2008. "No Scrutiny Whatsoever: Deconstitutionalization of Poverty Law, Dual Rules of Law, & Dialogic Default." *Fordham Urban Law Journal* 35(3) (April):629–72.

Novak, William J. 1996. *The People's Welfare: Law & Regulation in Nineteenth-Century America*. Chapel Hill: University of North Carolina Press.

———. 2022. *New Democracy: The Creation of the Modern American State*. Cambridge, MA: Harvard University Press.

Open Secrets. 2019. "Open Secrets Industry Profile: Real Estate, Year 2019 (Online Database)" (www.opensecrets.org/federal-lobbying/industries/summary?cycle=2019&id=F10).

Perez, Andrew and Joel Warner. 2022. "Democrats Took Big Real Estate Money, Then Let the Eviction Ban Expire." *Jacobin*, August 3, 2021 (https://jacobin.com/2021/08/democrats-eviction-moratorium-expiration-real-estate-industry-money-interests-lobby-biden-pelosi-superpac-donations).

Peterous, Siona. 2022. "Maxwell Frost on Why He Isn't Worried About Being the First Gen Z Member in Congress." *Vox*, November 29 (www.vox.com/podcasts/2022/11/29/23482867/maxwell-frost-florida-midterm-elections-2022-gen-z-congress).

Pistor, Katharina. 2019. *Code of Capital: How the Law Creates Wealth and Inequality*. Princeton: Princeton University Press.

———. 2020. "Limited Liability is Causing Unlimited Harm." *Project Syndicate*, February 5 (Commentary) (www.project-syndicate.org/commentary/limited-liability-corporate-shares-by-katharina-pistor-2020-02?barrier=accesspaylog).

Powell, Lewis. 1971. "Confidential Memorandum: Attack on the American Free Enterprise System." *Reclaim Democracy* (https://reclaimdemocracy.org/powell_memo_lewis/).

Purdy, Jedediah. 2018. "Beyond the Bosses' Constitution: The First Amendment and Class Entrenchment." *Columbia Law Review* 118 (November):2161–86.

Rahman, K. Sabeel and Hollie Russon Gilman. 2019. *Civic Power: Rebuilding American Democracy in an Era of Crisis*. New York: Cambridge University Press.

Raymond, Elora L., et al. 2016. "Corporate Landlords, Institutional Investors, and Displacement: Eviction Rates in Single-Family Rentals." *Federal Reserve Bank of Atlanta, Atlanta Community and Economic Development*, Discussion Paper No. 2016–4, December 1.

Regan, Milton C., Jr. 1985. "Community and Justice in Constitutional Theory." *Wisconsin Law Review* 1985:1073–133.

Sassman, Wyatt G. 2021. "Community Empowerment in Decarbonization: NEPA's Role." *Washington Law Review* 96(4):1511–66.

Shaw, Donald. 2019. "How the Real Estate Industry Masks Its Campaign Donations." *Sludge*, February 1 (https://readsludge.com/2019/02/01/how-the-real-estate-industry-masks-its-campaign-donations-through-the-internet/).

Sitaraman, Ganesh. 2022. "Industrial Policy, Warfighting, and the Creation of the Modern American State." *Notice & Comment* (blog), *Yale Journal of Law and Regulation & ABA Section of Administration & Regulatory Practice*, July 28 (Symposium on William Novak, New Democracy: The Creation of the Modern American State) (www.yalejreg.com/nc/symposium-novak-new-democracy-08/).

Somin, Ilya. 2014. "Foot Voting, Federalism, and Political Freedom." Pp. 110–54 in *NOMOS LV: Federalism and Subsidiarity*, edited by James Fleming and Jacob Levy. New York: New York University Press.

———. 2020. *Free to Move: Foot Voting, Migration, and Political Freedom*. New York: Oxford University Press.

Steinzor, Rena. 2015. *Why Not Jail? Industrial Catastrophes, Corporate Malfeasance, and Government Inaction*. New York: Cambridge University Press.

Stop Corporate Capture Act. 2022. "H.R. 6107–117th Congress: Stop Corporate Capture Act." *Reposed Legislation*, December 4 (www.GovTrack.us.www.govtrack.us/congress/bills/117/hr6107).

Sutton, Jeffrey S. and Ilan Wurman. n.d. "The Structure of the Constitution." *Federalist Society* 86 (website course video series). Retrieved December 5, 2022 (https://fedsoc.org/no86/course/constitutional-law-structure).

U.S. Dept. of Justice, Office of Legal Policy. 1988. "The Constitution in the Year 2000: Choices Ahead in Constitutional Interpretation." (Report to the Attorney General).

Vagianos, Alanna. 2020. "Covid-19's Looming Eviction Crisis Will Devastate Women." *HuffPost*, December 11 (www.huffpost.com/entry/covid-19-eviction-crisis-women_n_5fca8af3c5b626e08a29de11).

West, Robin. 2014. "A Tale of Two Rights." *Boston University Law Review* 94: 893–912.

2

VULNERABILITY THEORY AND ACCESS TO JUSTICE

Elaborating Possibilities for Legal System Design

Andrew Pilliar

Vulnerability theory has been considered in a wide range of social institutions, including marriage (Fineman 2015), families (Marvel 2015), health professions (Delgado 2021), and business (Grear 2016), among others. Ultimately, as Martha Fineman has often reminded us, vulnerability theory speaks to the need to reform many aspects of the role of the state. Accordingly, vulnerability theory should have much to say about virtually any sphere where the state structures and affects human life. It is a bit surprising, therefore, that despite some exceptions (MacDowell 2018), there has not been more explicit discussion of vulnerability theory's implications for the legal system. As the organizing and operative mode by which governments which adhere to rule of law principles give effect to the role of the state, legal systems are prime locations for analysis rooted in vulnerability theory.

This is perhaps all the more surprising given the increasing attention to so-called access to justice problems in recent years. Often used to describe the degree to which people are able to use legal services to prevent or resolve disputes, access to justice has become an important point of research, policy reform, and advocacy for legal scholars and those in cognate disciplines (Albiston and Sandefur 2013).

This chapter unfolds as follows. Part One provides background on access to justice by setting out some provisional definitions for the term, then exploring empirical work which helps to illustrate the scope and dimensions of access to justice problems within and across societies. This part also provides an opportunity to consider and frame how to think about the legal system (or legal systems) for the purposes of this chapter. Part Two situates discussion of vulnerability theory and explores possible connections and points of tension with access to justice scholarship. This provides an opportunity to compare

DOI: 10.4324/9781003323242-4

vulnerability theory with some other theoretical approaches that have been brought to bear on legal systems, such as responsive law and the capability approach. Part Three draws on the preceding two parts to explore how the theoretical posture of vulnerability theory could affect policies and operations within legal systems. That is, what would a legal system based on vulnerability theory look like? The chapter concludes with some observations of how some of these implications are already beginning to change legal systems.

1. Background on Access to Justice

a. What Is "Access to Justice"?

Access to justice is a topic that has gained increasing attention within the legal profession and among policymakers in recent years (McLachlin 2007; Sandefur 2016). To be fair, concerns about access to justice are not new. The very first paper published in the *Law & Society Review* in 1966 focused on the issue of access to justice and poverty (Carlin, Howard, and Messinger 1966). Over the ensuing decades, a significant amount of sociolegal research has been devoted to topics of access to justice, sometimes explicitly evoking that phrase, sometimes not.[1] In addition to this research attention, access to justice has been invoked in policy reform efforts ranging from the development and delivery of legal aid to reforms of court rules and procedures (Woolf 1996; LSC 2022).

Yet the field of access to justice runs the persistent risk of being underdefined. In the early 1980s, Austin Sarat (1981) argued that while access to justice is a "rhetorical symbol of undeniable power and attractiveness" (p. 1911), it nevertheless naively offers a quixotic and misplaced goal that is unrealizable in liberal societies where the state, society, and political order "derives its legitimacy from the popular perception that it honors the rights of individuals" (p. 1924). Access to justice can be a normatively vague term, which imports a significant risk of its being used without explaining its implicit assumptions and normative commitments.

In recent years, scholars such as Rebecca Sandefur (2019) have led a renaissance in access to justice research that offers a broad but explicit definition of access to justice. While "access to justice" has often been described as a problem "for the legal profession" (McLachlin 2007), access to justice problems are more properly understood as problems and crises for the people who experience them. This human focus, rather than a system focus, is a necessary shift in how we think about access to justice. Sandefur has described access to justice in the following way:

> When the relevant substantive and procedural norms govern resolution, that resolution is lawful and we have access to justice, whether or not

> lawyers are involved in the resolution and whether or not the problem comes into contact with any kind of dispute-resolving forum. Access to justice is a good in itself.
>
> *(p. 51)*

This definition suggests that access to justice requires fidelity between how people act and what the law both entitles them to and requires of them. As Gillian Hadfield (2010) has noted, we live in a "law thick world," meaning that law increasingly encumbers aspects of daily life (p. 133). As Martha Fineman has observed, law has been and continues to be omni-present in shaping our institutions, such as the family, the market, property, employment, and so on. Law "determines the nature of the relationships between individuals within these essential social institutions, such as parent/child, employer/employee, shareholder/consumer, and so on" (Fineman 2019:365–6). Clearly, meaningful access to justice cannot simply be access to courts. It must include substantive access to information and services that not only help to resolve disputes, but also allow people to benefit from rights and resources. This means that access to justice cannot focus exclusively on dispute resolution, but rather should focus on how legal tools should be deployed to improve well-being.

This also has implications for what we include in definitions of the "legal system" or "legal institutions." In this chapter, in keeping with some of these recent trends in access to justice scholarship, I will use the terms legal system and legal institutions interchangeably and broadly. That is, in my conception legal institutions include not only courts, but also the means of producing and distributing legal knowledge. This includes legal service providers and public legal education organizations. I also define legal service providers in a broad sense to include not only lawyers but also paralegals, notaries public, and other paraprofessional roles. I extend this even further to include regulators of legal service providers and legal education institutions, such as law schools. This broad definition of the legal system and legal institutions is intended to catch not only the paradigmatic example of courts, but also the institutional ecosystem that supports the "law thick world." It is intended to highlight the many and varied ways that the iceberg of law and legality, which determines so many of our social institutions yet so often lies outside our awareness, pokes above the waterline into view.

b. How Common Are Access to Justice Problems?

In recent years, an increasing body of well-designed research has demonstrated the ubiquity of justiciable problems in many countries (Sandefur 2016). Justiciable problems describe significant problems with a legal aspect, whether that legal aspect is perceived by those who experience the problems (Genn 1999). They can include disputes with neighbours, family separation, eviction, consumer complaints, disputes about government benefit entitlement, and so on. Increasingly, researchers in jurisdictions around the world have demonstrated that civil justice problems are ubiquitous, that members of marginalized or disadvantaged populations experience relatively higher rates of civil justice problems and negative consequences flowing from those problems, that most people will not interact with a lawyer or court to address their problem, and that the most important reasons that people do not "go to law" include believing that law does not provide a viable solution (Sandefur 2016:443–4).

Taking recent Canadian research as an example, almost 50% of adults experience at least one justiciable event over a three-year period (Farrow et al. 2016). Further, a minority of those who experience these problems seek the assistance of a lawyer or other legal professional to deal with these problems. These justiciable problems also tend to cluster and are not evenly distributed throughout the population (Currie 2007). Other countries have reported similar rates and trends (Sandefur 2016).

Another emerging trend from this unmet legal needs research relates to the relative importance of different access to justice barriers. Contrary to received wisdom, while the cost of legal services is a significant barrier for many, it is not the sole or dominant barrier. Instead, not seeing the legal system as a way to resolve problems appears to be a more common barrier (Sandefur 2016).

Recently, access to justice scholars Pascoe Pleasence and Nigel Balmer (2019) have elaborated the concept of "legal capabilities" as an analytically useful way to assess the extent to which people have knowledge about and comfort with the law in order to access information and services. They describe legal capabilities as "the disparate capabilities required for people to have opportunity to resolve problems fairly, including to make decisions 'about whether and how to make use of the justice system' "(p. 141). This concept provides the first psychometrically tested way of assessing how people approach legal matters at the individual level. As Pleasence and Balmer suggest, "[l]egal capability is central to opportunities and choices about how to handle problems" (2019:141).

These findings have significant implications for efforts to improve access to justice. Yet, it has been unclear what types of reforms should result in the wake of these findings.

2. Situating Vulnerability

Against this backdrop of ubiquitous—though unevenly distributed—access to justice problems, vulnerability theory provides a potent call for more responsive justice institutions and practices.

Vulnerability theory seeks to reimagine the legal subject on the basis of humans being both physically embodied and socially embedded. This gives rise to the reality of universal vulnerability over the life-course. In the face of this vulnerability, we must consider the nature and distribution of resources that contribute to resilience. As Martha Fineman has written, "[w]hile a vulnerability analysis begins with a description of universal vulnerability, it is the particularity of the manifestations of vulnerability and the nature of resilience that are of ultimate interest. Resilience is the critical, yet incomplete, solution to our vulnerability" (2017:146). This recognition of the role of resilience compels us to consider how social institutions contribute to the creation and distribution of resources for resilience. This in turn calls for widespread assessment and reform of state institutions.

One of the most important features of vulnerability theory is its suppleness in being both universal in scope and attentive to particularity. That is, because vulnerability theory sounds in the nature of human embodiment and the unavoidable fact of vulnerability over the life-course, it is a theoretical posture that can lay claim to being relevant and applicable to literally every single human person who has ever lived. At the same time, vulnerability theory can and does recognize the multifaceted nature of vulnerability: vulnerability "is experienced uniquely by each of us and this experience is greatly influenced by the quality and quantity of resources we possess or can command" (Fineman 2008:10). The nature of resilience in the face of this universal vulnerability is particular, and that particularity is a reflection of how "we are positioned differently within a web of economic and institutional relationships" that structure our vulnerability and resilience (Fineman 2008:10; Fineman and Grear 2016:2).

Martha Fineman has suggested that vulnerability theory requires a reorientation of governmental priorities to respond to shared vulnerability. She states that an "imperative would be placed on the legislature and the executive in the first instance: the mandate to be more responsive to and reflective of vulnerability" (Fineman 2008:20). Fineman names two of the three branches of government, but does vulnerability theory have implications for the third branch, the judicial branch? Legal institutions are aspects of the state. As such, they must be included in any thinking about the responsive state. Of course, legal institutions as defined in this chapter are not coextensive with the judicial branch of government. Vulnerability theory's implications for the judicial branch, in particular, will be discussed later in this chapter. Yet legality and legal mechanisms shape and structure the relations between people and the state, between people and corporate entities, and among people in many ways. At the very least, they offer a mechanism to help ensure that promises made by the legislature and the executive are properly given effect in the lives of the people. It is necessary, then, that vulnerability theory also has something to say about how legal institutions are structured and operate to support and enhance resilience. This includes ensuring that systems of justice and legality are actually, and not just formally, accessible to people within society.

Critiques of vulnerability theory have questioned whether and how the theory can be operationalized (Kohn 2014), resisted the theory's "post-identity" approach (Cooper 2015; MacDowell 2018), and suggested that the theory "provides little guidance as to how to prioritize among vulnerable subjects when allocating limited financial resources and political capital" (Kohn 2014:11, 13).

The following two sections will discuss vulnerability theory and two other approaches that have implications for legal institutions. First, I will compare vulnerability theory's call for a responsive state with Philip Selznick and Philippe Nonet's concept of "responsive law." Second, I will explore some conceptual differences and similarities between vulnerability theory and the capability approach outlined by Amartya Sen. Doing so lays a foundation for a more robust consideration of what vulnerability theory offers for reconstructing legal institutions.

a. Vulnerability Theory and Responsive Law

What does a responsive state imply for justice institutions? In 1978, Philippe Nonet and Philip Selznick (2001) proposed "responsive law" as a way to recast jurisprudence in order to make law and legal systems more responsive to social needs. While it is possible that Nonet's and Selznick's "responsive law" may have only superficial similarity to Fineman's call for a more responsive state, it is worth examining the two concepts to understand the depth of relationship between the two.

For Nonet and Selznick, responsive law was a continuation of the work begun by the legal realist movement (2001:73). Responsive law endeavoured to "[o]pen up the boundaries of legal knowledge . . . [and] [l]egal institutions were to give up [their] insular safety . . . and become more dynamic instruments of social ordering and social change" (p. 74). They describe responsive law in the following terms:

> A responsive institution retains a grasp on what is essential to its integrity while taking account of new forces in its environment. To do so, it builds upon the ways integrity and openness sustain each other even as they conflict. *It perceives social pressures as sources of knowledge and opportunities for self-correction.* (emphasis in original)
>
> *(2001:77)*

Nonet and Selznick imagined that as legal institutions increased their fidelity to justifiable purposes in legal reasoning—instead of strictly abiding by and adhering to precedent and formalism—they would make legal institutions more open, flexible, and political. But while this would help to make legal institutions more responsive to social circumstances, it could also threaten their institutional integrity. This, in turn, meant that "the integrity of the legal order [would] depend on the design of more competent legal institutions" (p. 78).

Selznick has written elsewhere that one of the positive attributes of legality (and what he terms the "morality of cooperation") is that it "abhors arbitrary judgment and constraint, presses for justifications, invokes the authority of agreed-upon purpose, and values the competent participant . . . [and in so doing] finds its warrant in the contribution it can make to human growth and self-realization" (1969:25).

Writing about her conception of a responsive state, Fineman has asserted:

> True equality of opportunity carries with it the obligation on the state to ensure access to societal institutions that distribute social goods, such as wealth, health, employment, or security is generally open to all and that the opportunities these institutions provide are evenly distributed so that no person or groups of persons are unduly privileged while others are disadvantaged to the extent that they can be said to have few or no opportunities.
>
> *(2008:256–7)*

Fineman has suggested that "[s]ociety and its institutions can address [the accumulated harms experienced by people] through law and policy that positions vulnerability as the organizing principle and seeks to alleviate these implications" (2010:268). In this view, societal institutions can:

> Collectively form systems that play an important role in lessening, ameliorating, and compensating for vulnerability. Together and independently they provide us with resources in the form of advantages or coping mechanisms that cushion us when we are facing misfortune, disaster, and violence. Cumulatively these assets provide individuals with resilience in the face of our shared vulnerability.
>
> *(p. 269–70)*

Legal institutions can and should help to foster resilience. Conceptualizing the role of legal institutions as one of contributing to resilience differs from traditional conceptions of legal institutions which elevate fidelity to the rule of law above other values. But as Selznick and Nonet noted, responsive law necessarily involves a broadening of the animating values within the legal system, in order to make that legal system more responsive to social needs and realities. It also suggests that the legal system should develop further institutions to help ensure that it is able to perceive social trends and developments that require a response from the legal system.

Fineman notes that the state is intimately involved in the creation, sustenance, and distribution of many of the institutions and resources that allow people to be resilient in the face of vulnerability (2010:272). This involvement creates a positive obligation on the state to ensure that these resources are distributed "with attention to public values, including equality or justice, or objectives beyond private or profit motivation" (p. 272). This is true of justice institutions no less than other aspects of the state.

The responsive state described by Fineman may seem quite different from the responsive law described by Nonet and Selznick. Whereas Fineman envisions a state that responds to human vulnerabilities in order to shore them up and promote resilience, Nonet and Selznick appear to be talking about an abstract change in jurisprudential approaches. Yet, there are some key commonalities between these two visions of responsiveness, and they lie in questioning how that responsiveness should be achieved. Both Fineman and Nonet and Selznick perceive state mechanisms that are more agile and porous in how they receive afferent information about social conditions, and both raise important questions about how that information should be imparted to the state institutions which should act. There is a consonance between Selznick's view of law as playing a role (at least sometimes) in contributing to "human growth and self-realization" and Fineman's call for responsive state institutions to equitably provide resources to bolster "resilience in the face of our shared vulnerability." In other words, both require us to imagine new ways of gathering, sorting, and using the right information about how to make states more responsive to people.

b. Vulnerability Theory and the Capability Approach

In describing how a responsive state should act, Martha Fineman has indicated that such a state "has a responsibility to structure conditions in which individuals can aspire to meaningfully realize their individual capabilities as fully as possible" (2010:274). Fineman's description bears some resemblance to stated goals of the capability approach, famously elaborated by Amartya Sen and others, which has been described as having a core "focus on what people are effectively able to do and to be; that is, on their capabilities" (Sen 1999; Robeyns 2005:94). Given this apparent similarity and the recent emergence of legal capability research, which is based on the capability approach, it may be useful to consider what these two theoretical postures have in common, as well as their differences (Pleasence and Balmer 2019:141).

Further, since the capability approach has been adapted to develop tools and projects which are deployed in society, examining the capability approach may have instrumental value for vulnerability scholars, given some critiques of vulnerability theory being difficult to adapt to practice.

The capability approach was initially described by Amartya Sen (1999) in the context of development economics. It has attracted significant scholarly attention in multiple fields, and has also influenced the design and use of tools to evaluate and shape public policy (Robeyns 2005:93–6). Sen's capability approach has been described as a "multidimensional approach to well-being . . . which moves away from an income-based perspective of well-being (utilitarian) and instead emphasizes the nonmaterial (that is, social, cultural, and political) aspects of human well-being" (Gigler 2015:15). It offers "a paradigm—loosely defined—that can be used for a wide range of evaluative purposes" (Robeyns 2005:96). As such, the capability approach "specifies an evaluative space and this does not amount to a theory of justice" (Robeyns 2005:96). Björn-Sören Gigler (2015) elaborates further:

> What matters, according to Sen, is what people are capable of being or doing with the goods to which they have access. A person's "capability" refers to the alternative combinations of functionings that are feasible for her or him to achieve. Capability is thus a kind of freedom: the substantive freedom to achieve combinations of alternative functionings—or, less formally put, the freedom to achieve various lifestyles.
>
> *(p. 15)*

To explore some similarities and differences between vulnerability theory and the capability approach, a recent study by Gigler provides a useful point of focus. Gigler's study explored and evaluated the use of information and communications technologies by Indigenous communities in Bolivia. This study is appropriate for discussion in this chapter because it contains a well-developed theoretical grounding along with detailed fieldwork and policy recommendations.

Gigler explicitly draws on Sen's conception of the capability approach, in contrast to some other conceptions such as those of Martha Nussbaum. Importantly, Gigler describes and uses examples of evaluation frameworks that have been deployed under the theoretical umbrella of the capability approach. These evaluation tools attend to the particular capabilities of the research participants and are attentive to their embeddedness within various social networks and relational contexts. As Gigler explains, "the capability approach evaluates people's well-being directly (indicators of quality of life) rather than indirectly through measures of inputs or means, such as higher incomes or consumption" (2015:25). This can avoid using identities as proxies for evaluating and assessing the effects of policies and institutions on people.

Gigler also points out that in Sen's capability approach, it is essential "that value judgments about the priorities of development have (a) to be made by individuals and society themselves and (b) to be made explicit by the theoretical framework" (p. 26). Doing so attempts to keep power in the hands of those being studied. Sen's approach calls for:

> An "evaluative exercise" in which individuals and society hold public discussions and engage in democratic processes. This is the reason that Sen,

> in contrast to Nussbaum and Alkire, never defines a specific list of "basic capabilities," deliberately leaving this open to be defined by the local context and people's priorities.
>
> *(Gigler 2015:26)*

This seems consonant with vulnerability theory. For a responsive state to properly understand how to best contribute to resilience in different people in different places at different times, it is necessary to approach and enquire from—and to build mechanisms for meaningful ongoing relationships with—those people. In doing so, it would be wise for responsive state institutions to approach subjects with a holistic curiosity and humility in attempting to understand the nature of particular vulnerabilities. This requires an openness on the part of responsive state institutions in order to hear what is needed to buttress vulnerabilities as they appear for different people, in different communities, across the life-course (Kohn 2014).

There are important differences between the capability approach and vulnerability theory. For example, while Sen's capability approach is described as a kind of "substantive freedom," Fineman's vulnerability theory is explicitly an attempt to displace liberal individualism and the "prevailing ideologies of autonomy, self-sufficiency, and personal responsibility" that inform so many contemporary legal, economic, and political principles (Fineman 2008:10). Sen's capability approach has been criticized for being too individualistic and not paying enough attention to social groups (Navarro 2000). Ingrid Robeyns has defended the capability approach from these critiques on the basis that it does not engage in ontological individualism, or what she describes as the position "that only individuals and their properties exist, and that all social entities and properties can be identified by reducing them to individuals and their properties" (2005:108). Robeyns admits, however, that the capability approach embraces "ethical individualism," which she defines as making a claim "that individuals, and only individuals, are the units of moral concern" (p. 107). Robeyns also acknowledges that the capability approach may not pay sufficient attention to social groups, and suggests that "the capability approach should engage more intensively in a dialogue with disciplines such as sociology, anthropology, history, and gender and cultural studies" (p. 109). In contrast, vulnerability theory has assailed approaches that eclipse "the needs, functioning, and nature of society, and make[] the individual the only relevant measure for justice" (Fineman 2019:351).

Vulnerability theory and the capabilities approach also differ in the role they expect of the state. While vulnerability theory "does not prescribe a specific form of state organization, [it] does call for a state that is responsive to universal human needs and for the reorganization of many existing structures" (Fineman 2019:342). In contrast, while Sen's capability approach provides a way to conceptualize and evaluate things like state institutions, it does not necessarily focus on claims of the government or the state (Robeyns

2005:105). This difference may reflect the different goals of vulnerability theory and the capabilities approach. While vulnerability theory provides a theoretical posture that should animate state goals and actions, Sen's capability approach is more limited in providing an "evaluative space" rather than a theory of justice.[2]

Another important difference between the two approaches is the universal touchstone embedded within vulnerability theory. Vulnerability theory speaks to the universal nature of embodied vulnerability that is undeniable of all humans. This provides an opportunity for solidarity that may be absent from capability-based approaches. This also emphasizes the importance of relationality in vulnerability theory which arguably does not have as prominent a place in the capability approach (Luna 2009:129). The importance of universality and solidarity to vulnerability theory should not be understated. As Delgado (2021) and others have noted, theoretical frameworks that do not emphasize the universal nature of human vulnerability risk reinscribing they dynamic of an autonomous and invulnerable self in contrast to a vulnerable "other" (p. 159). Indeed, this is a critique that Fineman herself has noted, writing that "this targeted group approach to the idea of vulnerability ignores its universality and inappropriately constructs relationships of difference and distance between individuals and groups within society" (Fineman 2012:85).

While there are important differences between the two approaches, there is much that vulnerability theory and the capability approach have in common. Acknowledging this provides an opportunity for vulnerability theory proponents to build on some of the successes of the capability approach and to share common aims. One significant commonality between the two approaches is that each attempts to put a realistic understanding of humans at their core. Sen has described the capability approach as:

> Essentially a "people-centered" approach, which puts human agency (rather than organizations such as markets or governments) at the centre of the stage. The crucial role of social opportunities is to expand the realm of human agency and freedom, both as an end in itself and as a means of further expansion of freedom. The word "social" in the expression "social opportunity" . . . is a useful reminder not to view individuals and their opportunities in isolated terms. The options that a person has depend greatly on relations with others and on what the state and other institutions do.
>
> *(Drèze and Sen 2002:6)*

Similarly, vulnerability theory aims to displace the abstract and fictional autonomous liberal subject with a more accurate legal subject: the vulnerable subject (Fineman 2008:2). In doing so, vulnerability theory emphasizes not only the universal reality of vulnerability over the life-course, but is also attentive to the nature of people as both embodied and embedded in social institutions and relations (Fineman 2017:143).

There is opportunity for proponents of vulnerability theory and of the capability approach to build on this shared concern for placing people at the core in reforming social institutions. For vulnerability theorists, the capability approach may provide useful tools and approaches when considering how to operationalize vulnerability theory, given the capability approach's track record of deployment in empirical research and evaluation studies across a number of fields. For proponents of the capability approach, vulnerability theory offers a more complete, over-arching theoretical framework in which to work, and it also presents a framework which shores up some of the frailties of the capabilities approach when it comes to critiques of being too individualistic. I am not attempting to elide vulnerability theory and the capability approach in this paper. Rather, I am suggesting that increased dialogue between these two approaches is merited. Further, research on access to justice problems may provide a focal point for such future engagement.

I have suggested elsewhere that pervasive access to justice problems call for a new conception of the justice system which moves beyond defending the rule of law and toward promoting the well-being of the people who seek to use the legal system. I have described this paradigm as "person-centred access to justice" (Pilliar 2022). The next section explores how vulnerability theory might transform person-centred access to justice into reality.

3. Realizing Person-Centred Access to Justice

Person-centred access to justice relies on vulnerability theory to illustrate how legal institutions should be reformed and operated. One way of conceptualizing access to justice using vulnerability theory is to recast the legal system as one that can and should contribute to the well-being of those who engage with the system.

It is important to note that, in describing a "person-centred conception" of access to justice based on shared vulnerability, the onus lies on our social and societal institutions to respond to our shared vulnerability. This should not be understood as an individualized responsibility. As Janet Delgado (2021) notes in discussing vulnerability theory and patient-centred care in the health professions, "[w]hen highlighting vulnerability as *the* human condition, the Vulnerability Theory focus [is] not on the individual level, but on social responsibility" (p. 158). Moreover, this focus on social responsibility "must not only transcend the specific interests of particular individuals and groups but also have concern for the intergenerational needs of society . . . [it] must be intergenerational and directed to the systems of institutions and relationships developed by a society to maintain general human well-being and flourishing" (Fineman 2019:359–60).

What does vulnerability theory call for in legal institutions? The legal system offers an opportunity to not only respond to particular vulnerabilities, but to attempt to restructure the very "web of economic and institutional relationships" in which we find ourselves (Fineman 2008:10). In so doing, legal tools can respond to vulnerabilities at both the particular and systemic levels. This is a rare institutional capacity, and one that should be more explicitly recognized.

One way in which vulnerability theory should inform changes to the legal system involves reconsidering the values which inhere in our legal system. This could proceed by modifying how the legal system conceives of or deals with the rule of law as an animating value (or set of animating values, if we understand the rule of law to be a bundle of separate values). A full consideration of this suggestion is beyond the scope of this chapter, but the movement from autonomous law to responsive law described by Nonet and Selznick provides a potential pathway. Nonet and Selznick (2001) have suggested that in moving toward responsive law:

> The ideal of legality needs to be conceived more generally and to be cured of formalism . . . [t]o press for a maximum feasible reduction of arbitrariness is to demand a system of law that is capable of reaching beyond formal regularity and procedural fairness to substantive justice.
>
> *(p. 108)*

That is, while the rule of law remains an important set of values, the content of those values is expanded beyond formalism in order to include values of substantive justice. And indeed, this movement from autonomous rule of law norms toward responsive rule of law norms is arguably apparent in some recent caselaw. For example, in *Fraser v. Canada (Attorney-General)*, a majority of the Supreme Court of Canada reaffirmed substantive equality as the "animating norm" of section 15 of Canada's Charter of Rights and Freedoms (2020). The Court held that "[s]ubstantive equality requires attention to the full context of the claimant group's situation, to the actual impact of the law on that situation, and to the persistent systemic disadvantages that have operated to limit the opportunities available to that group's members" (para. 42). In so doing, the Court moved beyond merely formal or procedural analysis to a more perceptive and more contextual analysis.[3]

Efforts to make legal institutions attentive to the insights of vulnerability theory by making them more responsive require changes not only to the substantive content of law, but also to how legal systems operate and, indeed, what we consider to *be* legal institutions.

Vulnerability theory applied to access to justice calls for developing new types of justice institutions that can bolster resilience in the face of legal problems. A starting point might be the understanding, demonstrated by recent empirical access to justice research, that one of the most important access to justice barriers is information insufficiency—believing that a problem cannot be solved but must be borne (Sandefur 2016). Another important insight is that most people do not go to legal institutions for problems that have a legal aspect (Pleasence and Balmer 2019). Building on these insights, a vulnerability-informed response to access to justice problems might lead to the creation of holistic advice institutions as a novel type of social institution. These institutions could help people understand and find their way to resilience-enhancing resources in order to mitigate their particular vulnerability at different points across the life-course. Some of those resources might be legal in nature, such as access to legal information or legal advice, but others would not be. These institutions would provide a locus to assess whether resilience-conferring resources were being appropriately distributed to each person. The focus of these institutions would be on the needs of the person, rather than on the specialization of the system.[4]

In suggesting that these institutions be holistic—effectively relegating legal problems to one among a range of life problems that people experience—I have drawn significantly on vulnerability theory's conception of different resilience assets. Martha Fineman has discussed the different classes of assets that are necessary to countervail against vulnerability. These include physical assets, human assets, social assets, ecological or environmental assets, and existential assets (2016:22). Fineman has suggested that we should consider the different types of "assets or resources that societal organizations and institutions can provide" (p. 22).

Encouragingly, some examples of holistic advice institutions already exist. Most notably, the Citizens Advice organization in the United Kingdom, as well as similarly named organizations in some other countries, provides "confidential advice online, over the phone, and in person, for free" (Citizens Advice n.d.). These organizations, formally operated as a set of networked charities, offer advice and information across a range of topic areas (including legal ones), independent of government (Richards 2001; Kirwan 2016).

Expanding these holistic advice institutions will require careful thought about institutional design to be effective. These might include formal separation between service providers and the government, due to the potential conflict between people claiming state support and the state itself. The strong protection afforded to lawyer-client privilege to ensure that clients are able to be completely forthright with their lawyers might serve as a model for those working in advice institutions. Another functional necessity will be service providers with high levels of relational competence—being able to effectively meet people where they are to understand what resources they need (Kirwan 2016).

Another area in which vulnerability theory could inform changes to legal institutions to improve access to justice is how legal aid functions. While the precise nature of legal aid programs differs among jurisdictions, some common elements appear. Legal aid programs were created throughout the twentieth century, often as elements of welfare state reforms or expansions (Currie 2006; Brooke 2017; Gordon 2019). Legal aid programs provide state funds for lawyers, either employed by legal aid programs or working independently, to represent clients who are unable to retain lawyers. In some jurisdictions, rights to state-funded counsel have been constitutionalized, at least in some circumstances.[5]

But in assessing whether individuals are entitled to legal aid, there are two near certainties. First, personal financial means are a significant part of the analysis. Where it is available at all, legal aid is often provided only to individuals who experience significant levels of poverty (Currie 2006). Second, legal aid generally provides only the services of a lawyer to successful applicants (Gordon 2019). In many cases, these legal services are limited in scope and extent by the terms of legal aid agreements.[6]

What might a legal aid program informed by vulnerability theory look like? Several answers stand out. We might imagine a much more holistic assessment of need based not only on personal finances, but on an evaluation of the asset classes—physical, human, social, ecological, and existential—that Fineman has suggested as a way to understand particularized vulnerability. While this type of assessment would be more complicated than simply assessing financial eligibility, it would offer a more nuanced way to understand the needs of prospective legal aid recipients and to evaluate when legal aid resources are most called for. To demonstrate how this kind of analysis could be done, we might examine the methods of the capability approach studies described in the preceding section to get an idea about how this might function. We might also draw on existing examples of particularized assessments of capacities and needs, such as individualized education plans or personalized pre-sentencing reports (Tremblay and Belley 2017; Hebert 2017).

Further, legal aid resources could be better tailored to the particular needs of each individual seeking assistance. For example, an individual with a well-established social support network might need assistance to defend against a criminal charge, and a legal aid lawyer might be what that person needs. On the other hand, an otherwise similar individual without any social supports might require, in addition to a legal aid lawyer, resources to help cultivate a social support network. In this case, legal aid could provide not only a lawyer, but also connections to local community organizations. This also suggests a more universal role for legal aid. Rather than being seen as an institution for those without economic resources, legal aid could be understood as a universal institution, where the supports provided vary. For someone with sufficient financial assets, a free lawyer may not be what is needed. But a peer support network for those experiencing divorce may be helpful if that person does not have sufficient social assets. Indeed, a broad vision of the holistic advice institution described above could subsume expanded legal aid within it to create a kind of law centre as community nexus. Lawyers and other legal service providers could create relationships and even co-locate with service providers, non-legal professionals, and other community organizations who are well-positioned to help people cultivate resources in different asset classes. While some community-embedded lawyers already do this as a matter of course, and while there are some excellent examples of this type of holistic, law centre as community nexus approach, these should be the norm, not the exception.[7] This has implications for the selection and training of legal service providers, which is discussed in more detail below.

To be clear, improved and new legal institutions are not a panacea for equity problems. Sometimes, people need housing, healthcare, and other resources that can aid resilience, and access to someone to help advocate for those resources is a paltry substitute for the resources themselves. But improved justice institutions provide a means by which people can seek to hold each other and states accountable for those things they require to bolster their resilience.

How might a holistic assessment proceed in practice? In her critique of vulnerability theory, Nina Kohn (2014) writes that "as a practical matter, unless each individual was subject to a personalized vulnerability assessment, a person's level of vulnerability would necessarily have to be determined on his or her group identity" (p. 13). As I mentioned above, there are real world examples of assessment tools that proceed on an individualized basis, rather than on the basis of group identity (Tremblay and Belley 2017). Martha Fineman has described the nature of distinguishing among individuals in a vulnerability analysis in the following way:

> In a vulnerability analysis, the basis for distinguishing some individuals from better positioned but equally vulnerable individuals in the first instance would revolve around questions of access to sufficient resources, with a deficit indicating they lacked the resilience that is necessary to address human vulnerability. Significantly, the initial emphasis here is on the distribution or allocation of resources and the structures within which they are produced. This suggests that the first question to be considered is whether institutional, not individual, functioning is inadequate. This inquiry shifts the focus to state and social responsibility because it recognises that a deficit in resources often reflects an institutional or societal failing more than an individual one.
>
> *(2017:147)*

In the context of holistic legal aid, this vulnerability analysis might be slightly modified. The legal aid providers might first attend to the specific resilience needs of the person seeking legal aid in order to help them proceed. Thinking in a capabilities approach context, the legal aid office would seek to bolster the individual's capabilities so that they could bring forth their legal claim in a way that would seek to address and remedy institutional functioning.

In suggesting that legal aid assessments should be more holistically based, it is true that resources might be expended on the process of holistic evaluation that could otherwise be put to use in directly providing legal aid. But the value of the holistic assessment speaks to the value of the vulnerability approach more generally. In conducting a review of Legal Aid Ontario in 2008, legal scholar Michael Trebilcock commented on the fact that legal aid had come to be increasingly seen as of interest only to impoverished communities, rather than society as a whole. As a result, it became easier for successive governments to limit the funding of legal aid programs, since political support for those programs was limited to discrete communities (2008:74–6). A way to transcend this problem is to argue for, and make arrangements that are attentive to, shared and universal interests. This is one of the hallmarks of vulnerability theory. Accordingly, devoting resources to holistic assessment is not only in keeping with the universal yet particular nature of vulnerability but may also have political benefits by extending legal aid programs beyond a sub-population and keeping those programs attentive and responsive to all.

Vulnerability theory also calls for significant reforms in how legal services are delivered, and the competencies necessary for those who deliver them. Writing in the context of health professions, Janet Delgado has remarked:

> The most important aspect about vulnerability from the perspective of those seeking professional help is the relationship between the healthcare professionals and the patients who are coping with their vulnerability. This relationship is based on interpersonal aspects of care; that is in the ability to perceive the needs and understand the situation of vulnerability of the patient.
>
> *(2021:162)*

This comment is equally apposite for professionals tasked with delivering personal legal services. Yet lawyers rarely receive training in how to cultivate effective relationships of care with their clients. Rather than focusing solely on "thinking like a lawyer," legal education should seek to foster a diverse set of competencies that enable legal service providers to develop relationships with clients that will allow those legal service providers to help understand and respond to clients' particular vulnerabilities. Indeed, infusing legal service providers with an ethic of care should be part of the training of those legal service providers. Delgado has described this as the "relational turn" in professionalism (2021:161). There are some indications that lawyers, judges, and law schools are becoming more attentive to these relational tools; the recent increase in interest in trauma-informed practice skills for lawyers is one example of this trend (Katz and Haldar 2016).

Legal service providers selected for, trained in, and accountable to an ethic of care are more likely to foster resilience by working alongside clients rather than by presuming to dictate the client's best interests. This echoes similar calls for reformulations of lawyer competencies in recent years (Macfarlane 2017).

Finally, vulnerability theory suggests that the legal system must develop better institutional capacity to monitor and assess whether it is responsive to the needs of people. Notwithstanding the unmet legal needs studies discussed above, there are few if any permanent institutional structures that analyze whether and how people are using the legal system to resolve their problems. In describing vulnerability theory and the responsive state, Martha Fineman has described it as a theory "in which the state is theorised as the legitimate governing entity and is tasked with a responsibility to establish and *monitor* social institutions and relationships that facilitate the acquisition of individual and social resilience" (Fineman 2017:134; emphasis added). In the context of the legal system, this monitoring function requires legal institutions to play a role in supervising not only the formal structure of laws and legality but also monitoring how people make use of or avoid legal systems. And in doing so, the focus of the scrutiny should be on ensuring that the legal system plays a positive role in the equitable creation and distribution of resilience-conferring resources.

4. Conclusion

This chapter has explored how vulnerability theory could inform efforts to make legal systems more responsive to universal human vulnerability, and in so doing help to distribute resilience-enhancing resources within society. Recent research on access to justice problems around the world demonstrates that access to justice problems are pervasive and that they are inequitably distributed in society, and it has shown some of the negative effects that these justice problems have on those experiencing them. Although these access to justice problems are significant for the people experiencing them, taken in aggregate they also demonstrate patterns of systemic dysfunction that call for resolution. In thinking about how the significant promise of vulnerability theory should be brought to bear on the legal system and legal institutions, it is helpful to consider points of consonance and similarity between vulnerability theory and some other theoretical approaches that may help to operationalize vulnerability theory in the context of legal systems. This chapter has explored two of those in particular: Philip Selznick and Philippe

Nonet's vision of responsive law, and the capability approach described by Amartya Sen.

Ultimately, I have argued that vulnerability theory's implications for the legal system necessitate changes to the very institutions that we consider to be part of the legal system. These include creating new ways in which the legal system can act in a responsive way in order to augment the resilience resources that people possess. While this requires action at the level of individuals, the legal system is perhaps uniquely placed in that claims can transcend individual interests and concerns and give rise to systemic changes. For this reason, the legal system is well-placed to demonstrate how supporting individuals and collectives can generate systemic responses. Just as vulnerability theory has the paradoxical capacity to encompass the universal and the particular, so too do reforms to our legal institutions carry the promise of being both responsive to particular claims while also presenting a framework that regulates social interactions everywhere. There is much that vulnerability theory can offer to those interested in reforming the legal system to improve access to justice.

Notes

1 For example, searching among all Law & Society Review articles between 1966 and 2021, the term "access to justice" appears in 128 separate articles.
2 Some capability approach theorists, notably Martha Nussbaum, go further than Sen in this regard and have attempted to make the capability approach a theory of justice (Nussbaum 2011).
3 This move was, however, criticized by some of the dissenting judges. See, e.g., paras. 146, 216–27.
4 While I have described these as a "new" type of social institution, there are models around the world that currently offer something like this type of service. Citizens Advice in England and Wales and citizens advice bureaux in some other countries are prime examples (Citizens Advice n.d.).
5 See, e.g., *Gideon v Wainwright,* 372 U.S. 335 (1963) in the United States; *R v Rowbotham* (1988), 25 OAC 321, and *New Brunswick (Minister of Health and Community Services) v G.(J.)* (1999), 3 SCR 46 in Canada.
6 See, e.g., *Single Mothers' Alliance of BC Society* v *British Columbia*, 2019 BCSC 1427 at paras 9–38.
7 For examples of holistic or "team based" approaches, see Bronx Defenders (n.d.) in the United States; and Parents Legal Centres (Legal Aid BC n.d.; Hrymak 2022:29) in Canada.

Reference List

Albiston, Catherine R. and Rebecca L. Sandefur. 2013. "Expanding the Empirical Study of Access to Justice." *Wisconsin Law Review* 2013:101–20.

Bronx Defenders. n.d. "Holistic Defense." Retrieved November 30, 2022 (www.bronxdefenders.org/holistic-defense/).

Brooke, Henry. 2017. *Bach Commission on Access to Justice Appendix 6: The History of Legal Aid: 1945–2010.* London: Fabian Society.

Carlin, Jerome E., Jan Howard, and Sheldon L. Messinger. 1966. "Civil Justice and the Poor: Issues for Sociological Research." *Law & Society Review* 1:9–89.

Citizens Advice. n.d. "Who We Are and What We Do." Retrieved November 30, 2022 (www.citizensadvice.org.uk/about-us/about-us1/introduction-to-the-citizens-advice-service/).

Cooper, Frank Rudy. 2015. "Always Already Suspect: Revising Vulnerability Theory." *North Carolina Law Review* 93:1339–79.

Currie, Ab. 2006. "Down the Wrong Road—Federal Funding for Civil Legal Aid in Canada." *International Journal of the Legal Profession* 13:99–116.

———. 2007. *The Legal Problems of Everyday Life the Nature, Extent and Consequences of Justiciable Problems Experienced by Canadians*. Ottawa: Department of Justice.

Delgado, Janet. 2021. "Vulnerability as a Key Concept in Relational Patient-Centered Professionalism." *Medicine, Health Care and Philosophy* 24:155–72.

Drèze, Jean and Amartya Sen. 2002. *India: Development and Participation*. Oxford: Oxford University Press.

Farrow, Trevor C. W., Ab Currie, Nicole Aylwin, Les Jacobs, David Northrup, and Lisa Moore. 2016. *Everyday Legal Problems and the Cost of Justice in Canada: Overview Report*. Toronto: Canadian Forum on Civil Justice.

Fineman, Martha Albertson. 2008. "The Vulnerable Subject: Anchoring Equality in the Human Condition." *Yale Journal of Law & Feminism* 20:1–23.

———. 2010. "The Vulnerable Subject and the Responsive State." *Emory Law Journal* 60:251–75.

———. 2012. "Elderly as Vulnerable: Rethinking the Nature of Individual and Societal Responsibility." *Elder Law Journal* 20:71–112.

———. 2015. "Vulnerability and the Institution of Marriage." *Emory Law Journal* 64:2089–91.

———. 2016. "Equality, Autonomy, and the Vulnerable Subject in Law and Politics." Pp. 13–27 in *Vulnerability: Reflections on a New Ethical Foundation for Law and Politics*, edited by Martha Albertson Fineman and Anna Grear. New York: Routledge.

———. 2017. "Vulnerability and Inevitable Inequality." *Oslo Law Review* 4:133–49.

———. 2019. "Vulnerability and Social Justice." *Valparaiso University Law Review* 53(2):341–69.

Fineman, Martha Albertson and Anna Grear. 2016. "Introduction: Vulnerability as Heuristic—An Invitation to Future Exploration." Pp. 1–11 in *Vulnerability: Reflections on a New Ethical Foundation for Law and Politics*, edited by M. A. Fineman and A. Grear. New York: Routledge.

Fraser v. Canada (Attorney-General), SCC 28 (2020).

Genn, Hazel. 1999. *Paths to Justice: What People Do and Think About Going to Law*. Oxford: Hart.

Gigler, Björn-Sören. 2015. *Development as Freedom in a Digital Age: Experiences of the Rural Poor in Bolivia*. Washington, DC: World Bank.

Gordon, Robert W. 2019. "Lawyers, the Legal Profession & Access to Justice in the United States: A Brief History." *Daedalus* 148:177–89.

Grear, Anna. 2016. "Vulnerability, Advanced Global Capitalism and Co-Symptomatic Injustice: Locating the Vulnerable Subject." Pp. 41–60 in *Vulnerability: Reflections on a New Ethical Foundation for Law and Politics*, edited by Martha Albertson Fineman and Anna Grear. New York: Routledge.

Hadfield, Gillian K. 2010. "Higher Demand, Lower Supply? A Comparative Assessment of the Legal Resource Landscape for Ordinary Americans." *Fordham Urban Law Journal* 37:129–56.
Hebert, Alexandra. 2017. "Change in Paradigm or Change in Paradox? *Gladue* Report Practices and Access to Justice." *Queen's Law Journal* 43:149–74.
Hrymak, Haley. 2022. *Creating Safety in BC Courts: Key Challenges and Recommendations.* Vancouver: Rise Women's Legal Centre.
Katz, Sarah and Deeya Haldar. 2016. "The Pedagogy of Trauma-Informed Lawyering." *Clinical Law Review* 22:359–93.
Kirwan, Samuel. 2016. "The UK Citizen Advice Service and the Plurality of Actors and Practices That Shape 'Legal Consciousness'." *The Journal of Legal Pluralism and Unofficial Law* 48:461–75.
Kohn, Nina A. 2014. "Vulnerability Theory and the Role of Government." *Yale Journal of Law & Feminism* 26:1–26.
Legal Aid BC. n.d. "Parents Legal Centres." Retrieved November 30, 2022 (https://legalaid.bc.ca/legal_aid/parents-legal-centres).
LSC (Legal Services Corporation). 2022. *The Justice Gap: The Unmet Civil Legal Needs of Low-Income Americans.* Washington, DC: LSC.
Luna, Florencia. 2009. "Elucidating the Concept of Vulnerability: Layers Not Labels." *International Journal of Feminist Approaches to Bioethics* 1:120–38.
MacDowell, Elizabeth L. 2018. "Vulnerability, Access to Justice, and the Fragmented State." *Michigan Journal of Race & Law* 23:51–104.
Macfarlane, Julie. 2017. *The New Lawyer: How Clients Are Transforming the Practice of Law, Second Edition.* Vancouver: UBC Press.
Marvel, Stu. 2015. "The Evolution of Plural Parentage: Applying Vulnerability Theory to Polygamy and Same-Sex Marriage." *Emory Law Journal* 64:2047–88.
McLachlin, Beverley. 2007. "The Challenges We Face." Address delivered at the Empire Club of Canada, Toronto, March 8 (www.scc-csc.ca/judges-juges/spe-dis/bm-2007-03-08-eng.aspx).
Navarro, Vicente. 2000. "Development and Quality of Life: A Critique of Amartya Sen's *Development as Freedom.*" *International Journal of Health Services* 30:661–74.
Nonet, Philippe and Philip Selznick. 2001. *Law and Society in Transition: Toward Responsive Law.* New Brunswick, NJ: Transaction. Originally Published 1978.
Nussbaum, Martha. 2011. *Creating Capabilities: The Human Development Approach.* Cambridge: Harvard University Press.
Pilliar, Andrew. 2022. "Filling the Normative Hole at the Centre of Access to Justice: Toward a Person-Centred Conception." *UBC Law Review* 55:149–202.
Pleasence, Pascoe and Nigel J. Balmer. 2019. "Justice and the Capability to Function in Society." *Daedalus* 148:140–9.
Richards, Jean. 2001. *Inform, Advise and Support.* Cambridge: Lutterworth.
Robeyns, Ingrid. 2005. "The Capability Approach: A Theoretical Survey." *Journal of Human Development* 6:93–117.
Sandefur, Rebecca L. 2016. "What We Know and Need to Know About the Legal Needs of the Public." *South Carolina Law Review* 67:443–60.
———. 2019. "Access to What?" *Daedalus* 148:49–55.
Sarat, Austin. 1981. "Book Review: Access to Justice by Cappelletti and Garth." *Harvard Law Review* 94:1911–24.

Selznick, Philip. 1969. *Law, Society, & Industrial Justice*. New York: Russell Sage.
Sen, Amartya. 1999. *Development as Freedom*. New York: Alfred A. Knopf.
Trebilcock, Michael. 2008. *Report of the Legal Aid Review 2008*. Toronto: Ministry of the Attorney General.
Tremblay, Philippe and Stéphanie Belley. 2017. "Individualized Education Plans in Canada: A Comparative Analysis." *International Journal for Cross-Disciplinary Subjects in Education* 8:3017–24.
Woolf, Harry. 1996. *Access to Justice: Final Report to the Lord Chancellor on the Civil Justice System in England and Wales*. London: H. M. Stationery Office.

PART II

Role of Social Movements in Vulnerability Theory

3

TOWARD A RESPONSIVE LANDSCAPE

The Role of Social Movements in Vulnerability Theory

Kathryn Abrams

Introduction

I am an appreciative consumer of vulnerability theory. I see great value in the project of thinking from our embodied state in a way that centers and normalizes—rather than shields and exceptionalizes—our inescapable vulnerability to the corporeal challenges of youth, disease, aging, and a range of environmental challenges, and our inevitable dependence on other human beings and social institutions (Fineman 2020). I share its urgent call for a "responsive state" that presumes and regulates in the anticipation of this kind of human subject, fostering the resilience of that subject by providing access to resources—physical, human, social, environmental, and existential (Fineman 2010).

Yet I have not situated my recent work within vulnerability theory. This has been largely because of what I have chosen to study: in recent years, my work has focused on the emergence and trajectory of a particular social movement (Abrams 2022). Social movements have been analyzed through a variety of frames from sociology, political science, and, more recently, legal scholarship. Vulnerability theory has also acknowledged the role of social movements as part of the "infrastructure" of the responsive state: a source, as Martha Fineman (2010) has explained, of social resources, along with unions, affinity groups, and political organizations. But social movements have not yet been a primary focus of vulnerability theory; nor have social movement theorists in the law or adjacent disciplines given systematic thought about the light vulnerability theory sheds on social movement activity. In this chapter, I aim to strengthen this dialogue: I ask what viewing social movements through the lens of vulnerability theory might contribute

DOI: 10.4324/9781003323242-6

to scholarship in both domains. Social movements foster the resilience of their participants, all of whom encounter vulnerability, which may be given particular shape or intensity by the specific circumstances they illuminate and protest. Sometimes this cultivation of resilience is a specific goal of social movement activity; in other cases, it is a generative by-product, which is sometimes taken for granted as scholars focus on the legal or political goals of mobilization. Focusing on these resilience-enhancing effects makes clear the connection between social movements and goals of vulnerability theory. Once this link is made, many vital questions emerge: how do social movements relate to the work of the responsive state in buffering vulnerability and fostering resilience? What new questions, or areas for research, might their foregrounding in vulnerability theory suggest?

In this essay, I explore these questions. In Part I, I describe the movement I studied—a movement of undocumented immigrants, mobilizing against state-sponsored hostility and immiseration in the state of Arizona. The work of this movement illustrates how social movements can foster the resilience of their participants, in many of the ways highlighted by vulnerability theory. Given this role, I ask, in Part II, how social movements relate to the responsive state and other institutions that buffer vulnerability and build resilience. In Part III, I ask what new directions and inquiries the exposition of these relations suggests for vulnerability scholars. My primary goal is to foster a conversation between vulnerability and social movement scholars about the role of this kind of collectivity in fostering resilience and forming a more responsive *landscape* in and around a responsive state.

I. Learning From Social Movements: Cultivating Resilience in Arizona

The term "social movement" encompasses many forms of collective action, and has been defined variously by social movement theorists and activists themselves (Snow et al. 2019; Diani 1992). My own use of the term in this section draws on a number of elements common among these definitions. In what follows, the term "social movement" refers to the coalescence and sustained collective action of a group of people with a shared grievance; this collective action is aimed at making that grievance visible, identifying its source(s) (often though not always a form of state action or inaction) and resisting or proposing action to address that grievance, through appeals to the public, institutional, or governmental actors. Movements may work through the activity of dedicated organizations, or may function through looser or more transient collaborative structures. Most perform some combination of functions such as soliciting participation, motivating, informing, preparing, and coordinating the activities of participants, and establishing networks that can be used to inform the public. They are not state-created entities but neither are they untouched by state regulation, as I will explain below.

I studied a particular movement: a movement of immigrants—increasingly led by undocumented people—that emerged in response to state and local hostility in Arizona (Abrams 2022). Arizona had implemented a policy of "attrition through enforcement," a series of laws withdrawing state benefits and imposing law enforcement surveillance that aimed to make undocumented residents so miserable that they would return to their countries of origin. This effort culminated in the state's notorious statute SB 1070, which criminalized undocumented presence and employment, imposed penalties on citizens for transporting or harboring undocumented immigrants, and authorized any state law enforcement official, in the course of any legal stop, to ask for the papers of any person they had a "reasonable suspicion" might be undocumented.[1] In the state capital, Phoenix, these legislative edicts were enforced with particular severity by Sherriff Joe Arpaio, who exercised his power by conducting workplace raids and neighborhood saturation patrols, in which anyone who could not produce papers could be subject to detention and possible deportation. The undocumented community struggled under curtailment of employment and loss of in-state tuition for college-bound undocumented youth; undocumented residents were terrorized by the raids in their workplaces and patrols in their neighborhoods. Many observers judged the prospects for resistance to be dim because the visibility entailed by acts of protest could trigger already intensified, state-assisted immigration enforcement. Thousands of undocumented immigrants, in fact, left the state.

Yet over a period of several years a social movement began to coalesce and mobilize against these oppressive measures (Abrams 2022). At first, lacking dedicated immigrant rights organizations, this emerging effort relied on the leadership of former Chicano activists and co-ethnic allies in churches, labor unions, and Latino cultural centers. It utilized neighborhood and other word-of-mouth networks and garnered publicity for its events from Spanish language media. Constellations of immigrants and allies mounted initial tactics of resistance—such as a hotline, a copwatch operation, and practices of neighborhood self-defense—that not only pushed back on intrusive surveillance but built solidarity and capacity in immigrant communities.

After the passage of SB 1070 brought an influx of funding and infrastructural assistance from supporters outside Arizona, organizations dedicated to immigrant rights and to supporting the voice and leadership of undocumented people began to form. These organizations—some of which were themselves founded or led by undocumented people—ranged from the informal and community-based to the more professionalized; some did and some did not draw on training and mentorship national immigrant-led organizations. These social movement organizations utilized several specific practices to support the political confidence of undocumented participants (Abrams 2022), a group that faced distinctive barriers to activism given their wariness of public visibility and their uncertainty—amplified by state hostility—about whether people lacking legal status could be effective and legitimate political claims-makers.

Organizers used the practice of experiential storytelling to change the minds of the public and decisionmakers, and to persuade each prospective participant that they had a vital resource they could share (Abrams 2022). The distinctiveness of experiential storytelling as a political asset spoke to the legitimacy and the potential efficacy of their participation; its unique benefits also gave them a motivation for overcoming fears of public visibility. Storytelling, honed as a practice of introduction and mutual support within organizations, became a means by which undocumented activists could engage the public at meetings, rallies, and legislative proceedings.

Organizers also utilized tactics of "performative citizenship": they assigned undocumented people roles of public responsibility that were conventionally performed by citizens (Abrams 2022). For example, undocumented youth served in large numbers to canvas neighborhoods, register prospective voters, and turn out those registered to vote. This practice utilized resources that youth already possessed—they could share their stories on the doorstep of prospective voters to motivate participation—but it also fostered in participants new forms of knowledge (about the ballot issues, the structure of local government, or the dynamics of electoral accountability) and new skills (face-to-face persuasion, data entry, working on teams) that would serve them in their continued activism. Moreover, their growing understanding of local electoral politics and their sense that their committed service in roles historically reserved for the most committed citizens helped to establish them both internally and externally as legitimate political participants. And as they engaged with voters in their neighborhoods, they also began to feel a greater sense of social membership—shared experience, investment, and goals—in the communities they canvassed. As undocumented activists gained political confidence through activities that utilized strengths and built capacity within political institutions, they were also emboldened to engage in more resistant or contentious political action: protesting state hostility or federal inaction through direct action and civil disobedience (Abrams 2022).

A vital resource in all of these efforts was the emotional experience of solidarity with other participants (Abrams 2022). By observing and engaging with others who faced similar challenges, new participants learned what immigrants were capable of—and that they might therefore be capable of—even without legal status. As they worked and mobilized together, they experienced an energy and a force that exceeded the sum of their individual efforts. And they came to believe, as they frequently witnessed in practice, that the support of the collectivity could keep them safe when they engaged in what they might otherwise view as risky public action. Not only were enforcement efforts more likely to target anonymous individuals than those who were part of an active visible community; collective action was often successful in securing the release of those placed in immigrant detention—for civil disobedience, working without papers, or other reasons. The combination of these practices built a robust movement capable of voice, resistance, and strategic response to changes in government policies (Abrams 2022).

Many analyses—including my own—have focused on the contributions that this and other immigrant social movements have made in garnering public support for DACA or other programs for undocumented youth; fighting detention and deportation; and growing diversifying state electorates by registering Latino voters. But if we step outside the immediate frame of political engagement, we can see that the movement I studied also provided—and many social movements provide—vital resources for cultivating the personal and political resilience of participants. Within a short span of years, a group of people beset by state hostility and uncertain about their own capacity for resistance emerged as confident, knowledgeable, and effective political claims-makers. The next question is how to distinguish and amplify these effects within the framework of vulnerability theory.

II. Social Movements and Vulnerability Theory: Three Questions

A. *Do Social Movements Help to Meet Human Vulnerability?*

I begin from the insight, drawn from vulnerability theory, that "the counterpoint to vulnerability . . . is resilience" (Fineman 2010:269), understood as "capabilities, skills, resources, support, a sense of belonging, emotional strength and so on [that] is "gained over the life course, within [] social institutions and relationships" (Fineman 2020:28). The value of the responsive state, and the infrastructure of social institutions that it superintends, is that it provides resources for resilience that buffer or ameliorate vulnerability, making human beings within its purview better able to sustain the inevitable effects of youth, illness, disability, or aging, and more agile in adapting to external shocks or changes. The resources provided by a responsive state and surrounding institutions comprehend such categories as the material, social, human, environmental, and existential (Fineman 2010). Social movements are very much a part of this landscape: we can look at social movements in terms of their specific political objectives: that is, as responding to the group-specific injuries of their members, and fostering among those members political confidence, agency, and efficacy. But if we step outside the immediate frame of political engagement, we can see that the movement I studied provided—and many social movements provide—the very kinds of resources for resilience that vulnerability theory describes. The immigrant activists I studied have utilized these resources in their lives in ways that extend beyond political activity, to the navigation of challenges created by inevitable bodily dependence over the human life course.

The most obvious contribution of the movement was the *social* resources it generated. Organizations serving undocumented immigrants helped them to understand and feel that they were part of a community, and that they could draw strength, emotional support, and even material resources from others, when they faced challenges. These lessons had particular value to undocumented people because their fear of visibility had often caused them to live in isolation from others, even within their own communities. But social movement activity assisted participants not simply in their lives as undocumented people, but as human beings more generally. Their strong connection to others, and their experience of interdependence and solidarity as a source of strength, helped participants to feel less alone and more willing to draw on collective resources as they navigated the inevitable ups and downs of embodied existence—much as individuals might rely on members of their family.[2] These social resources strengthened participants as they faced fear, illness, and economic hardship during the pandemic. They turned to community-based and online networks for moral support, and used organizational structures to create food banks and disseminate information about vaccines.[3] Families who found themselves without their primary wage-earners through illness or layoffs utilized some of the same online vehicles for garnering community support—and even raising funds—that they had used to help those facing the detention of family members.

The movement also bolstered the human resources, or human capital, of its participants. In the first instance, this meant that they could be effective as activists: they developed the confidence that they could contribute as political claims-makers, though their lack of citizenship made them atypical participants and deprived them of the formal ties to elected representatives on which many social movements rely. But this same human capital bolstered their confidence, made them capable problem solvers, and increased their ability to collaborate with others, all skills that—as many activists told me—served them in other facets of their lives. These skills served them in their employment (where some cited clearer direction and greater leadership), in their education (where they made more set goals and made more autonomous decisions), and in managing family responsibilities,[4] including the provision of care of dependent others. Youth became better able to guide and motivate siblings. Parents who had been engaged in social movement activity became more involved in their children's schools and more effective advocates on their children's behalf (Terriquez 2011).

Over time the generativity of social and human resources fostered by this movement enabled it to provide material physical resources as well. This was true not only in terms of formal fundraising or innovative, community-based uses of platforms such as GoFundMe, but in terms of islands of community-based infrastructure that were inspired or instigated by the movement. Community health clinics—that handled minor injuries and performed diabetes and blood pressure screening—emerged from the collaboration between movements and allies such as medics. Community gardens became a vehicle for fostering solidarity and providing fresh produce to areas without ample grocery access. Food banks, which became a staple of some undocumented organizations during the pandemic, supplemented this provision of nutritional needs.

In addition, the movement provided existential resources. Mobilizing to right wrongs done to immigrants and discovering a deep sense of community not only provided the meaning necessary to turn people wary of visibility toward public action. It also gave participants a broader sense of meaning and value in their lives, which enabled them to withstand ongoing material hardship, bodily illness and susceptibility, and the loss of loved ones—whether to aging and death or to detention and deportation.[5]

Though in one sense the resilience fostered by these forms of social movement resources could be described as political—it enables participants to function as confident political claimants who can respond to the vicissitudes of their legal and political environment—my research suggests that this resilience also serves immigrants in responding to vulnerabilities created by embodiment throughout the life cycle, and to the effects of external forces—pandemics, natural disasters, economic downturns—on their embodied existence.

None of this analysis demonstrates that social movements will be—in any given case—a buffer to human vulnerability, or will provide resources for resilience. But it suggests that they have the *potential* to do so and, as such, deserve the closer attention of vulnerability theorists.

This potential leads to a further inquiry. The capacity of social movements to support the resilience of their members—even as they advocate for those members through their engagement with the decisionmakers and with members of the public—suggests that they fit squarely within Vulnerability theory. They perform a function that is vital to respond to the human susceptibility rooted in the body. But this then raises the question of their relationship to the more familiar engines of resilience in vulnerability theory, most notably the responsive state. The relationship of social movements to the state can affect their ability to foster, and the means through which they foster, resilience; their activity can shape the state's ability to support resilience as well. The following section will investigate the relationship between social movements and the responsive state—or more accurately, the relation between them as part of a larger, responsive landscape of state and non-state institutions.

III. How Does the Work of Social Movements Relate to the Activity of the Responsive State?

Vulnerability theory begins from a notion of human vulnerability, rooted in the susceptibilities of the body; and from there, it asks how the state might be reconceptualized in a way that incorporates this notion of the subject, and functions to meet and buffer that vulnerability with resources for resilience (Fineman 2010). In more recent vulnerability scholarship, the notion of the responsive state not only encompasses government at the highest levels of law-making or programmatic initiation. It includes a variety of "infrastructural" social institutions, which include the family, systems providing education or health care, and market institutions such as corporations or other employers, which have regulatory relations with the state. The state brings many of these institutions into being; it can also dissolve them. Such institutions operate within regulatory frameworks created through law. These frameworks serve to transfer resources for resilience from the state to the social institution (as when Congress creates an agency responsible for administering certain kinds of benefit); they may to protect the cultivation of resilience that occurs within these institutions from internal disruption or external threat. Understanding the role of social movements in vulnerability theory means not only understanding their relation to the responsive state, but understanding the ways in which they may function similarly to—or differently from—these other institutions, on a terrain vulnerability theorists seek to direct toward greater responsiveness. I will focus on three attributes, which shape the relations of social movements to the responsive state. These attributes, of course, vary among social movements; the *genus* itself is broad and heterogeneous. But my hypothesis, which will be tested as more specific studies of social movements in vulnerability theory unfold, is that these attributes may be more pronounced, as a general matter, for social movements than for many other institutions within the responsive landscape. I will ask what the qualities mean for the way social movements interact with the state, and support resilience, and how exploring these features might suggest new directions for vulnerability theory.

The first, which concerns legal relations with the state, is the nature of the regulatory framework within which social movements operate. There is reason to expect that that this framework is less dispositive of the life course of social movements, and less dense, as compared with many of the infrastructural institutions thus far examined within vulnerability theory. The second, which concerns political relations with the state, is the oppositional posture of many social movements toward state actors and institutions. The third concerns relations within social movements themselves: they are characterized not by the "inescapable and appropriate inequality" that characterizes relations between parents and children, doctors and patients, and teachers and students, but rather by relations of mutuality and solidarity. To the extent these features may distinguish social movements from more familiar infrastructural institutions, they may also shape different kinds of relations to the responsive state.

A. Density and Effects of Regulatory Frameworks

In vulnerability theory, the notion of the responsive state encompasses a variety of "infrastructural" social institutions, which include the family, systems providing education or health care, and market institutions such as corporations or other employers, which have regulatory relations with the state. Regulatory frameworks give shape and content to those relations, and they may affect the capacity of infrastructural institutions to foster resilience among the human beings they serve.

Legal enactments, the operation of legal processes, or the fulfillment of legal conditions bring many of these institutions into being: families assume legal form through marriage or adoption; school systems are constituted by law; governmental agencies are created to address particular tasks or social needs. State action can also transform or terminate such institutions. Infrastructural entities also function, on an ongoing basis, within the regulatory frameworks created by law. These frameworks shape the ability of such institutions to perform their appointed tasks: schools to develop curricula, or corporations to produce their products or services, or respond to the interests of their stakeholders. These regulatory frameworks may also be part of the way that infrastructural institutions address vulnerability: they affect the transfer of resources for resilience from the state to the social institution (as when Congress creates an agency responsible for administering certain kinds of benefits, or funds certain resilience-enhancing programs). Such frameworks, Fineman has argued, might also be used to protect the cultivation of resilience that occurs within these institutions from external disruption or threat (Fineman 2020).

Like these social institutions, social movements are also touched by state structures of regulation. This is particularly true of social movements that function through dedicated organizations. Those that wish to provide to prospective contributors the tax benefits of a non-profit form must comply with the constraints on their behavior (for example, non-partisanship in relation to elections) imposed by the federal tax code. Those who wish to employ paid staffers as well as volunteers must abide by strictures of employment law. Even the many social movements that function through loose or informal structures, or do not seek 501(c)(3) status, must navigate between trespass and traffic regulations, on the one hand, and constitutional protections that enable them to rally, demonstrate, or voice grievances to government officials, on the other. The state also holds a monopoly of force, and a control over other sanctions that can shape the choices of social movement actors. The movement that I studied constantly weighed the risk that arrest, for participants who revealed their undocumented status or participated in civil disobedience or other disruptions, could render participants subject to detention or deportation.

But the regulatory frameworks through which the state touches social movements are in many cases less foundational or less dense for social movements than is the case for some other "infrastructural" institutions. Although social movement emergence may be sparked or facilitated by legal action (Almeida 2019; Meyer 2004), under US law, the state does not formally bring social movements into being, as it does marriages or corporations. And while state cooptation or repression may hasten the decline of social movements (Bloemraad and Voss 2020), the state does not formally dissolve them. Social movements may consider generally applicable state laws and sanctions as they weigh their tactical options; but legal frameworks do not set goals or standards; oversight by or accountability to government entitles by social movements is the exception rather than the rule.[6]

For social movements, the law (and the state behind it) is less an originary force, or a framework that directs or structures daily operations, than a target of intentional action. Although some social movements seek to foster a sense of identity or reshape cultural understandings, many specifically aim to change the law or other features of state policy. They address a failure of legal action, or legal action they see as prejudicial or unjust. This points to a second way in which social movements diverge from some other institutions Fineman identifies as "infrastructural."

Oppositional Stance

Social movements view themselves, to varying degrees, as "outsiders" to power; they often approach the state from a posture of grievance or critique. Their goal is to produce change—sometimes transformative change—in the way that the state and its instrumentalities function. This stance is often expressed through tactics as well as strategy. The most dramatic, publicly visible mobilizations of social movements—large protests, direct action events, or instances of civil disobedience—take place outside of state institutions, albeit sometimes with the goal of influencing what happens within them.[7]

This oppositional role separates social movements in some respects from the state and its agencies, grantees, and policymakers. Social movement participants rarely perceive themselves as part of the state's structure—whatever the impingement of laws on their practical decision-making—though participants may have a sense of affiliation with the polity, or certain of its traditions, or see state actors as accountable to them (Abrams 2022). This last perception by social movement participants—of state accountability to oppositional demands—illustrates a means by which oppositional action can be connected to greater state responsiveness. Oppositional positioning, and the substantive commitments that underlie it, can incite state responsiveness not simply to the immediate goals of the organization, but to human vulnerability more generally. One of the most interesting campaigns I observed during my time in Arizona was the 2016 campaign for Proposition 206, in which an immigrant rights organization, Living United for Change in Arizona (LUCHA), led a successful statewide effort to pass an initiative that provided for an increase in the minimum wage and sick leave for Arizona workers (Abrams 2022). This initiative undoubtedly provided material support to undocumented workers, substantial numbers of whom worked at minimum wage jobs, by providing a higher minimum wage and sick leave which had not been available before. But by advocating for Prop 206's benefits, LUCHA broadly demanded that the state account for human vulnerability—in this case, the need for adequate material support and care when facing illness– of all Arizona workers and their families.

Solidaristic Relations

One final respect in which social movements may be distinct from other institutions on the responsive landscape is the kinds of relationships they cultivate among members. Infrastructural social institutions, as Fineman explains, are built around specific social relationships—such as parent/child, teacher/student, doctor/patient, or employer/employee. These relationships are characteristically relationships of "inescapable and appropriate inequality" (Fineman 2020:31). The institutions within which they operate may foster the resilience of the less powerful partners by recognizing responsibilities on the part of the more powerful partners (although they may also function in ways that undermine this goal). Social institutions must also be alert to the circumstances of the more powerful partners because these parties too can become vulnerable—indeed the social institutions themselves can become vulnerable—through the care they provide to the less powerful party. Legal frameworks, articulated by the state at the inception of such institutions, or imposed as the state seeks to advance particular goals, may serve to define the relationship between the specific partners—parent and child, or employer and employee—and what constitutes justice between them. The state may also respond, through legislation or through the courts, to institutions' own efforts to define these relationships.

Although some social movements may be characterized by a hierarchical relation between participants and a charismatic leader, and most involve (transient) forms of hierarchy, as new participants are socialized by more experienced organizers to their movement roles, they are not primarily structured around relationships of "inescapable and appropriate inequality," as for example between parent and child, or teacher and student. Rather, they generate resources for resilience quite specifically, through relations of solidarity. Participants' shared experience and goals—including, in some cases, their shared opposition to the state—unite them as equals and commit them to mutual support. Immigrants in the movement that I observed gained strength by recognizing that there were others who shared their experience, on whose steps toward resistance they could model their own activism, and who would fight to protect them (for example, from detention and deportation) in their contentious encounters with the state (Abrams 2022). Through experiences of solidarity they gained the capacity to respond to personal susceptibilities, and external challenges. This is a different engine of resilience, with its own distinctive susceptibilities: to hierarchies that might unsettle the sense of mutuality or solidarity, through subtle shifts in the dynamic of leadership or forms of self-serving or corruption; to external pressures that constrain the ability of participants to protect and support each other. These risks might occasion a different kind of intervention or support from a responsive state.

IV. Directions for Vulnerability Theory

These elements may distinguish social movements from other "infrastructural" institutions, or they may suggest a spectrum of relations between other entities that provide resources for resilience and the responsive state: these relations may be different, for example, for families than for corporations; and different for public schools than for health care organizations. But they raise a final question worth considering: what new insights or inquiries might we foster by observing and analyzing these features of social movements, or this part of the spectrum of institutions that offer support for resilience?

First, institutions whose relations to the state are more oppositional, or less the relation of a part to the whole, may help move the state itself toward greater responsiveness. This is an argument that Risa Lieberwitz has made about unions—which may themselves be viewed as a kind of social movement. They may rely on resources from the state, including the promulgation of particular legal rules, to support the resilience of their members; but they also press state actors toward broader policies that serve the goals of responsiveness. This same role can sometimes be played to a greater or lesser degree, by entities from school systems to corporations that center their efforts on advocacy that urges the state toward greater supports for human resilience.

This dynamic of oppositional pressure can help scholars to understand more about how states become more responsive. Much attention within vulnerability theory has been devoted to the content of responsive state policy, or the ways that a responsive state forms and supports those infrastructural institutions that surround it. But more attention could be devoted to those processes through which a state comes to embrace more responsive policies. Analysis of social movement campaigns can help to illuminate these processes. Though not all social movements advocate for policies that buffer vulnerability, those movements that support such policies—like the work of LUCHA in support of Arizona's Prop 206—can illustrate the processes of persuasion, and the assertions of power, through other entities may press a state to embrace more responsive policies.

Second, institutions that are based on relations of mutuality may experience distinct kinds of vulnerabilities, and the state may need to work with them in different ways to address these vulnerabilities. With respect to institutions based "inescapable and appropriate inequality," Fineman has observed that states do not always address such necessarily unequal relationships in a way that conduces to justice between the paired parties. In the context of some infrastructural institutions, she argues, extant liberal legal frameworks have failed to foster the resilience of the less powerful partner but have left such partners to fend for themselves, by presuming a fiction of equality. Examples include the structuring of the employment relation around an individualist, egalitarian fiction of contract, and the doctor/patient relationship around a related fiction of informed consent (Fineman 2020).[8] In Fineman's view, the role of a responsive state is not to perpetuate such fictions, but to center the inequality in such relationships and investigate "how justice can be achieved—and the vulnerability of all parties addressed—across these unequal relationships" (Fineman 2020:20). This requires the state to be attentive to "the rules and practices governing relationships of inevitable inequality" (Fineman 2020:32), a focus that includes both rules operating inside the social institution and rules imposed by the state that bear on these institutional pairings.[9] A responsive state can also achieve justice in relation to inescapably unequal relationships through a more forward-looking, pro-active role: it could involve itself in "questions of institutional design so that the inequality within social relationships is handled justly within these institutions" (Fineman 2020:21).

How the state could support, or fail to support, an institution whose relations are constituted by mutuality or solidarity, is a distinct and largely unexplored question. Perhaps the role of the responsive state in this context would be less concerned with questions of institutional design. Perhaps it would be less pro-active than protective, guarding the social movement against interventions—from the unintended effects of legal rules to the pointed hostility of legal or other actors[10]—that might disrupt or attenuate this solidarity and the resilience it fuels. Or perhaps the state might nurture that solidarity itself, through regulation that protects organizations against corruption or impositions of hierarchical leadership that threaten mutuality. These possibilities might productively be explored by vulnerability scholars.

Finally, focusing on the role of social movements in fostering resilience among vulnerable subjects may shift the conceptualization or metaphors that we use to think about the relations between the state and other potentially responsive institutions. Fineman's metaphor of the *infrastructure of the responsive state* captures aptly the centrality of the state to many forms of human flourishing, the distinctive powers that it holds, the importance of the transformation required to align it with a vision of a vulnerable human subject. But the language of a *responsive landscape* may more accurately evoke the range of institutions—with variable attributes, characteristic strengths and vulnerabilities—that serve to foster human resilience.

Notes

1 Support Our Law Enforcement and Safe Neighborhoods Act of 2010, S 1070.
2 "Family" was sometimes metaphor used by immigrant groups in Arizona to describe the close and interdependent relationships among participants.
3 As I continued to follow the electronic platforms (websites, Facebook pages, Twitter accounts) used by Phoenix immigrant rights organizations with which I'd worked throughout the pandemic, I saw these platforms used to generate community awareness about the distribution of vaccines, or to announce the work of foodbanks.
4 While not a central finding of my research—which was focused on political action—these broader effects were a recurrent theme in the interviews I conducted with undocumented activists, primarily between 2012 and 2017.
5 There was one particularly painful episode during my research when a promising and highly engaged young activist was killed in a motorcycle accident. From the scores of activists who attended his funeral, to the repeated use of the phrase "rest in power" to pay tribute to his life, movement participants not only provided his grieving family with social support, but reminded them that his life had meaning and value in part because of the political struggles in which he had engaged.
6 Perhaps for this reason, social movements in the US are more often considered to be part of "civil society," that is, "voluntary organizations of citizens and other residents that aim to articulate common interests, inform the public, or advocate changes in policy" (Ingram 2020), rather than a part of the state. But my understanding is that Fineman uses the term "infrastructure" (of the responsive state) in a more encompassing way.
7 Jane Mansbridge (2001) describes the consciousness that underlies and animates these features of social movements
8 Fineman (2020) observes that the law conventionally treats children as dependent and not of equal capacity, but this is treated as a departure from the usual presumption of equality in social relationships.
9 Hila Keren (2021) gives an example of how this role might work in the employment context. She argues that employers' insistence on mandatory arbitration clauses drains, rather than fosters, the resilience of employees, by preventing them from challenging unfair employment practices in courts of law, and, more importantly, by preventing them from coming together through class actions to do so. The deprivation of both the opportunity to seek recourse, and the support and solidarity of others in doing so, drains resilience from workers, making them feel helpless and isolated, and creates excess resilience in employers, whose hand is strengthened by the inaccessibility of vehicles for complaint. She observes that the

state role has thus far been limited to judicial action validating the use of arbitration clauses. See Keren (2020). But she argues that it should be directed instead to supporting the resilience of comparatively disempowered employees by enabling access to collective proceedings. See Keren, Resilience Drainage, supra.

10 During the period of my research in Arizona, the federal government sometimes litigated on behalf of undocumented immigrants, and occasionally on behalf of undocumented immigrant organizations, in the face of hostility by Arizona's state government or local law enforcement. Although in some cases it was more concerned with protecting federal plenary power over immigration, see e.g., Arizona v. United States, 567 U.S. 387 (2012) (holding that several provisions of Arizona's anti-immigrant law SB 1070 amounted to an independent state immigration policy in violation of federal plenary power over immigration), in other cases federal court holdings suggested a more direct concern with protecting the well-being of immigrants within those organizations, see e.g., Arizona Dream Act Coalition v. Brewer, 757 F.3d 1053 (9th Cir. 2014) (striking executive order by which the governor denied drivers' licenses to DACA recipients).

Reference List

Abrams, Kathryn. 2022. *Open Hand, Closed Fist: Practices of Undocumented Organizing in a Hostile State*. Berkeley, CA: University of California Press.

Almeida, Paul. 2019. "The Role of Threat in Collective Action." Pp. 43–62 in *The Wiley-Blackwell Companion to Social Movements*, 2nd ed., edited by David Snow, Sarah Soule, Hanspieter Kriesi, and Holly McCammon. Oxford: John Wiley & Sons.

Arizona v. United States, 567 U.S. 387 (2012).

Arizona Dream Act Coalition v. Brewer, 757 F.3d 1053 (9th Cir. 2014).

Bloemraad, Irene and Kim Voss. 2020. "Movement or Moment? Lessons from the Pro-Immigrant Movement in the United States and Contemporary Challenges." *Journal of Ethnic and Migration Studies* 46(4):683–704.

Diani, Mario. 1992. "The Concept of Social Movement." *The Sociological Review* 40(1):1–25.

Fineman, Martha Albertson. 2010. "The Vulnerable Subject and the Responsive State." *Emory Law Journal* 60:251–75.

———. 2020. "Reasoning from the Body: Universal Vulnerability and Social Justice." Pp. 17–34 in *A Jurisprudence of the Body*, edited by Chris Dietz, Mitchell Travis, and Michael Thomson. London: Palgrave Macmillan.

George Ingram. 2020. "Civil Society: An Essential Ingredient of Development." *Brookings Institution*, April 6 (www.brookings.edu/blog/up-front/2020/04/06/civil-society-an-essential-ingredient-of-development/).

Keren, Hila. 2020. "Divided & Conquered: The Neoliberal Roots and Emotional Consequences of the Arbitration Revolution." *Florida Law Review* 72(3):575–638.

———. 2021. "Resilience Draining and the Role of Private Law." In *Vulnerability Theory Symposium*, September 13. Law and Political Economy Project (https://lpeproject.org/blog/beyond-neoliberalism-allocating-resilience-through-corporate-law).

Mansbridge, Jane. 2001. "The Making of Oppositional Consciousness." In *Oppositional Consciousness: The Subjective Roots of Social Protest*, edited by J. Mansbridge and A. Morris. Chicago: The University of Chicago Press.

Meyer, David. 2004. "Protest and Political Opportunities." *Annual Review of Sociology* 30:125–45.

Snow, David, Sarah Soule, Hanspieter Kriesi, and Holly McCammon. 2019. "Introduction Mapping and Opening Up the Terrain." Pp. 1–16 in *The Wiley-Blackwell Companion to Social Movements*, 2nd ed., edited by D. Snow, S. Soule, H. Kriesi, and H. McCammon. Oxford: John Wiley & Sons.

Support Our Law Enforcement and Safe Neighborhoods Act of 2010, S. 1070 (SB 1070). 49th Leg., 2d Reg. Sess. (Ariz. 2010).

Terriquez, Veronica. 2011. "Schools for Democracy: Labor Union Participation and Latino Immigrant Parents' School-Based Civic Engagement." *American Sociological Review* 76(4):581–601.

4

LAW, PUBLIC POLICY, AND SOCIAL MOVEMENTS TO SUPPORT AND STRENGTHEN INDIVIDUAL AND COLLECTIVE INTERESTS OF LABOR

Risa L. Lieberwitz

I. Introduction

Vulnerability theory stresses the role of the State to respond to universal human needs and to create a political, economic, and social institutional infrastructure to ensure that all members of the society have adequate resources to meet universal individual and social needs. This includes health, safety, sustenance, shelter, education, and fulfilling, well paid work, which are essential to the ability of individuals to have a good life and are foundational to creating a democratic society.

This chapter analyzes the obligations of the responsive State regarding the employment relationship, addressing the following questions: what is the nature of universal human needs in the context of the employment relationship? What is the nature of the State's obligation to respond to those needs in ways that address the individual and collective interests of workers? How does this State responsibility advance the public interest in expanding and deepening democracy in all political and economic institutions? The chapter will focus most closely on the State's responsibility to respond to individual universal needs and to support social movements that strengthen the individual and collective interests of workers in private sector employment.

I. The Role of the State to Provide for the Public Welfare

A. The Vision of the Responsive State

To fulfill its responsibility to respond to universal human needs, the State has an obligation to use its power to create and support institutions that

DOI: 10.4324/9781003323242-7

provide resources for addressing needs for material and social well-being, such as health care, food, housing, employment, and child care. But what are the necessary conditions for creating a responsive State? To begin, the vision of the good society must have at its core the interrelated nature and interdependence of individual and collective well-being. As individuals, we each have basic needs that include sustenance, shelter, safety, health care, education, and self-expression. As social beings, we each have basic needs to engage in meaningful relationships with family, friends, schoolmates, co-workers, and as members of organizations. The responsive State will create a political and economic institutional infrastructure to ensure that all members of the society have sufficient resources to meet these universal individual and social needs.

The role of the collective—through actions and activism of organizations—is integral to both supporting the creation of a responsive State and pressuring the State to fulfill its responsibilities. Social movements for economic, political, and social justice are made up of organizations that build grassroots pressure on the State to respond to human needs for material and social well-being. Thus, there is a reciprocity between the State and social movements. The State can rely on them to strengthen collective demands for social justice, which the State can then respond to in carrying out its obligation to meet universal human needs. This relationship between the responsive State and social movements is also integral to the democratic process, as the legal infrastructure must ensure that such organizations are able to participate effectively in the political process.

When it comes to the workplace, there is a reciprocity between the responsive State and the labor movement to provide for individual and collective needs. A strong labor movement is essential for advancing the collective interests of labor and the public interest to build a democratic society. Labor unions can pressure the State to pass laws, such as legislation for a living wage, paid leave, and retirement benefits, which improve material conditions for workers. Labor unions also bring democracy to the workplace through collective action, including collective bargaining, which makes progress toward greater equality in distribution of power and wealth in the economy. The laws of the responsive State, therefore, must create and enforce positive rights of employees to form and join labor unions and the ability of unions to carry out their role in bringing democracy to the workplace.

B. The Reality of the Unresponsive State in the U.S.

The vision of a responsive State is far from the reality of the U.S, where the contradictions of liberalism and neoliberalism have shaped the role of the State vis-à-vis universal human needs and social and economic relationships.

The contradictions of liberalism and neoliberalism are structural and systemic, as democratic political institutions co-exist with and serve the interests of capitalist economic institutions (Lieberwitz 2022:322–5). Although liberal and neoliberal ideology asserts that the State should play a limited role in the economic system, in reality, the State's network of interlocking and mutually supporting laws and public institutions creates and maintains this domination of capitalist interests (Lieberwitz 2022). Some state actions directly subsidize business; others are indirect subsidies such as tax laws and exemptions from regulations. At the same time, the ideology of limited State intervention in market forces is used to justify the lack of public benefits for individuals and the lack of State regulation of business to protect workers and the public welfare. Instead, the role of government is defined as intermittent and partial, whether in the form of financial assistance to individuals or regulation of business practices. Thus, liberal ideology functions as a cover to hide the reality of an active State that provides political and financial resources and support to capitalists, which enables them to expand and maintain their power and wealth. The same ideology is used to justify the State's limited provision of public goods to individuals and weak support of labor unions and other social justice organizations. These contradictions, if left unchallenged and unchanged, will never result in a State that is responsive to the needs of the working class. Nor will the society be one that can be called democratic, as the State will ultimately respond to the interests of capital rather than supporting the ability of individuals, social institutions, and organizations, like unions, to fully participate in a democracy.

The social and economic inequalities in the U.S. reveal the results of liberal structures, institutions, and policies, which have been worsened by neoliberal policies of deregulation and privatization initiated by the Reagan administration in the 1980s. In 2010, the top 10 percent in the U.S. controlled 77 percent of all wealth, leaving the bottom 90 percent with only 23 percent (Mishel et al. 2012:376). This inequality has been maintained, with the top 10 percent in the U.S. in 2022 controlling 68 percent of all wealth, and the lowest 50 percent of earners owning only 3.2 percent of the total wealth (Statista Research Department, November 1 2022). From June 2009 through September 2021, average hourly earnings for private sector production and nonsupervisory employees increased 40.3 percent, while after-tax corporate profits increased 133.7 percent (Keating 2022). There is an inverse relationship between the unionization rate and the inequality wealth gap in the U.S. As union density in the private sector has declined, falling to 7 percent in 2021 (Shierholz et al. 2022), inequality has risen (Equitable Growth 2020). As in prior years, the public sector unionization rate remained higher, at 37.6 percent in 2021 (Shierholz et al.).

II. The Role of the State in the Employment Relationship

A. The "Private Welfare" System in the U.S.

The U.S. has always had a weak public welfare system, beginning with the New Deal legislative model of government provision of partial relief from economic hardship. The minimum standards of New Deal legislation, such as the minimum wage, have not kept people out of poverty, let alone provided a decent standard of living. The U.S. is an outlier among industrialized nations in failing to adopt public policy providing for the most basic of universal needs, including national health care, publicly supported child care, paid sick leave, vacation benefits, or adequate retirement benefits. Instead, U.S. policy is based on a system of "private welfare" (Munger 2004:550–1) or of an "employee welfare state" (Charny 1996:1601), which relies on the private employment relationship rather than a public welfare state to provide for basic needs. This amounts to a public policy that substitutes employment-related benefits for a governmental obligation to ensure that all individuals have a minimal level of sustenance, housing, health care, paid sick leave, child care, other basic needs. In practice, therefore, much of employees' social protection is contingent on employment contracts or employers' voluntary actions.

This "laissez-faire benefit model" (Kochan and Shulman 2007:6) is based on the 1930s New Deal expectation that benefits would be linked to a "long-term, relatively stable employment relationship" (ibid). The model fails at multiple levels. Fundamentally, it denies the State's responsibility to protect the welfare of all individuals, whether they are employed or employable. Further, the State does not even shift responsibility to private employers, who are free to decide whether to provide benefits to workers. Rather, the model is based on a fictional "freedom of contract" in which an individual job applicant will negotiate with an employer about wages and benefits. This system works to the advantage of employers, as the "reserve army of labor" under capitalism maintains a steady stream of individual applicants and employees without power to negotiate individually, particularly under the U.S "employment at will" common law doctrine that gives employers unilateral power to hire or fire employees without just cause (Magdoff and Magdoff 2004). This system also pits workers against each other, enabling employers to demand the "ideal worker" who will accept a job at low wages and without benefits such as sick leave, health insurance, or child care (Zanhour and Sumpter 2022). Instead, the cost of such benefits is shifted to the family, where unpaid labor of caregiving, primarily by women, subsidizes the employer and boosts the employer's profits (ibid). Further, employers can increase their power and profits by sowing divisions among workers based on race, gender, religion, and national origin, for example, by paying white male workers poorly, but still higher than women, workers of color, and immigrants (Cunningham-Cook and Bayard 2022).

B. The Liberal Contradictions of the National Labor Relations Act

As New Deal legislation reveals, even a laissez-faire ideology of liberalism needs to incorporate democratic measures that provide a degree of legitimacy to the claim of "capitalist democracy" (Lipset and Marks 2001; Henry 2018). In the U.S., the legitimacy of a "private welfare" policy depends on ensuring that employees have the ability to act collectively to gain higher wages and benefits from their employers. Thus, the National Labor Relations Act (NLRA), enacted in 1935, was central to the cluster of laws of the New Deal. After World War II, the 35 percent private sector unionization rate created a strong base for collective bargaining for higher wages and benefits (Kochan and Shulman 2007:2). Further, with a sufficient level of unionization in a healthy economy, even non-union employers feel pressured to provide these social protections to their employees.

The collective labor power through unionization creates a more realistic basis for asserting that there is freedom of contract between employers and employees. However, in shifting the State's public welfare responsibility to private parties, the NLRA reinforces the link between benefits and employment, which necessarily excludes all individuals outside the employment relationship. Further, this system of "private welfare" weakens the potential of unionization to build on the floor of a public system of universal benefits. It also views unionization as primarily aimed at improving "bread and butter" items through collective bargaining, rather than as a collective force for democratizing the workplace. Such an instrumentalist view of collective bargaining is built into Congress's enactment of all New Deal legislation, including the NLRA, as part of its constitutional power to regulate interstate commerce. Section 1 of the NLRA declares U.S. policy "to eliminate the causes of certain substantial obstructions to the free flow of commerce and to mitigate and eliminate these obstructions when they have occurred by encouraging the practice and procedure of collective bargaining." This reveals the view of unionization as a means of stabilizing the underlying capitalist economic system. As the U.S. Supreme Court explained in upholding the constitutionality of the NLRA, providing employees with the rights to unionize, collectively bargain, and strike would increase the likelihood that the employer and union would seek to reach a contract without having a strike take place (*National Labor Relations Board v. Jones & Laughlin Steel Corp* 1937:45). Thus, the governmental policy protecting employee rights serves an instrumental goal of maintaining "industrial peace" that is essential to ensuring uninterrupted commerce (1937:42).

The democratic potential of the NLRA has also been undermined by legal structures that simultaneously support and undermine collective rights of labor (Klare 1978). Some early judicial interpretations and legislative actions provide examples of the contradictions at play. In 1944, in *J.I. Case v. NLRB*, the Supreme Court emphasized the redistributive nature of collective bargaining to serve the collective good of employees, stating, "The practice and philosophy of collective bargaining looks with suspicion on . . . individual advantages. . . . [I]ncreased compensation, if individually deserved, is often earned at the cost of breaking down some other standard thought to be for the welfare of the group, and always creates the suspicion of being paid at the long-range expense of the group as a whole" (1994:338–9). Yet, in 1938, in *Mackay Radio v. NLRB*, the Court decided that employers may lawfully "permanently replace" economic strikers, that is, employees striking over wages, hours, and terms and conditions of employment. With this decision, which was the first Supreme Court decision applying the NLRA after upholding its constitutionality, the Court made clear that its interpretations of the Act would ultimately serve the economic interests of capital. This early decision gave employers a powerful tool against unions. The threat of being permanently replaced lowers the likelihood of a strike, thereby increasing employer power in collective bargaining. If the union does call a strike, employers can permanently replace strikers as a way to weaken the strike or even to crush the union.

Congress amended the NLRA with the 1947 Taft-Hartley Act, which was aimed at curbing the power of unions, including the addition of a prohibition of secondary strikes and secondary boycotts (Labor Management Relations Act 1947). The Landrum-Griffin Act, passed in 1959, further strengthened the prohibition on secondary strikes and boycotts (Labor-Management Reporting and Disclosure Act 1959). Given the NLRA's structure of union organizing at the level of the firm, rather than on an industrial or sectoral basis, the secondary strike is a particularly important tool for a union to gain support from other unions and employees at other workplaces. Through such secondary activity, a union seeks to expand the scope of its strike to increase pressure on the employer. For example, if a union goes on strike during collective bargaining against a manufacturing employer (the primary employer), the employees at the supplier company (the secondary employer) might go on strike in solidarity with the striking employees at the manufacturing company. The secondary strike puts pressure on the primary employer to settle the strike. Secondary strikes thus have great potential for expanding the power of class-based labor solidarity by building alliances among unions and employees in multiple workplaces and by building public support for labor action. The legislative justification for prohibiting secondary strikes is based on a legal fiction that the secondary employer is a "neutral" party that should not be brought into the "primary dispute" between an employer and union. This legal perspective ignores the reality that primary and secondary employers choose their economic relationship for their mutual benefit, which also carries economic risk such as disruptions from labor disputes (Summers 1988:820–1).

The Taft-Hartley Act also takes aim at labor solidarity by statutorily limiting the scope of workers protected by the NLRA. Although the NLRA broadly defines "employee" as "any employee" (*National Labor Relations Act* 1935) the Taft-Hartley Act legislatively shifted the class line by excluding "supervisors" from the statutory definition of "employee" (*National Labor Relations Act* 1935). Taft-Hartley was enacted within months of a Supreme Court's decision finding that "foremen" or "lead men" were "employees" under the NLRA, given their common labor interests (*Packard Motor Car Co. v. NLRB* 1947). The Court affirmed the NLRB's decision recognizing that under employment practices in industrial production, foremen might still assign and direct the work of the rank and file, but had largely lost authority to participate in managerial decisions such as setting wages or disciplining employees (Seitz 1984:205–7, 230). The statutory exclusion of "supervisors" was based largely on Congress' view that employers should be able to demand undivided loyalty from individuals employed to carry out supervisory duties (Seitz 1984:241–2). The scope of the exclusion under Section 2(11), though, is very broad, defining supervisors as any individual who exercises any one of twelve supervisory duties in the interest of the employer, including assignment or direction of work, as well as duties with greater authority such as recommending wage increases or employee discipline (*National Labor Relations Act* 1935). In recent years, the Supreme Court and the NLRB have broadly interpreted the statutory definition of supervisors in ways that encompass many professional employees, such as lead nurses, who otherwise would be defined as "employees" with rights to unionize and collectively bargain (*National Labor Relations Board v. Health Care and Retirement Corporation of America* 1994; *National Labor Relations Board v. Kentucky River Community Care Inc.* 2001; *Oakwood Healthcare, Inc.* 2006). Thus, as the U.S. has shifted from manufacturing to being largely a service economy, legislative changes and judicial interpretations have shaped the NLRA to narrow the legal definition of the working class in ways that serve employers' economic interests in limiting the collective power of labor unions.

The contradictions of the liberal state have resulted in a combination of weak NLRA provisions and judicial statutory interpretations that maintain the status quo of outsized unilateral power in employers. Employers commonly engage in vociferous anti-union campaigns that intimidate employees and yet do not necessarily cross into unlawful statements or actions under the NLRA. Even for unlawful threats or actions such as discharging employees in retaliation for their engagement in union activities, such employer conduct is rewarded, in effect, by the NLRA's weak remedies (Lafer and Loustaunau 2020). Where a union does win an election to become the exclusive bargaining representative of the employees, the NLRA's remedies for employer refusals to collectively bargain or bad faith bargaining consist of an order to bargain in good faith—that is, nothing more than a slap on the wrist. Further, judicial deference to employers' "managerial prerogative" has severely narrowed the scope of bargaining (Rogers 1990:131–6). Combined with employer power to permanently replace strikers and the statutory prohibition on secondary strikes, the law creates and maintains structural obstacles to building collective labor power to move toward a democratic workplace.

Despite the severe problems of the limited scope of the NLRA and the conservative judicial interpretation of the Act, unionization in the U.S. has made a real difference in people's lives. Unionized workers earn 10.2 percent more in wages on average than nonunionized peers with similar education, occupation, and experience in the same sector (Shierholz et al. 2022). This reduces gender and racial/ethnic inequalities, as unionized women's hourly wages are 4.7 percent higher on average than for nonunionized women, black workers who are unionized earn 13.1 percent more than nonunion black workers, and Hispanic workers who are unionized earn 18.8 percent more than nonunion Hispanic workers (ibid). Unionized workers have better benefits than nonunion workers. Through collective bargaining, 95 percent of unionized workers are covered by employer-provided health insurance, as compared with 69 percent of nonunion workers; 92 percent of unionized workers have paid sick days, as compared with 77 percent of nonunion workers (ibid). Collective bargaining agreements also include workplace health and safety protections (ibid), require employers to have just cause for employee discipline, and set forth grievance/arbitration procedures for contract enforcement (Schwartz 2019).

Since the Reagan era, neoliberal policies of privatization and deregulation have undermined the positive impact of unionization and collective bargaining. With the 1981 Professional Air Traffic Controllers Organization (PATCO) strike when the Reagan administration discharged and permanently replaced more than 11,000 federally employed air traffic controllers and criminally prosecuted 71 controllers for engaging in an illegal strike under federal law (Fox 1985), the White House sent a clear message that the gloves were off in the attack on unions. In the private sector, employers increasingly used their power to break strikes by permanently replacing economic strikers, as in the Greyhound strike in 1983, the International Paper strike in 1987, and the New York Daily News strike in 1990 (LeRoy 1996:985–96; Brudney 1999:71–2). Under the conservative presidencies of George W. Bush and Donald Trump, the NLRB rolled back NLRA labor protections (McNicholas, Poydock, and Rhinehart 2019). In the public sector, the attacks on unions came through state legislative restrictions or repeals of public employee rights to unionize, the expansion of "right to work" law and policy through state legislation (Lieberwitz 2018), and the Supreme Court's *Janus* decision in 2018 holding that the First Amendment prohibits collective bargaining agreement provisions requiring covered public employees to pay their "fair share" of union dues (*Janus v. American Federation of State, County, and Municipal Employees* 2018).

The weakening of organized labor in the U.S. came, as well, from neoliberal policies favoring the free global movement of capital in search of cheap labor, while limiting the freedom of workers to immigrate (Silver 2003:137–8, 154–5). Given the "private welfare state" system in the U.S., the global flight of industrial manufacturing also means the loss of social protection through benefits won in collective bargaining. Employers have exploited the loss of a strong base of unionized jobs by restructuring the employment relationship, which has entailed a dramatic increase in contingent employment, with estimates that contingent employees comprise 30 to 40 percent of the workforce (Lobel 2017:56). Through this mechanism of expanding the ranks of part-time and temporary employees and "gig workers" often misclassified as independent contractors, employers have been able to avoid unions, lower wage rates, and cut back or eliminate benefits (Weaver 2021).

Not surprisingly, neoliberal policies have led to widening class-based divisions of wealth in the U.S. One example of the growing income gap is the skyrocketing of executive compensation as compared with wages and benefits that dropped for the working class. In the late 1970s, CEOs were paid about 30 times that of a typical worker (Mishel et al. 2012:175). In the year 2000, CEOs at large corporations were reported to have earned 419 times an average worker's pay. In 2021, it was estimated that, on average, CEOs received almost 400 times the annual average salary of their employees (Statista Research Department 2022).

C. Legislative Reforms to Move Toward a Responsive State

Creating a responsive State in the U.S. requires federal legislative reform to address the contradictions of the liberal/neoliberal legal and institutional structures that maintain the inequalities between capital and labor. This must include reform that moves the State toward fulfilling its obligation to provide for individual and collective needs of labor. As discussed in this chapter, the individual and the collective are interrelated in a society with democratic political and economic structures and institutions. Legislative reform to provide public goods to meet universal individual needs is an essential measure for moving toward political and economic democracy. The State's responsiveness to individual material needs shows an unconditional respect for all individuals and enhances collective values of democracy by providing the material foundation to enable all individuals to participate more fully in the society. In the labor context, the State's obligation to support workers' rights to act collectively is essential to bring democracy to the economic system, which in turn enhances individuals' ability to participate meaningfully in their workplace and the broader society.

To respond to universal material needs of individuals, legislative reform should strengthen the welfare state's provision of public goods rather than linking benefits to the employment relationship. Regardless of employment status or eligibility, all individuals need health care, shelter, sustenance, child care, elder care, income during periods of unemployment, and a good retirement income. The U.S. can learn from other countries' systems that provide State-supported benefits to all individuals in the society. Further, minimum standards for working conditions should be regulated based on standards for a good quality of life, including requirements that employers pay a living wage, provide a healthy and safe the workplace, pay sufficient compensation for workplace injuries, and apply "just cause" standards in hiring, discipline, and discharge.

Legislative reform must also fulfill the responsibility of the State to address the needs of workers for meaningful collective voice and power in the employment relationship. The recently proposed PRO Act (Protecting the Right to Organize Act) includes important reforms of the NLRA. Although the U.S. House of Representatives passed the PRO Act in February 2020 (H.R. 2474) and again in March 2021 (H.R. 842), the PRO Act was never taken up by the Senate. Despite this political setback, the PRO Act is important as a model of legislative reform that would strengthen the effectiveness of existing NLRA provisions, add new provisions to enhance the ability of workers to organize and engage in collective bargaining, and remove NLRA provisions that impede meaningful collective labor action. These reforms would address three key obstacles to union organizing under the NLRA. First, PRO Act provisions would reduce employers' power to coerce or intimidate employees during union organizing campaigns. These provisions include prohibiting employer "captive audience" anti-union meetings; streamlining and speeding up the process for holding union elections; strengthening remedies for employees and penalties on employers for violating workers' rights; and empowering the NLRB to order the employer to collectively bargain with the union if the employer interferes with a free and fair union representation election where the union initially had majority support (Giolito and Babson 2021; Education and Labor Committee 2021). Second, PRO Act provisions would expand the scope of employees with rights under the NLRA, including adopting a definition of "independent contractor" that would reduce misclassification of employees, providing undocumented workers with full remedies under the NLRA, and narrowing the definition of "supervisors" to those who exercise genuine managerial power (ibid). Third, the PRO Act would strengthen unions' power in collective bargaining, including allowing newly certified unions to seek arbitration and mediation to settle impasses in negotiations for their first collective bargaining agreement, removing the NLRA's prohibition on "secondary boycotts" or "secondary strikes," and overriding state "right to work" laws (ibid).

Legislative reforms for governmental provision of universal benefits to individuals, and for passage of the PRO Act, would advance the common good. Legislation creating individual entitlements for public goods recognizes the universal nature of such needs and the State's responsibility to provide them directly to all members of the society. This would also change the status quo that links such benefits to the employment relationship, which would enable individuals to exercise greater freedom to decide whether to accept or leave a job. This reform would also increase democratic participation at and away from the workplace. A legislative system of universal benefits would enhance the collective power of unions to engage in the political system to support laws that broaden the scope and raise the level of universal minimum benefits–for example, for legislation that provides for health care, paid vacation time, and tuition-free higher education. The democratic process would extend to unionized workplaces where collective bargaining could raise benefits above the statutory floor and expand the union's ability to bargain for other priorities such as increased job security, freedom of expression, and flexible work hours. Thus, State responsiveness to the universal individual needs is integrally related to advancing collective labor interests at the workplace. This would build a foundation of economic security for individuals to fully participate in a society, including the ability to make meaningful choices about pursuing education, family life, work life, leisure activities, civic and political engagement, and organizational activities (Fineman 2010).

Legislative reform such as the PRO Act is an integral part of expanding democracy by strengthening the legal protection of employees' ability to unionize and unions' ability to effectively represent collective labor interests. As important as "bread and butter" collective bargaining is for employees' individual and collective welfare, passing the PRO Act is about more than this–it is about creating the necessary conditions for economic democracy. By removing prohibitions on secondary strikes, the PRO Act would broaden the scope of protected worker solidarity across workplaces and industries. Additionally, at the level of the firm, collective bargaining increases employees' ability to express their individuality at the workplace. For example, the collective bargaining agreement places the burden on the employer to prove "just cause" for employment actions, such as discharge or discipline. This increases transparency in the decision-making process, requires objective job-related standards to be used, and can protect worker freedoms such as expression of their political views. Thus, such legislative reform is essential to fulfill the State's responsibility to bring democratic principles and practice to the workplace by supporting the ability of workers to act in solidarity for the common good, including respect, dignity, meaningful work, and a good and full life for all workers.

D. Recent Legal and Social Developments that Resonate With the Reforms of the PRO Act

The PRO Act will not be passed in Congress, given the state of politics in the U.S. But there are currently two interesting developments that reflect much of the spirit and substance of the PRO Act. The first development has taken place with the changes at the NLRB under the Biden administration. A majority–three of the Board's five members—support labor rights. Further, the new General Counsel of the NLRB is implementing a creative agenda to strengthen the enforcement of the NLRA.

Through the adjudication process, the current NLRB General Counsel, Jennifer Abruzzo, is bringing issues to the Board that reflect some of the proposals in the PRO Act, including two reforms that would strengthen employees' ability to freely choose whether to unionize. First, the General Counsel has argued that employer "captive audience" meetings violate employee rights to engage in and to refuse to engage in union activity (Memorandum GC 22–07 2022). This change could limit employers' ability to abuse their power to require employees to attend meetings to listen to employers deliver anti-union speeches. Even if the speeches do not cross a line into unlawful coercive statements, employers can make lawful speeches that are strongly anti-union—and thus use employer economic power to intimidate employees from voting for a union.

The General Counsel is also advocating for a change in Board legal doctrine that allows employers to refuse to recognize the union without a formal election. Currently, even if a majority of employees have signed union authorization cards stating that they want to be represented by the union, the employer can insist on a formal union election. In April 2022, the General Counsel filed a brief arguing that the Board should return to its earlier legal doctrine that the employer could insist on an election only if the employer has a good faith doubt that a majority of employees support the union (Kullgren 2022). Without evidence of a good faith doubt, the employer would be obligated to recognize the union as the collective bargaining representative of the bargaining unit of employees. Certainly, the lack of a good faith doubt would exist where an employer commits unfair labor practices in violation of the NLRA during a union campaign and then refuses to recognize the Union's evidence of majority support by the employees.

The second recent development is an organizational one—that is, the recent increase and expansion of unionization in workplaces that are not considered "traditional" occupations for unionization. In the period from October 2021 to June 2022, there was a 58 percent increase in union election petitions filed at the NLRB (Office of Public Affairs 2022). This is consistent with the rising positive U.S. public opinion of unions to a 71 percent approval rating, which is the highest rating since 1965 (McCarthy 2022). Over the past two years, workers have unionized across a range of businesses and employment settings, including successful union elections at the Amazon warehouse in Staten Island, multiple Starbucks locations, two REI department stores, and unionization in the technology sector at two Apple retail stores and in the video game industry at Activision Blizzard (Shierholz et al. 2022; Tarasov 2022; Novet 2022; Hofstaedter 2022). These developments show the interest in unionization by a new generation of workers across a range of occupations. Moreover, in all these examples, employees unionized in the face of vociferous anti-union campaigns by large, powerful employers (ibid).

III. Conclusion

Progress toward a democratic society requires a State that responds to human needs and supports and sustains political, economic, and social institutions that are central to individuals thriving in their work, civic, and personal lives. Making this democratic vision a reality in the U.S. must involve State political action, including legislative reform, which provides directly for individual material needs and that supports collective institutions for social justice, including labor unions. A strong labor movement can bring democracy to the workplace, which is essential to address the contradictions of liberalism/neoliberalism: the co-existence of authoritarian capitalist economic institutions and democratic political institutions.

The responsive State and social institutions can and should be mutually reinforcing democratic forces. No legislative reform will come about without social movements. In the labor movement, grassroots organizing together with unionization by established unions has resulted in a resurgence of interest in unionization in unexpected workplaces. The growth of unionization will strengthen the labor movement's power to lobby for legislative reform that responds to workers' universal material and social needs. Unions can lobby for legislation that expands public goods, such as health care, to be provided directly to all individuals without regard to employment status. Further, a stronger labor movement can more effectively lobby for legislation such as the proposed PRO Act, which would amend the NLRA to expand individual rights to organize and collective power through unionization. Such legislative reforms, in turn, will strengthen employees' ability to unionize and bring democratic processes to the workplace.

Reference List

Brudney, James J. 1999. "Book Review: To Strike or Not to Strike, Julius Getman, 'The Betrayal of Local 14: Paperworkers, Politics, and Permanent Replacements (1998)'." *Wisconsin Law Review* 1999:65–89.

Charny, David. 1996. "The Changing Workplace: The Employee Welfare State in Transition." *Texas Law Review* 74:1601–43.
Cunningham-Cook, Matthew and Marc D. Bayard. 2022. "In Bessemer and the South, Black Workers Hold the Key." *The American Prospect*, February 18 (https://prospect.org/labor/in-bessemer-and-the-south-black-workers-hold-the-key/).
Education and Labor Committee. 2021. "Press Release: Top Democrats Introduce Bill to Protect Workers' Right to Organize and Make Our Economy Work for Everyone." February 4 (https://edlabor.house.gov/media/press-releases/top-democrats-introduce-bill-to-protect-workers-right-to-organize-and-make-our-economy-work-for-everyone).
Equitable Growth. 2020. "How Strong Unions Can Restore Workers' Bargaining Power." *Washington Center for Equitable Growth*, May 1 (https://equitablegrowth.org/factsheet-how-strong-unions-can-restore-workers-bargaining-power/).
Fineman, Martha Albertson. 2010. "The Vulnerable Subject and the Responsive State." *Emory Law Journal* 60:251–75.
Fox, Neil. 1985. "PATCO and the Courts: Public Sector Labor Law as Ideology." *University of Illinois Law Review* 1985:245.
Giolito, Robert S. and Marshall B. Babson. 2021. "The PRO Act: Reforming American Labor Law and Practice." *ABA Committee on Practice and Procedure Under the NLRA*, March 5 (www.americanbar.org/groups/labor_law/committees/ppcom/pp_archive/2021/).
Henry, John F. 2018. "Reflections on the New Deal: The Vested Interests, Limits to Reform, and the Meaning of a Liberal Democracy." *Levy Economics Institute of Bard College*, Working Paper No. 905:1–32 (www.levyinstitute.org › *pubs*).
Hofstaedter, Emily. 2022. "REI Workers Just Unionized—Again." *Mother Jones*, August 25 (www.motherjones.com/politics/2022/08/rei-workers-just-unionized-again/).
H.R. 842—Protecting the Right to Organize Act of 2021. *117th Congress*. 2021–2022 (www.congress.gov/bill/117th-congress/house-bill/842).
H.R. 2474—Protecting the Right to Organize Act of 2019. *116th Congress*. 2019–2020 (www.congress.gov/bill/116th-congress/house-bill/2474).
J.I. Case Co. v. National Labor Relations Board, 321 U.S. 332 (1944).
Janus v. American Federation of State, County, and Municipal Employees, Council 31, 585 U.S., 138 S. Ct. 2448 (2018).
Keating, Aaron. 2022. "Economic Update: Workers' Wages and Corporate Profits." *Economic Opportunity Institute*, January 6 (www.opportunityinstitute.org/research/post/economic-update-workers-wages-and-corporate-profits/).
Klare, Karl E. 1978. "Judicial Deradicalization of the Wagner Act and the Origins of Modern Legal Consciousness, 1937–1941." *Minnesota Law Review* 62:265–339.
Kochan, Thomas and Beth Shulman. 2007. "A New Social Contract: Restoring Dignity and Balance to the Economy." Briefing Paper #184 *Economic Policy Institute*, February 22 (www.sharedprosperity.org/bp184/bp184.pdf).
Kullgren, Ian. 2022. "Revisit Card Check to Ease Union Organizing: NLRB Top Lawyer (1)." *Bloomberg Law*, April 12.
Labor Management Relations Act, ch. 120, 61 Stat. 140 (1947).
Labor-Management Reporting and Disclosure Act of 1959, Pub. L. No. 86–257, 73 Stat. 519.
Lafer, Gordon and Lola Loustaunau. 2020. "Fear at Work: An Inside Account of How Employers Threaten, Intimidate, and Harass Workers to Stop Them from Exercising

Their Right to Collective Bargaining." *Economic Policy Institute*, July 23 (www.epi.org/publication/fear-at-work-how-employers-scare-workers-out-of-unionizing/).
LeRoy, Michael H. 1996. "Lockouts Involving Replacement Workers: An Empirical Public Policy Analysis and Proposal to Balance Economic Weapons Under the NLRA." *Washington University Law Quarterly* 74:981–1057.
Lieberwitz, Risa L. 2018. "Contract as Public Law: The Public Nature of Collective Bargaining." Pp. 122–41 in *Vulnerability and the Legal Organization of Work*, edited by M. A. Fineman and J. Fineman. Oxford: Routledge.
———. 2022. "Corporatization of Higher Education: A Crisis of Labor and Democracy." Pp. 318–33 in *The Cambridge Handbook of Labor and Democracy*, edited by A. B. Cornell and M. Barenberg. Cambridge: Cambridge University Press.
Lipset, Seymour and Gary Marks. 2001. "How FDR Saved Capitalism." *Hoover Digest*, January 30 (www.hoover.org/research/how-fdr-saved-capitalism).
Lobel, Orly. 2017. "The Gig Economy & the Future of Employment and Labor Law." *University of San Francisco Law Review* 51:51–73.
Magdoff, Fred and Harry Magdoff. 2004. "Disposable Workers: Today's Reserve Army of Labor." *Monthly Review* 55(11) (April) (https://monthlyreview.org/2004/04/01/disposable-workers-todays-reserve-army-of-labor/).
McCarthy, Justin. 2022. "U.S. Approval of Labor Unions at Highest Point Since 1965." *Gallup*, August 30 (https://news.gallup.com/poll/398303/approval-labor-unions-highest-point-1965.aspx).
McNicholas, Celine, Margaret Poydock, and Lynn Rhinehart. 2019. "Unprecedented: The Trump NLRB's Attack on Workers' Rights." *Economic Policy Institute*, October 19 (www.epi.org/publication/unprecedented-the-trump-nlrbs-attack-on-workers-rights/).
Memorandum GC 22–04.2022. "The Right to Refrain from Captive Audience and other Mandatory Meetings." *Office of the General Counsel, National Labor Relations Board*, April 7 (www.nlrb.gov/guidance/memos-research/general-counsel-memos?search_term=captive+audience&year=2022&volume=-1&form_build_id=form-_Mk6yZdCx9xgcoRUKsxl8T5-ezuKV5NE5vLUUVUcemk&form_id=nlrb_case_decisions__search_form&op=Search).
Mishel, Lawrence, Jared Bernstein, and Sylvia Allegretto. *The State of Working America 2006/2007* (www.stateofworkingamerica.org/swa06-00-toc-exec-intro.pdf).
Munger, Frank. 2004. "The New Economy and the Unraveling Social Safety Net: How Can We Save the Safety Net?" *Brooklyn Law Review* 69:543–81.
National Labor Relations Act. 1935.49 Stat. 449, codified at 29 U.S.C. §§ 151–169.
National Labor Relations Board v. Health Care and Retirement Corporation of America, 511 U.S. 571 (1994).
National Labor Relations Board v. Jones & Laughlin Steel Corp., 301 U.S. 1 (1937).
National Labor Relations Board v. Kentucky River Community Care Inc., 532 U.S. 706 (2001).
National Labor Relations Board v. Mackay Radio & Telegraph Co., 304 U.S. 333 (1938).
Novet, Jordan. 2022. "Activision Employees Announce Second Union Ahead of Game Company's Sale to Microsoft." *CNBC*, July 19 (www.cnbc.com/2022/07/19/activision-blizzard-workers-forming-second-union-before-microsoft-deal.html).
Oakwood Healthcare, Inc., 348 NLRB 686 (2006).
Office of Public Affairs. 2022. "First Three Quarters' Union Election Petitions Up 58%, Exceeding All FY21 Petitions Filed." *National Labor Relations Board*,

July 15 (www.nlrb.gov/news-outreach/news-story/correction-first-three-quarters-union-election-petitions-up-58-exceeding).

Packard Motor Car Co. v. NLRB, 330 U.S. 485 (1947).

Rogers, Joel. 1990. "Divide and Conquer: Further Reflections on the Distinctive Character of American Labor Laws." *Wisconsin Law Review* 1990:1–147.

Schwartz, Robert M. 2019. "Using 'Just Cause' to Defend Against Unfair Discipline." *Labor Notes*, January 15 (https://labornotes.org/2019/01/using-just-cause-defend-against-unfair-discipline).

Seitz, Virginia A. 1984. "Legal, Legislative, and Managerial Responses to the Organization of Supervisory Employees in the 1940's." *American Journal of Legal History* 28(3):199–243.

Shierholz, Heidi, Margaret Poydock, John Schmitt, and Celine McNicholas. 2022. "Latest Data Release on Unionization is a Wake-up Call to Lawmakers." *Economic Policy Institute* January 20 (www.epi.org/publication/latest-data-release-on-unionization-is-a-wake-up-call-to-lawmakers/).

Silver, Beverly J. 2003. *Forces of Labor: Workers' Movements and Globalization Since 1870*. New York: Cambridge University Press.

Statista Research Department. 2002. "U.S. Wealth Distribution 2022." *Statista*, November 1 (www.statista.com/statistics/203961/wealth-distribution-for-the-us/).

———. 2022. "U.S. CEO-to-Worker Compensation Ratio of Top Firms 1965–2021." *Statista*, October 18 (www.statista.com/statistics/261463/ceo-to-worker-compensation-ratio-of-top-firms-in-the-us/).

Summers, Clyde W. 1988. "The First Fifty Years: Questioning the Unquestioned in Collective Labor Law." *Catholic University Law Review* 47:791–823.

Tarasov, Katie. 2022. "Unions are Forming at Starbucks, Apple and Google. Here's Why Workers are Organizing Now." *CNBC*, August 5 (www.cnbc.com/2022/08/05/why-starbucks-apple-and-google-are-unionizing-now-for-the-first-time.html).

Weaver, Julia H. 2021. "Two Sides of the Same Coin: Examining the Misclassification of Workers as Independent Contractors." *Georgia Law Review* 55:1355–82.

Zanhour, Mona and Dana McDaniel Sumpter. 2022. "The Entrenchment of the Ideal Worker Norm During the COVID-19 Pandemic: Evidence from Working Mothers in the United States." *Gender, Work & Organization*: 1–19. Doi:10.1111/gwao.12885.

PART III

Organizing the Economic Infrastructure

5

THE CORPORATION, VULNERABILITY, AND RESILIENCE

Lua Kamál Yuille

Introduction

Picture the stylized, idealized, contemporary American legal subject—the ordinary average Joe.

If you are honest, it is not hard to do. His story is familiar. Ellen Goodman called him Phil:

> He worked himself to death, finally and precisely, at 3:00 A.M. Sunday morning. . . . He worked six days a week. . . . He worked like the Important People. He had no outside "extracurricular interests," unless, of course, you think about a monthly golf game that way. To Phil, it was work. . . . At the funeral, the sixty-year-old company president told the forty-eight-year-old widow that the fifty-one-year-old deceased had meant much to the company and would be missed and would be hard to replace. The widow didn't look him in the eye. She was afraid he would read her bitterness and, after all, she would need him to straighten out the finances—the stock options and all that. . . . [W]hen he finally worked himself to death, at precisely 3:00 A.M. Sunday morning, no one was really surprised. By 5:00 P.M. the afternoon of the funeral, the company president had begun, discreetly of course, with care and taste, to make inquiries about his replacement. . . . He asked around: "Who's been working the hardest?"
>
> *(Goodman, 1979:18–19)*

Phil is Joe. Well, not precisely, but most of the details are unimportant: you may have sited your Joe in any region. You may have given him any level of education, basic or advanced. He may be married or single (though probably

DOI: 10.4324/9781003323242-9

married, with the requisite two-point-five children). He might be the boss, or a manager, or a workaday player. But invariably, the ordinary average Joe is a working man.

He is Ward Cleaver, the father in the iconic television series *Leave it to Beaver*. The Cleavers were considered the archetypal American family, and Ward was a briefcase-toting, white-collar professional. He dressed in a business suit, worked in an office, and had a secretary. He commuted to his job for a "big company" each day from the suburbs and returned in the early evening. He golfed on the weekends at the country club. He is the *Brady Bunch*'s Mike Brady, working at his drafting table from his home office, an architect at a respected firm at which he eventually becomes partner. He is even Archie Bunker, the patriarch of the revolutionary Norman Lear comedy *All in the Family*. Bunker was, and remains, the fetishized American blue-collar archetype. He was a dock worker who climbed the ladder to become a foreman, though he supplemented his company salary as a night-time taxi driver.

Joe is any of these men, and he is all these men. He is a company man. He relies on the company for the foundations of his existence and derives security—annual bonuses, semi-regular job promotions, a schedule that has him home for dinner most nights, and the promise of a secure retirement—and identity from his relationship and association with some business entity. Joe, law's *homo juridicus*, spends 40 hours a week working for a living. And "living" is an expansive concept. Joe's job is his primary source of income. Joe's job provides his health care. Joe's job is his main saving mechanism. Joe's job is an important site of interpersonal relationships, fellowship, and leisure. Joe's job even provides social standing.

And indeed, if Joe's job did not adequately provide all of these things and more, it would be considered a "bad" job, and Joe would provide a countertype. Instead of Ward Cleaver or Mike Brady, you have Al Bundy, the disaffected shoe salesman from *Married With Children*, who lacks the stability, autonomy, and status bestowed on the paradigmatic company man.

Through the company, because of the company, Joe becomes the paradigmatic liberal legal subject: autonomous, independent, self-sufficient—free. But the liberal legal subject is a fallacy. *Homo juridicus* is a myth. And the ordinary average Joe—like Ward, Mike, and Archie—is fiction. The company man is not autonomous, independent, or self-sufficient. Although his central relationships fail to generally be recognized as dependence, Joe relies unwaveringly on power, privilege, and assets afforded to him by the company. He is constitutionally, constantly vulnerable, and the company helps him confront that reality.

This chapter uses vulnerability theory, which views the human subject as universally and inevitably vulnerable (M. Fineman 2008), to develop this alternative perspective on the economic reality of a universalized *homo juridicus*. It outlines an account of the corporation as an institution to which the state has delegated a large measure of its responsibility to generate and distribute "resilience," i.e. those resources and assets that allow individuals to confront, adapt to, ameliorate the consequences of, compensate for, or contain the universal human condition of vulnerability.

I. Vulnerability, the Human Condition, and the Liberal Legal Subject

The fundamental characteristics of the human condition should be uncontroversial: "we all live and die within a fragile materiality that renders us constantly susceptible to both internal and external forces beyond our control" (M. Fineman 2008:9). At birth, *all* humans are, in and of themselves, defenseless. Advanced in age, they return (to greater or lesser degrees) to that state. And, throughout their lives, humans are persistently thrust into the position of dependence because of sickness, weather, child-bearing, child-rearing, occupational displacement, institutional transition, or any of an innumerable and often unpredictable influences on human life. This natural, unavoidable, and constant susceptibility is vulnerability, and it "arises from our embodiment" (M. Fineman 2010:267). People's fragile materiality—the fundamental vulnerability of the human condition—is not merely a gross physical descriptor. Vulnerability is equally a characteristic of the human mind, human emotions, and human institutions. As a result of the universal and constant condition, all people require protection, care, and support (M. Fineman 2015).

This is a descriptive and empirical observation. It says nothing more than that to be human is to be vulnerable. Vulnerability is ontological, not relational. It describes the fundamental nature of being and existence. It does not arise due to some deficiency or problem or attack or subordination or oppression or subalternity. It is an inevitable part of the terms of life. While we can attempt to lessen risks associated with or act to mitigate possible manifestations of our vulnerability, the possibility of harm—the vulnerability itself—cannot be eliminated (M. Fineman 2010).

This statement of the human condition depathologizes vulnerability, which is rhetorically associated with negative traits like poverty, dependence, otherness, and deficiency. As articulated here, vulnerability is not a problem, though it can have negative or positive implications. It is not pathological. It is not a temporally bounded status or a state to be resolved, fixed, or overcome. "[H]uman vulnerability is universal and constant—there can be no position of invulnerability. Vulnerability IS the human condition" (M. Fineman 2018:4).

While the vulnerability observation itself should be as uncontroversial as it is incontrovertible, its most immediate implication is: accepting vulnerability as the human condition means rejecting the idealized subject asserted in the liberal tradition—"autonomous, independent, and fully-functioning adult, who inhabits a world defined by individual interests, no societal responsibility, where state intervention or regulation is perceived as a violation of his liberty" (M. Fineman 2008:2).

In place of the "liberal legal subject," vulnerability theory demands law and socio-political-economic decision-making address itself to take into account, and serve, the vulnerable legal subject.

II. Understanding Resilience

This is not so for the very real vulnerable legal subject. The inescapability of vulnerability means that there is no state of invulnerability; there is only the possibility of resilience (M. Fineman 2010). Resilience, in turn, should be understood as the ability to adapt to, recover from, cope with, and mitigate the consequences of vulnerability. It is the capacity to recuperate from difficult experiences, setbacks, failures, and harms to which one is prone by virtue of being human (or embedded in a human institution). Resilience contemplates adaptability not only in the body's capacity to withstand and recover from harm or illness but also socially, psychologically, and economically.

Resilience has been defined in many ways. It is the ability to bounce back and continue to function after physical, mental, or relational setback. It is predicting, preventing, and minimizing the potentially disruptive consequences of vulnerability. It is the accumulation of sufficient resources to allow individuals to confront, adapt to, ameliorate, compensate for, or contain vulnerability (M. Fineman 2015).

Money is resilience. Wealth (as in sticky, auto-reproductive, generationally distributed financial resources) is resilience. Healthcare is resilience. Housing is resilience. M. Fineman has identified five categories of "assets" that offer resilience:

- Physical or material assets (e.g. transportation, mobile phone) are those that determine standards of living and ability to invest or respond to economic crisis;
- Human assets (e.g. education, health) are those gathered in terms of education or training that allow individuals to accumulate other assets, as well as provide for daily needs;
- Social or relational assets are the supports and safety net provided by family, professional associations, social networks, trade unions, church or charity groups, local community relationships;
- Ecological or environmental assets (e.g. clean water, healthy food, access to parks or woodland or rural environments, clean air); and
- Existential or deontological assets (systems of meaning like religion, culture, and art) give life meaning and offer solace, comfort, and purpose.

"Resilience is perceived as necessary to both confront life's challenges and to allow individuals to manage risk and to take advantage of life's opportunities and enjoyments" (J. Fineman 2017:26). These needs catalyze the creation of social relationships and institutions, like the family, schools, financial institutions, social institutions, and the corporation. Such institutions serve to mediate, compensate, and mitigate vulnerability through the accumulation of assets. Indeed, they are designed to perform that function.

In the dominant legal perspective, resilience is generally framed as an intrinsic, individual characteristic for which no one person or institution bears responsibility. One cannot demand resilience, and a lack of resilience is typically deemed an individual failing or a private problem. But it should be clear, the state and its institutions are crucial to the production of most of these resources. Unlike vulnerability, resilience is not an innate, constant condition. Instead, individuals accumulate the resources that confer resilience over time and within and through social institutions and relationships (M. Fineman 2010). Thus, resilience "is largely dependent on the quality and quantity of resources or assets that [a person] has at their disposal or command" (M. Fineman 2014:320). Physical, human, social, ecological, and even existential assets are produced by social institutions (regional or national government, markets, corporations, as well as the family) that are, in turn, constructed, structured, and/or mediated by the state. Therefore, a lack of resilience is a function of unequal the societal institutions and structures responsible for distributing and generating resilience and/or unequal allocations of privilege and power within those institutions.

To illustrate, think of inclement weather. When it rains, for example, everyone is susceptible to getting wet. However, their access to resources can determine the likelihood that a specific individual will actually get wet. Does the person have an umbrella? Impermeable clothing? Rain boots? Does the person have access to shelter and the privilege to choose to remain within that shelter until the rain were to pass? If a person does get wet, do they have access to the means to dry themselves? These "assets" help an individual cope with the rain. This is resilience and even this mundane example should make clear that it is the product of a "vast and interlocking network" of political and economic decisions that differentially distribute power and privilege.

Illness provides another simple example:

> [A]ll bodies are vulnerable to illness; however, individuals may have a range of differing resources in order to mitigate the effects of illness. . . . [R]esilience to illness and its effects are affected by laws on the cost, patenting and distribution of drugs, and the circumstances under which the state will pay for healthcare provision, private healthcare afforded through agreement with employers, care provided through private family

> arrangements, the way these roles are recognized by the state, as well as having a stable home, access to adequate nutrition and employment law that allows for time off work to recuperate.
>
> *(Travis 2019:305)*

Again, both the generation and distribution of resilience to illness is the product of a range of institutional choices, power, and privilege.

When vulnerability is understood as a universal constant, the question is not, "Who is more or less vulnerable?" Everyone is inevitably and always vulnerable, and that condition is not countable or measurable or changeable. Resilience is the only possible response to vulnerability. Thus, the central questions are: "Who is more or less resilient? How did they get that way? And, most important, where do you get resilience? In contemporary capitalist societies, the answer is, in large part, the corporation.

III. The Corporation as a Site of Resilience

Vulnerability theory provides a distinct lens through which to re-examine some core corporate conversations. Its reorientation around the vulnerable subject as the core unit of just societal ordering and resilience as the key task of government makes the central corporate law questions how and why corporations are the central institutions for the distribution of resilience. The foundation of that discussion requires at least some consideration of the question, "What is a corporation?" and "Why is the corporation?"

A. Conceiving of the Corporation

Determining the nature of the corporation occupies much of the law of corporations, but the strict legal answer is straight forward: a corporation is a legal entity with the characteristics defined by the law of the jurisdiction in which it was formed (Harper Ho 2012). In practice, that means the corporation is an entity:

- Engaged in business;
- With legal personality (i.e., the capacity and authority to own property, sue and be sued, and bear criminal responsibility) separate from its constituents;
- Afforded limited liability for owners and managers;
- Characterized by shared ownership by investors of capital;
- Managed through delegated authority; and
- With transferability of ownership interests.

But the legal answer—which should be uncontroversial—is not particularly instructive.

That is because the question "what is a corporation?" really seeks to understand the fundamental nature of the choice to organize economic activity using the unique institution grant it considerable power: Why have corporations? Who do they serve? To whom are they accountable?

1. Under Corporate Theory

There are no universally accepted answers to such existential, "nature of the corporation" questions. Instead, the nature of the corporation is a conversation, debate, and polemic that "extend[s] far back into history" (Hamilton 1971:980, citing *Case of Sutton's Hospital*, 1613). Prevailing corporate theory offers varying accounts, most of which offer thin, stylized characterizations of corporations that do little to engage the rich and complex reality of the corporation as an institution.

In *Trustees of Dartmouth College v. Woodward* (1819), the United States Supreme Court laid out what would become known as artificial entity theory:

> A corporation is an artificial being, invisible, intangible, and existing only in contemplation of law. Being the mere creature of law, it possesses only those properties which the charter of its creation confers upon it. . . . Among the most important are immortality, and, if the expression may be allowed, individuality; properties, by which a perpetual succession of many persons are considered as the same, and may act as a single individual. They enable a corporation to manage its own affairs, and to hold property without the perplexing intricacies, the hazardous and endless necessity, of perpetual conveyances for the purpose of transmitting it from hand to hand. It is chiefly for the purpose of clothing bodies of men, in succession, with these qualities and capacities, that corporations were invented, and are in use.
>
> *(p. 636)*

From this perspective, corporations exist to facilitate whatever ends the state (which grants the corporate charter) concludes benefit society (Ripken 2009). That idea eventually came to be understood to mean commerce or economic development, but today the Supreme Court admits a wide range of potential benefits—anything that is lawful—even if the default remains economically oriented.

In contrast, the real or natural entity perspective posits that, rather than the progeny of government fiat, corporations are the result of the natural tendency of individuals toward collective action (Blair 2013). Under this view, the corporation is "an organic social reality with an existence independent of, and constituting something more than, its changing shareholders" (Blumberg 1990, as cited in Blair 2013:806).

The aggregate theory, animating the Supreme Court's description of the corporation as an "association[] of citizens" (*Citizens United v. FEC* 2010:356), understands the corporation as "a group of otherwise disaggregated natural persons joining together by agreement to mutually pursue a private endeavor" (Johnson 2012:1142). That same perspective—that the corporation is not a real entity but a convenient fiction—underlies the popular contractarian perspective of the nature of corporations. Under this perspective, the corporation is "a shorthand for the complex arrangements of many sorts that those who associate voluntarily in the corporation will work out among themselves" (Easterbrook and Fischel 1989:1426).

Present debates, conversations, and polemics surrounding the nature of the corporation are best characterized as concerned primarily not with defining or understanding corporations but with determining which understanding best meets society's needs. That question, it should be clear, is wholly normative (Yuille 2017).

This reality is starkly clear when reflecting on the United States Supreme Court's most prominent engagements with the existential debate in a generation: *Citizens United* and *Hobby Lobby*. In an operative legal sense, *Citizens United v. FEC* (2010) overturned the long-established practice of regulating corporate political speech. Normatively, the court determined that corporations have essentially the same First Amendment rights as natural persons, so corporate campaign spending cannot be restricted. Four years later, in *Burwell v. Hobby Lobby Stores, Inc.* (2014), the Supreme Court invalidated the contraceptive mandate provision implemented under the Affordable Care Act (a federal statute that broadly expanded access to healthcare), as violating the First Amendment's free exercise right. This operative determination flowed from the Supreme Court's normative conclusion that for-profit corporations are entitled to exercise religion.

The debate that followed each of these decisions, though shrouded in the language of corporate personhood and corporate purpose, essentially centered on the propriety and value of offering First Amendment protection to corporations and corporate decision-making. Consistent with the Supreme Court's long-standing trend, neither decision adopted expressly a theory of corporate personhood or purpose (Mayer 1990). Instead, it justified its *Citizen United* holding by reference to its evaluation of the importance to political discourse—it is "vital"—of the corporate voice (2010:365). Hobby Lobby justifies its opinion on the importance of religious freedom.

Crucially, all these perspectives largely leave the corporation (or its constituents) to determine the corporation's vocation. That is, whatever the corporation is, it does what it wants.

2. Under Vulnerability Theory

Notwithstanding corporate theory's uncertainty about the nature of the corporation, vulnerability theory—looking to uncontroverted histories and historiography—provides a clear understanding of the nature and purpose of the corporation: The corporation is a site of resilience. The corporation emerged as a functionary of the state specifically to serve resilience generating functions. In exchange for an evolving set of benefits (profits, limited liability, etc.), groups of investors would be charged with tasks within the domain of the state's authority and responsibility.

Although something like the corporate form can trace itself to antiquity, the modern corporation emerged with capitalism. Prior to the seventeenth century, corporations were introduced in Europe as not-for-profit entities to build institutions, like hospitals and universities, for the public good. They had constitutions detailing their duties overseen by the state.

In the seventeenth and eighteenth centuries, The East India Company, the Verenigde Oostindische Compagnie, the Virginia Company, the Geoctrooieerde Westindische Compagnie, the Companhia Geral do Brasil, the Plymouth Company, and other chartered companies were delegated the work of European colonization in exchange for the financial spoils of the endeavor. These chartered companies were mandated to increase trade and economic prosperity, and they were expected to provide employment, housing, medical, educational, and governmental services in their trading localities. The Verenigde Oostindische Compagnie's powers, for example, expressly included the right to wage wars and colonize territories, as well as to imprison and execute people. At the same time, however, the rhetoric of their founding charters was framed by notions of public good for their European constituencies, and their socially beneficial activities were not simply for public relations but were the very reason for their continued existence. Later, charters began to be granted to carry out more and more functions that were either previously carried out by the state or that became necessary with the emergence of capitalism—banking, insurance, water works, real estate, infrastructure (e.g. bridge building). In those early days, the corporation existed in a clear hierarchical collaboration with the State, and corporations were obligated to be responsive to the legitimated arbiter of power.

Only in the nineteenth century did corporations begin to shift away from the strict limitations of their legislature-approved charters. States began granting free incorporation in certain industries. And, in 1896, New Jersey passed a statute allowing corporations to define the scope of their charters themselves, independent of the government. This sort of freedom was first introduced in England in 1844. Eventually, general, free incorporation would be the standard, and the formal link between the corporation and state-monitoring of its social contribution would be broken.

Through this development, the corporation evolved into the ideal liberal subject. And the market-fetishized capture of the corporate regulatory space led to the development of the corporation and corporate-esque entities (e.g. the limited liability partnership and the limited liability company) away from this cooperative, accountable relationship with the state.

B. Corporate Resilience

The same market fetishization has led to the delegation of more and more resilience functions from the state to corporations. Corporations are increasingly dominant in all aspects of social, political, and economic life. As early as the 1930s, Adolf Berle and Gardiner Means recognized this entrenchment of the corporation as a profoundly powerful socio-economic institution. Today, corporations dominate the key categories of resilience generating assets, either directly having been assigned the responsibility for distributing those assets internally or indirectly by corporatizing the production of resilience generating assets.

1. Corporate Resilience Distribution

Perhaps the clearest example of the corporation's role in resilience distribution is the employment relationship. Census data suggests that the United States is a "a nation of employees working for large companies, often very large ones" (Francis 2017:para. 2). Some 71% of workers are employed in the private sector, and just 0.4% of firms employ over half of those workers. Berle and Means likened these mega-corporations to mini-sovereigns, exercising the authority and wielding the influence of the state (Berle and Means 1991). While they are not expressly granted the extensive powers of, say, the East India Companies, they are responsible for distributing the main sources of resilience.

The embodied nature of the human condition leaves people vulnerable to physical and mental harm, sickness, and injury. The ability to resist, recover from, and manage such harms when they arise depends largely on access to proper medical care. Left out of Franklin Delano Roosevelt's expansive "new deal," the provision of health insurance in the United States was delegated to private employers and insurance companies. At its peak, employer-sponsored health insurance covered more than 70% of non-elderly Americans (National Center for Health Statistics 2021). Through the employment relationship, corporations are distributing the material assets of resilience.

Where the state provides only a minimal "social safety net" and privatizes the production of resilience assets—that is, when the state consigns to the market the distribution of most sources of resilience—then people must purchase those assets. That makes money the central resilience mechanism.

And, in turn, salary and wages (which constitute about 70% of Americans' reported income) become indispensable to resilience. Again, and more centrally, through the employment relationship, corporations are distributing the material assets of resilience.

From the status of worker to the nature and conditions of the employment, work has always been recognized as a central generator of social relations. Adam Smith and Karl Marx both recognized the extent to which people's attitudes and behaviors take shape out of the experiences they have in their work" (Kanter 1993:3). People adapt their hopes, dreams, and values to their work lives. People seek and develop relationships and social networks through work (Schultz 2000). Jobs create people and the corporation is the quintessential people producer, allocating key existential and social assets of resilience.

2. Corporate Resilience Production

In a privatized, market economy, the corporation is not solely an institution through which resilience is distributed in the employment relationship. Corporations are also the chief manufacturers of resilience. Corporations dominate American economic life well beyond employment. They literally make and sell the tools of resilience.

Reflect on your surroundings, your daily needs. How much of the "stuff"—the goods and services—that you rely on to survive is directly or indirectly related to a corporation? The health insurance distributed within the corporation's employment relations is sold by a corporate insurance company that, in turn, intermediates the purchase of healthcare from (largely) corporatized healthcare and pharmaceutical providers. Banking and financial services that allow individuals to manage and use the money necessary to purchase other material resilience assets (from clothes to transportation to housing) are sold by corporate banks. Corporate technology and social media companies—like Apple, Facebook, or Tinder—provide virtual spaces and digital tools, by and in which social and relational assets are cultivated and maintained.

There is no resilience category that is uniformly accessible without the interposition of a corporation. Access to public land is managed in whole or in part by privately contracted corporate management companies and concessionaires. Utilities vital to people's basic shelter needs (water, energy, waste) are routinely provided by for profit corporations with no obligation or incentive to maximize access. Education is increasingly privatized through developments like the charter school movement; and, even where the state has retained primary authority over education, contemporary curricula public school curricula are overwhelming created and sold by corporations. Most people must purchase sustainable, healthy food from a corporation. For more than 15% of Americans (and counting), this includes clean water, which can be obtained only from a corporate seller. Even faith and spirituality are vended by large corporations on the religious equivalent of a home shopping network.

The role of corporations as the main producers of the assets of resilience is a direct function of market-fetishism. The dominate ideology contends that the imagined "private" sector will produce the essential assets of resilience more efficiently than any state-based process.

3. Corporate Resilience Protection

Corporations allocate and manufacture resilience. But the corporation remains a human institution. As such, it is vulnerable. Human institutions, they are subject to decay, manipulation, corruption, and decline:

> [S]ocietal institutions are not foolproof shelters, even in the short term. They may fail in the wake of market fluctuations, changing international policies, institutional and political compromises, or human prejudices. Even the most established institutions viewed over time are potentially unstable and susceptible to challenges from both internal and external forces.
>
> *(M. Fineman 2010:256)*

Such vulnerability is evident in the corporation. They are subject to capture, market disruption, regulatory pressure, market fluctuation, reputational harm, insolvency, and so on.

The state has, however, proactively bestowed upon the corporation a range of resilience assets. Indeed, "without the protection of a dense network of laws enforced by public governments, the largest American corporation could not exist for a day" (M. Fineman 2017:146). Through the corporate form, the law enabled the business entity to exist in perpetuity. Corporate law recognizes juridical personhood of the corporation, enabling their "taking and granting property, of contracting obligations, and of suing and being sued" ("Corporation Aggregate," *Halsbury's Laws of England*). The corporation's separation of ownership and control mitigates prohibitive costs of broad multilateral collaboration. Limited liability ensured that possibility of investors, while the state also created specialized markets to ensure investment liquidity.

These constitutional, structural assets of corporate resilience were complemented by a range of norms designed to minimize transaction and agency costs associated with the complicated corporate from. For example, broad fiduciary duties that require corporate manager to act in the best interests of the corporation and its shareholders—even if operationally weak—generate investor confidence and managerial discipline to protect the corporation from major sources of instability. The "business judgement rule," which creates a presumption of managerial fiduciary compliance, protects the corporation from vexatious litigation and empowers perceived desirable managerial risk taking.

What is more, corporate law evolves with relative speed to respond to new or unanticipated sources of vulnerability. For example, when in the 1980s American corporations faced a wave of hostile takeovers, corporate law across jurisdictions sanctioned a range of new mechanisms—most famously the shareholder rights plan, or poison pill—designed to permit otherwise impermissible defensive actions. In less than a decade, the majority of U.S. jurisdictions adopted some version of a benefit corporation statute in response to concerns from social entrepreneurs about liability for integrated and expansive (or ambitious) corporate social responsibility programs.

The conventional explanation for the generous allocation of resilience to the corporation has been to allow and support economic market activity that would less likely occur without such resilience. The normative call of vulnerability requires a much more robust justification of these choices.

IV. Toward a Responsive State Approach to the Corporation

Ellen Goodman's (1979) The Company Man—styled as a eulogistic reflection on a corporate executive whose work became, quite literally, his life (and death)—was intended as a critique of modern corporate culture, which colonizes and consumes the lives of its dispensable constituents. Like Ward, Mike, and Archie, Phil relied on the company for the assets and resources necessary to confront the realities of life—the company was his only source of resilience. Phil, "who worked himself to death finally and precisely at 3:00 a.m. Sunday morning—on his day off" (1979:18) is not, however, presented as an ideal. He is a warning, a cautionary tale. Beware, urges Goodman. The corporation on whom you rely, the corporation you need, it does not need you back. When you are gone the company president will "discreetly of course, and with care and taste" (p. 19), begin post haste the inquiries about your replacement. Underlying Goodman's warning are the questions that become clear when the resilience function of the corporation is laid bare.

This chapter started from the proposition that humans—each and every one—face a constant, immutable but dynamic and unquantifiable condition of vulnerability. The only response to that condition is resilience (that is, the development of mechanisms that allow individuals to confront, survive, mitigate, and even avoid the consequences of that vulnerability). Resilience is, in turn, produced within and through institutions and relationships that confer privilege and power. Using that heuristic, the chapter identified the corporation as a central institution used to allocate and distribute resilience.

Like the fact of vulnerability as the human condition, this is a descriptive and empirical observation. And, like the fact of vulnerability, it has important implications. When we take vulnerability as a universal constant, the existential corporate questions become: how is the corporation generating resilience? For whom is the corporation generating resilience? Why has the corporation been selected as the dominant institution for the distribution and management of the major mechanisms of resilience? And why—among other vital resilience generating and allocating institutions—are corporations themselves granted such extraordinary assets of resilience?

Recognizing the corporation's role in resilience provides a useful, more contextualized heuristic for exploring and examining the structures and strictures of privilege and disadvantage in an economy dominated by corporate power. But it also creates space for normative demands: so long as vulnerability is the constant, universal human condition, the organizing logic of the state, the central justification of government, and the primary purpose of all its ancillary human institutions must be the building of resilience.

Organized, purposeful, institutionalized, equitable, and democratic resilience generation and distribution is affected through a "responsive state." Through the law the state creates and maintains a network of institutions and the social identities contained within them (M. Fineman 2015). By continuously monitoring, evaluating, updating, and reforming its institutions, a responsive state provides and supports the institutions that help create such resilience (M. Fineman 2015). This notion complicates prevailing critiques of the corporation, but it also opens space for enriched regulatory demands on the institution.

The organizing principle of the corporate law regime is enabling. Although they do not consistently achieve those aims, corporate law rules are—often explicitly—intended to minimize transaction costs, manage agency costs, encourage investment, and support entrepreneurship. Resting on the presumption that the profit motive is the only stable and uniform business interest; those rules aim corporate commitments to that end. An intransigent managerial culture has built up around this legal structure.

The corporation's resilience-generating role fundamentally undermines these settlements. Profit, for example, may provide a useful reward or incentive structure for corporate behavior. But—maybe—the *purpose* of the corporation is resilience generation and distribution. That is, if the state consistently and increasingly delegates resilience functions to the corporation, then it is reasonable to conclude that the aim of the state in chartering corporations is to serve this role. Resilience may not be a byproduct of corporate activity; it is the primary task. And, if that is the case, the corporate law lacks any meaningful accountability heuristics for assessing a corporation's resilience performance.

That the corporation *should* play a central role in generating and distributing resilience is hardly clear. Indeed, outlining the myriad ways the state has delegated its responsibility to corporations may rather be an indictment of the state's abdication of its fundamental purpose. And an equitable, democratic approach of the responsive state may demand regression of corporate privilege, power, and authority.

The core intervention of vulnerability theory is threefold: (1) appreciate that vulnerability (i.e., susceptibility to attack, shock, and harm) is not a pathology to be fixed, repaired, or prevented but a basic and indelible characteristic of humans and human institutions. (2) recognize that the only meaningful response to the universal, constant human condition of vulnerability is resilience (i.e., the resources and mechanisms that facilitate recovery or insulation from the effects of vulnerability). and (3) demand that the role of the state must be to respond to vulnerability by producing, reproducing, and allocating mechanisms of resilience.

This chapter accepted that core intervention to interrogate the central functions of the corporation in the social and material constitution and reproduction of individuals and communities and make two claims: first, it suggested that the corporation (or, more accurately, the business enterprise) has become the main structure through which resilience is generated and distributed. The corporation's influence is expansive. Housing, health care, food, education—these most basic resilience mechanisms are dominated by corporatized power. The corporate space has also become the mediator of the types of networked relationships that constitute the core of informal and invisible sites of resilience, including kinship and friendship. And resilience itself has become the most popular good and service produced by business enterprises.

Reference List

Berle, Adolf A. and Gardiner C. Means. 1991. *The Modern Corporation and Private Property*. 2nd ed. New York: Routledge.

Blair, Margaret M. 2013. "Corporate Personhood and the Corporate Persona." *University of Illinois Law Review* 2013(3):785–820.

Burwell v. Hobby Lobby Stores, Inc., 573 U.S. 682 (2014).

Citizens United v. FEC, 588 U.S. 310 (2010).

Easterbrook, Frank H. and Daniel R. Fischel. 1989. "The Corporate Contract." *Columbia Law Review* 89(7):1416–48.

Fineman, Jonathan. 2017. "A Vulnerability Approach to the Private Ordering of Work." Pp. 13–33 in *Vulnerability and the Legal Organization of Work*, edited by M. A. Fineman and J. W. Fineman. New York: Routledge.

Fineman, Martha Albertson. 2008. "The Vulnerable Subject: Anchoring Equality in the Human Condition." *Yale Journal of Law and Feminism* 20:1–23.

———. 2010. "The Vulnerable Subject and the Responsive State." *Emory Law Journal* 60:251–75.

———. 2014. "Vulnerability, Resilience, and LGBT Youth." *Temple Political & Civil Rights Law Review* 23:307–30.

———. 2015. "Equality and Difference—The Restrained State." *Alabama Law Review* 66:626–45.

———. 2017. "Introducing Vulnerability." Pp. 1–10 in *Vulnerability and the Legal Organization of Work*, edited by M. A. Fineman and J. W. Fineman. New York: Routledge.

———. 2018. "Injury in the Unresponsive State: Writing the Vulnerable Subject into Neo-Liberal Legal Culture." Pp. 50–74 in *Injury and Injustice: The Cultural Politics of Harm and Redress*, edited by A. Bloom, D. M. Engle and M. McCann. Cambridge: Cambridge University Press.

Francis, Theo. 2017. "Why You Probably Work for a Giant Company, in 20 Charts." *The Wall Street Journal*, April 6 (www.wsj.com/graphics/big-companies-get-bigger/).

Goodman, Ellen. 1979. "The Company Man." Pp. 18–19 in *Close to Home*, edited by E. Goodman. New York: Simon and Schuster.

Hamilton, Robert W. 1971. "Corporate Entity." *Texas Law Review* 49(6):979–1009.

Harper Ho, Virginia E. 2012. "Theories of Corporate Groups: Corporate Identity Reconceived." *Seton Hall Law Review* 42(3):879–952.

Johnson, Lyman. 2012. "Law and Legal Theory in the History of Corporate Responsibility: Corporate Personhood." *Seattle University Law Review* 35:1135–64.

Kanter, Rosabeth Moss. 1993. *Men and Women of the Corporation*. 2nd ed. New York: Basic Books.

Mayer, Carl J. 1990. "Personalizing the Impersonal: Corporations and the Bill of Rights." *Hastings Law Journal* 41(3):577–667.

National Center for Health Statistics. 2021. "Private Health Insurance Coverage Among People Under Age 65, by Selected Characteristics: United States, Selected Years 1984–2019." *Center for Disease Control* (www.cdc.gov/nchs/data/hus/2020-2021/HIPriv.pdf).

Ripken, Susanna Kim. 2009. "Corporations Are People Too: A Multi-Dimensional Approach to the Corporate Personhood Puzzle." *Fordham Journal of Corporate and Financial Law* 15:97–177.

Schultz, Vicki. 2000. "Life's Work." *Columbia Law Review* 100(7):1881–964.

Travis, Mitchell. 2019. "The Vulnerability of Heterosexuality: Consent, Gender Deception and Embodiment." *Social & Legal Studies* 28(3):303–26.

Trustees of Dartmouth College v. Woodward, 17 U.S. 518 (1819).

Yuille, Lua Kamál. 2017. "From *Corpo Economicus* to *Corpo Sapiens*." *University of Louisville Law Review* 55(2):163–202.

6

MARKET CITIZENSHIP, RESILIENCE DRAINAGE, AND THE ROLE OF PRIVATE LAW

Hila Keren and Ronit Donyets-Kedar

Introduction

Conventional legal thinking associates public law with the vertical relationship between the state and its members while reserving the horizontal relationship between members of society to private law. While the state's role in the sphere of public law is relentlessly discussed and debated, its functions in the domain of private law are routinely framed as minimalist. By and large, state acts pertaining to the latter realm are branded interventions that must be kept to exceptional situations.

In what follows, we use vulnerability theory to critique this fundamental legal approach, which informs both liberalism and, more recently, neoliberalism. We have three general goals in doing so. The first is to re-configure the state's duties vis-à-vis its members' interactions with each other (the horizontal axis). The second is to demonstrate the normative power of vulnerability theory, both in general legal analysis and in the particular context of laws that shape the economic arena. The third is to enhance this normative power by further developing a central tenet of the theory—the state's duty to allocate resilience across society equitably.

Our path towards achieving those general goals is tripartite. We first take up the conventional divide between what is considered "public" versus what is perceived as "private" to justify our focus on private law and define the principal terms used in our discussion. Applying vulnerability analysis, we explain why we better replace this bifurcated outlook with a more holistic approach. Calling this approach "market citizenship," we highlight the marketplace as a crucial area in which social membership is formed, shaped, and must be protected. The most necessary protection, we argue, is from market

DOI: 10.4324/9781003323242-10

actors that exploit powers awarded to them via private law to deplete others' capabilities to cope with life's challenges. We utilize vulnerability theory's vocabulary to define this harmful behavior as "resilience drainage," asserting that the state has an obligation of the highest order to prevent it.

The next two sections demonstrate *how*—as a normative matter—the state can and should suppress resilience drainage and protect market citizenship for all. Following our emphasis on fields of law branded "private," we open from contract law and close with corporate law.

Regarding contract law, resilience-oriented analysis guides us to propose a revival of the Thirteenth Amendment's right "to make and enforce contracts." We see this as an urgent state response to unfortunate but common market behavior in which businesses humiliate people perceived as "Others," by either refusing to deal with them or mistreating them as they seek to participate in the market.

As to corporate law, the vulnerability approach leads us to redefine the most fundamental principles of corporate separation and corporate purpose. Such reform, we argue, is sorely needed to cope with businesses owned by religious market actors that use corporations to evangelize the marketplace at the expense of users who do not live by the most traditionalist views of those owners.

All told, we make a novel claim regarding the state's impact on human resilience and the significance of private law. The duty to equitably allocate resilience among people and social institutions cannot be fully satisfied through direct state grants of resources. The state must also pay attention to and assume responsibility for how the resilience it provides is being used. Concretely, because the state confers significant resilience on *some* market actors through its private law, it should use this law's principles and doctrines to prevent beneficiaries from draining the resilience of other market users. It must maintain market citizenship for all.

I. The Private-Public Divide and the Role of Private Law

One of the implications of the liberal and neoliberal underpinning of law is the affirmation and perpetuation of the public-private divide. According to this dominant paradigm, the state's role is to secure and foster what is framed as public interest while setting the private sector free to promote self-interest and the economy via an idealized free market (Donyets-Kedar 2017a). A bifurcation of the legal world follows. Under the private-public dichotomy, laws related to private interactions are not supposed to address public issues. Instead, the paradigm assigns the responsibility to promote the public interest to areas of law considered "public," with our constitutional law as a leading example.

This conventional division of labor makes private law's role appear narrow and devoid of social impact. Seemingly, private law operates to allow people to fulfill their self-interest, free will, and individual freedom. The legal creation and protection of important private tools such as contracts and corporations are prime examples that we discuss below. For now, however, our point is different. A body of law decidedly focused on fostering autonomy and supporting individualistic behavior creates the illusion that whatever people achieve in the private domain is merely their own accomplishment. Indeed, liberal and neoliberal views celebrate the ideals of personal merit and independence. They also present them as achievable with very minimal, if ever noticed, help from the state or its laws.

Drawing on vulnerability theory, our first point of disruption regards the myth surrounding market success. The theory's name highlights its descriptive critical insight that vulnerability is universal: all humans, and the institutions they establish, are inevitably vulnerable (Fineman 2008). Contra liberalism and neoliberalism, no one is independent or entrepreneurial enough to become and remain successful alone (Fineman 2000). Instead, people's survival, accomplishments, and well-being heavily depend on state-conferred resources and society's structure. This structure—provided through laws and social institutions—determines the level of ability to cope with inescapable vulnerabilities. To illustrate, no one can avoid sickness, but recovery hinges on access to quality health services. For that reason, vulnerability theory defines and highlights *resilience*—the resources available for coping with inescapable vulnerability—as an essential building block of a just society (Fineman 2020).

Applying those ideas to the private-public divide and the assumptions underlying the conventional framing of private law makes a striking difference. Against leading myths, it forces us to acknowledge the significant resilience that private law confers upon its regular beneficiaries—businesses. No celebrated entrepreneurial project, we insist, arose to success without heavy reliance on sources of resilience such as the ability to make and enforce contracts and the capacity to invest and solicit investors under the protections of corporate law. These examples, which will be discussed below, demonstrate how private law itself offers resilience to private businesses, despite being an arm of the public state.

This type of resilience allocation also calls untrue the perception of the private arena as one in which the state is—and should be—minimally involved. Instead, since the state is already active via its private law on behalf of businesses and other repeating market actors, it cannot selectively and asymmetrically relinquish its so-called public duties to all other members of society.

On this point, and in a critical normative move, vulnerability theory assigns the state the responsibility of responding to the endless manifestations of human vulnerability, envisioning and prescribing what it calls *the responsive state* (Fineman 2010). Accordingly, the main role of the responsive state is to engage in equitable *resilience allocation* (Fineman 2020). This demand alone presents a significant normative deviation from the private-public divide and the confined role it attributes to private law. Under liberal and even more under neoliberal dominance, the state should stay away from the market on behalf of the myth of freedom. Thus, any state activity in the private zone is met with considerable hostility, negatively framed as an intervention that must be minimized (Keren 2020). By contrast, a resilience-oriented approach should lead to an expectation for greater, not lesser, state involvement. Since the state is already very active in the private arena—highly (if unnoticeably) engaged in enhancing some actors' resilience—it ought to be monitoring the impact of its resilience allocation on others present in the same arena. Under this view, state regulations that apply to private actors and their exchanges cannot be limited to promoting liberty, market efficiency, and competition, as the conventional paradigm suggests. Instead, other-regarding values such as justice, equality, and fairness, to name a few, should be integrated into private law rather than being solely relegated to public law.

The next step we take focuses on the constraints that must be imposed on private actors via private law. The commonly accepted division of labor between public and private norms functions as a shield for those pursuing economic power: since they are invited to pursue self-interest, and are sometimes even ordered to disregard the public good, they are implicitly allowed to do so at the expense of others. Indeed, legal doctrines within private law tend to ignore situations in which private actions turn injurious to others or the public interest (Donyets-Kedar 2017b). Through compartmentalization, we argue, private law neglects the impact that market competition, mainly carried through utilizing contracts and corporations, has on persons' well-being and the health of their physical and social environment. Protected by a badge of "privacy," people and legal entities are allowed a free pass to consider only self-interest, as long as they are in compliance with the very thin demands of private law. Their relentless wealth accumulation is presumed legitimate, even at the expense of essential human needs and public interests. Those impacted, in turn, are supposed to fend for themselves and never look to the state for help. When exploited by wealth maximizing actors, they are subject to victim blaming mechanisms, made responsible to take care of themselves, and judged for not pulling themselves up by their bootstraps, as the metaphor goes (Keren 2020).

Such a tendency of private law to ignore the misuse of power by its primary beneficiaries cannot survive the scrutiny offered by vulnerability analysis. Thus, building on the general tenet of state obligation to engage in equitable resilience allocation, we add here the more specific concept of *resilience drainage* (Keren 2021). Descriptively, what we call resilience drainage is the behavior of using state-conferred resilience to undermine the resilience of others. Normatively, we argue that the role of private law in a responsive state must include the active prevention of such resilience drainage.

We plan to elaborate further using the right to make and enforce contracts, as well as the principle of corporate separateness as specific examples, but in preparation for this discussion, we argue here that the private-public divide, in and of itself, perpetuates the ability of private actors to use the powers conferred upon them via private law in a manner harmful to others. This paradigm yields legal insensitivity to how interactions narrowly and misleadingly framed as mere economic relations profoundly influence our society.

Once one defines vulnerability as the mark of the human condition, and thus the equitable distribution of resilience as the core task of law, the divide between private and public loses much of its logic. Instead, the vulnerability approach guides us to recognize that socially embedded institutions—private or public—are legal constructs. They are never isolated, and they always impact levels of resilience around them. Accordingly, they either exploit and enhance vulnerability, perpetuating societal power imbalances, or award others with resources that build resilience. Their effect on resilience levels does not flow from or hinge on their classification as private or public. Consequently, we question not only the private-public divide but also the ensuing splits between market and state, economy and society, and—most importantly—private and public law. We also follow the theory in framing the market as an institution vital to the accumulation of resilience (Fineman 2020) and claiming that for that reason, it is essential to consider normative reforms *in all areas of law*, not just those focused on civil rights. Accordingly, we focus here on private law as a central zone within which resilience allocation occurs. Generally, we argue that such a vulnerability-inspired focus has much normative power. It can and should drive us to reconsider and reshape leading principles of private law particularly to prevent the damaging phenomenon of resilience drainage.

Our normative aspiration is to outline a type of responsive private law that creates and protects market citizenship for all. Note that the term market citizenship is coined to overcome the private-public divide as it intentionally integrates the "private" market with the "public" nature of citizenship. As defined by one of us in previous works, the term stands for the bundle of rights and duties that come with living in a market society and using legal tools such as contracts and corporations (Keren 2022). Defining market citizenship and committing to protecting it is a reminder that participation in the marketplace entails more than privileges and access to profits. Instead, it is the role of the responsive state to ensure—by all means, including private law—that all its members have access to market rights and adhere to their duties; that no one uses market powers to undermine the market citizenship of others.

In the coming two sections, we demonstrate how contract law and corporate law can be used to combat resilience drainage and promote market citizenship. We do so by presenting as a case study the behavior of businesses that use their contractual and corporate powers to impose and disseminate their owners' ideological or merely prejudiced objections to engaging with others in the marketplace. With a focus on contracts and contract law, we first address the issue of general resilience drainage that takes place when various disfavored groups, some but not all protected under nondiscrimination laws, suffer market exclusions or severe mistreatment. Then, while focusing on corporate law, we discuss the more specific case of businesses that drain the resilience of others due to their owners' religious objections. Here, the rejections and attacks target mainly women and LGBTQ+ people. Both in the general and the specific manifestations of the phenomenon, state-supported contractual tools, and corporate protections are misused to inflict severe harm on people. Using the vulnerability typology we have developed so far, seasoned market actors have engaged in resilience drainage while breaching the duties that come with their market citizenship.

The following sections delve into the phenomenon of market behaviors that, without any connection to the transaction at hand, express hostility to some people due to features of their identity. We do so to illuminate further the normative power of vulnerability theory. In general, the theory offers liberation from the limited and limiting view of private law's role. Then, with private law tools that include concrete doctrines of contract and corporate law, it can better secure equitable resilience allocation, prevent resilience drainage, and foster true market citizenship for all. We first take up contract law and then turn to corporate law.

II. Resisting Resilience Drainage via Contract Law

In this section, we demonstrate the normative power of vulnerability analysis by discussing how contract law—as a leading field of private law—could and should be deployed to prevent resilience drainage and support market citizenship for all.

A. The Problem: Market Rejections and Humiliation

Life in this day and age cannot proceed without a host of market interactions. We must depend on the market for income, housing, transportation, food, medical treatments, and more. We also turn to the marketplace for less necessary goods and services; for example, when we purchase travel services for joy or browse and shop as a social or familial activity. The problem is that while numerous people enjoy these forms of market participation and take them for granted, others risk immense suffering when they try to do the same. Their ability to partake in the market is constrained not by the limits of their own means or capabilities but by how wrongfully providers and counterparties treat them.

Far too often, individuals are assaulted in the marketplace—refused a service, followed and searched while shopping, yelled at when trying to insist on their rights, harassed and ridiculed, ignored while others are cared for, terminated from their job, evicted from their housing, abandoned by a rideshare driver, and more (Keren 2023). These hostile events stem from various reasons related to one or more characteristics disparaged by aggressive market actors: gender, race, weight, disability, gender identity, parenthood, foreign accent, height, sexual orientation, and more.

Despite this great variety of reasons, a significant and painful pattern emerges, featuring some key elements. First, the incidents occur at the heart of the market, in the various settings that comprise the marketplace: work, housing, transportation, retail, and other types of transactional exchanges of goods or services for pay. Second, the events entail adverse treatment of people who engage or attempt to engage in ordinary market activities. They are being refused, insulted, rejected, or excluded, notwithstanding their undisputed *economic* ability to engage in the transactions they seek. Third, the aggressions are intentional and sometimes carefully calculated. In them, the mistreating parties openly express disdain toward their counterparties. Fourth, the offenses target traits that have nothing to do with the exchange at hand but have much to do with other aspects of the mistreated parties' core identity.

What this pattern suggests is that complete, stable, safe, and effortless market participation—enjoyed by many and celebrated by liberal and neoliberal philosophies—is far from being available to all. It exposes that true market membership is only the rule for standard-able-bodied heterosexual and cisgender white men. At the same time, people perceived—for one reason or another—as "others" are at constant peril of severe market mistreatment. However, by and large, conventional law fails to respond to this phenomenon, thereby legitimating the harm it entails—one it is yet to be properly conceptualized.

Much of this failure stems from what we already discussed: any state intervention in the market is made merely via "public" laws—here, nondiscrimination laws—and is treated with hostility due to its perceived attack on "private" freedoms. But, even when applying nondiscrimination laws is considered, the result is highly disappointing, leaving most of the harm in place. As a general matter, the leading legal response is limited by the very framing of the issue of these market aggressions as "discrimination." This narrow outlook makes redress depend on a complex and confusing patchwork of nondiscrimination norms, imposing endless hurdles on those damaged in the marketplace under a hopelessly fragmented analysis that is unsympathetic to their plea.

Consider the following leading obstacles. First, most nondiscrimination norms that pertain to the market cover only certain enumerated groups, leaving many others exposed or questionably and inconsistently covered. Examples include fat people, LGBTQ+ individuals in many jurisdictions, individuals with foreign accents, and more. Second, even for enumerated groups, such as racial minorities, establishing a legal claim is a deeply frustrating uphill battle. Courts have applied well-established protections, such as those awarded under Title II of the Civil Rights Act of 1964, narrowly and erratically. They approved, for example, practices such as following and monitoring shoppers of color, giving inferior seating and service to diners of color, and offering second-rate accommodations to minority guests (Thomas 2021). Courts also released from the Act's prohibitions significant segments of the market, including retail stores as large as Walmart, airplanes, banks, most barbershops, and more (Thomas 2021; Jones 2020). Third, as part of the legal chaos, businesses in some specific market sections have been trying to escape nondiscrimination laws for concrete reasons, for example, because they operate in the wedding industry but object to same-sex marriage (Keren 2022) or because they run an app-based online business and thus are not subject to laws such as the Americans with Disability Act (*Martinez v. San Diego County Credit Union* 2020).

Last and most significant, even those with cognizable discrimination claims and the ability to prove them face another considerable hurdle: a struggle to get legal remedies for the injury. Some nondiscrimination laws relevant to market behavior specifically deny redress for events that had already ended, limiting remedies to injunctions and declarations and excluding compensation (U.S. Department of Justice 2022). More broadly and crucial to the discussion of resilience that follows, nondiscrimination laws have increasingly limited access to damages for emotional harm. Recently, the Supreme Court decided, in *Cummings v Premier Rehab Keller* (2022), that businesses that receive Federal funding and therefore are particularly obliged to refrain from discrimination do not owe damages for causing emotional suffering by breaching their duty. This approach is clearly an offshoot of the artificial separation of the economic sphere from the human condition. Indeed, in many cases, businesses and even Supreme Court Justices defend a right to exclude clients based on the free-market logic that no harm is involved in this behavior when the goods or services can be purchased elsewhere (Keren 2023).

B. A Vulnerability-Based Response

Unlike mainstream legal analysis, vulnerability theory offers sophisticated new tools to comprehend the problem of market aggressions and normatively allows us to develop a far more adequate legal response. It first helps avoid the shortcomings of the nondiscrimination paradigm, reframing the general normative goal as reaching beyond the battle against what current law classifies as discrimination. Instead, the theory "does not seek equality, but equity" (Fineman 2017:143). This radical shift, facilitated by the focus on the universal need for resilience, is far more inclusive than our current legal regime and enables caring for *everyone* who suffers rejection or harassment in the marketplace. Such inclusiveness relieves us from the limits of identity-based safeguards, including burdensome classifications, ongoing debates regarding which groups deserve protection, and the ensuing risk of pitting marginalized groups against each other. Thus, for instance, when an employer insults female employees for being "fat," forcing them to weigh themselves in his presence (*Reynolds v. Robert Hasbany* 2018), a vulnerability approach makes room for redress that does not exist in most jurisdictions.

Significantly, vulnerability theory explains why the troubling pattern of market maltreatment deserves a much stronger legal response. Once we view the world through the lenses of resilience allocation, we can see how market attacks are acts of severe resilience drainage. In them, seasoned market actors use their market powers to deplete their counterparties' resilience. Because vulnerability analysis frames the market as an institution vital to resilience accumulation (Fineman 2020), it becomes evident that limitations on accessing the marketplace—or participating in it in a dignified manner—deplete resilience. This problem is particularly severe in a privatized and hyper-capitalist society like ours, where lack of access to quality goods and services carries dramatic economic and other tangible damages, from job loss to inferior health care. Moreover, the dominance of neoliberalism *outside* the economic sphere, and the evaluation of everything that matters, including social status and self-esteem, by market metrics, makes things much worse (Brown 2015).

A resilience-based analysis also highlights what current laws ignore or marginalize: emotional harm. Because emotional resources are vital to coping with life's challenges (Abrams and Keren 2013), this analysis demands full accounting for the emotional damage many suffer in the marketplace as they try to participate in it. Since self-worth and social belonging are vital to human survival, businesses' refusal to contract with people due to who they are (their race, weight, or gender identity, for example) presents an immense risk. The emotion of humiliation serves the role of alerting humans to this risk. As many studies evidence, humiliation is a particularly intense and long-lasting emotion (Jogdand, Khan, and Reicher 2020). As such, humiliation is also known to lead to considerable health problems, including anxiety, symptoms of post-traumatic stress disorder, and clinical depression (Torres and Bergner 2012; Chen et al. 2008; Otten et al. 2017). In the gravest cases, these medical problems can lead to suicidal ideation and even death (Klein 1991). Given those dreadful consequences, it is clear how the deliberate infliction of humiliation through market boycotts and other acts of harassment dangerously drains people's resilience. Unlike existing laws, vulnerability analysis conceptualizes this harsh reality as relevant to law and normatively significant to shaping a response.

So, having insisted on the magnitude of the problem, what should this legal response be? Here, we argue, the normative strength of the vulnerable theory comes again to the fore. In the face of explicit and often brutal acts of resilience drainage, vulnerability analysis speaks loudly against leaving things in the hands of private market actors and calls for a state response. This is so, not because the state desires to impose its specific social agenda at the expense of freedom, as the myth goes. Rather, it is the result of the state's ongoing obligation to respond to universal vulnerability by maximizing the resilience of people and institutions. As we said earlier, since the state always participates in conferring resources critical to accumulating resilience, it must create and maintain an equitable allocation of such resources. Such duty, we argue, cannot be fully discharged vertically by fair distribution of resources by the state to its members. Instead, the task should also include monitoring the horizontal relationship between market participants to ensure that the state's most resilient members do not exploit their powers to undermine others' resilience.

In legal terms, the state's duty to monitor what happens in the market and ensure the marketplace serves as a source of resilience for everyone can be traced to the Thirteenth Amendment. This often-neglected Amendment, together with the cluster of statutes that sought to implement it, can offer a valuable platform for a vulnerability-inspired solution. These constitutional norms can be centralized and then re-read as making the promise of what we call here market citizenship for all. They have the power to instruct legislators and courts to make sure that every member of society has the same ability to partake in the market and enjoy its benefits.

This proposed path to market citizenship starts with treating contracts as critical to civil standing, as suggested by the explicit promise that everyone shall have a right to "make and enforce contracts" (42 U.S.C. §§ 1981–1986; Keren 2005; Wolff 2002). It continues by expanding the promise's reach, interpreting it also to reflect state commitment to protecting individuals' ability to use contracts "to make and pursue meaningful life decisions" (Tsesis 2021). And, as some scholars further suggested, such decisions require the universal capacity of all people to "buy and sell when they please," (*Jones v. Alfred H. Mayer Co.* 1968), thus commanding recognition—within contract law—of a general principle of "freedom TO contract" (Keren 2005). Professor Robin West explained the rationale behind these demands when she wrote: "participation in the commercial sphere [is] a vehicle for inclusion in civil life in market economies" (West 2019:185).

But formal access and mere participation are hardly enough if we are to adopt more than a narrow economic approach. It is, therefore, significant to recall that the Thirteen Amendment additionally empowered a legislated right to "full and equal *enjoyment*" of public accommodations. Although this remarkable insistence on enjoyment is presently almost invisible, the holistic focus on resilience proposed here highlights its importance (Sepper 2021; Leong 2021; François 2021). While the right for full and equal enjoyment was included in legislation later deemed unconstitutional (*United States v. Stanley* 1883) many states have adopted the statutory language (Sepper 2021:577–8). And most importantly, the constitutional debate induced a salient clarification that even without special legislation, at least some businesses must serve "all unobjectionable persons who in good faith apply for them" (*United States v. Stanley* 1883:25).

Embracing a commitment to prevent resilience drainage, we argue that all these historical sources can generate a robust market principle and further demonstrate vulnerability theory's practical normativity. Concretely, we suggest putting together the pieces of the above language to reconstruct a broader constitutional principle of market citizenship. To this end, consider the following phrasing: "all unobjectionable persons who in good faith apply for" (*United States v. Stanley* 1883:3) goods and services shall have "a right to make and enforce contracts" (42 U.S.C. §§ 1981–1986) to obtain such goods and services with "full and equal enjoyment" (18 U.S.C. § 242).

Notably, the newly phrased principle relates directly to several unwarranted limitations that present courts impose through a narrow interpretation of existing laws. First, in terms of scope, everyone is entitled to the rights covered by the principle regardless of affiliation with certain protected groups. Second, the principle broadly pertains to all market activities based on contracts, allowing us to cope with market actors that try to exploit existing loopholes. Third, the proposed formulation protects more than economic transactions, emphatically demanding that the entire market process—before, during, and after the exchange, and even without a deal—would be dignified rather than humiliating. If nothing less, this process-focused approach nullifies the claim that no harm is done as long as the market can offer alternatives. Instead, it responds to much more than economic damage, forbidding *any* harm to others' resilience, including the drainage of emotional reserve and the depletion of a sense of belonging.

Most important to our argument here, a vulnerability reconstruction of a constitutional principle that defines and protects market citizenship invites and authorizes changing the way the state operates not only nondiscrimination laws but also *private* law—particularly the law that governs contracts. Allow us to illustrate briefly.

As one of us has discussed elsewhere, the most appropriate tool within contract law to curtail market attacks that humiliate and drain resilience is the principle of good faith. Following European legal systems (Miller and Perry 2013:690–1), American contract law adopted the duty to handle the contractual process with good faith to maintain its morality (Summers 1982; Markovits 2004; Miller and Perry 2013:725). As a result, both the Uniform Commercial Code (2011) and the Restatement (1981) declare this principle as broadly applying to all contracts. Further, although the principle in its American version does not have its full original power, it is still considered one of the pillars of our law of contracts (Miller and Perry 2013:690).

The principle of good faith can and should straightforwardly apply to the many market aggressions that occur while the parties have already established contractual relationships. For example, when a landowner evicts someone for being transgender, contract law must respond to the evident drainage of resilience. Particularly, the duty to perform contracts in good faith should be applied, leading to classifying the hostility as a breach of contract that carries liability. While good faith should easily offer protection when the humiliation happens after contractual relationships are formed, applying the principle to protect those denied or assaulted during the pre-contractual phase is admittedly more complex. In those scenarios, the legal problem is that, unlike the civil-law world, "common-law systems have always been reluctant to recognize a duty of good faith in the pre-contractual stage" (Miller and Perry 2013:700). And yet, significant exceptions exist, and there is an increasing willingness to impose pre-contractual duties (Kessler and Fine 1964:408; Eisenberg 2000:1811–13; Farnsworth 1987:273–85).

The state of existing law notwithstanding, vulnerability analysis offers a compelling normative claim that the principle of good faith *should* be expanded to cover the pre-contractual stage. Indeed, we ought to treat refusals to deal with others for no contractual reason, including mistreating them until they give up and leave, as bad faith in contracting (Keren 2005). The fact that some businesses are perfectly ready and willing, as part of their business model, to profit from serving unlimited amounts of people they find unobjectionable is most relevant here. In contractual terms, businesses are making a promise that originates from their market presence and heavy use of the contractual system. Albeit implicitly, they promise to consider potential contractual partners fairly (Barak 1996). Therefore, while they do not have to transact with individuals who do not accept the terms of the exchange, they cannot legitimately reject people who would.

Drawing on vulnerability theory, we argue that the state that allocates resilience to businesses by letting them benefit from an effective contractual system must *condition* the use of this system on adhering to inclusiveness. It should demand market actors to use the entire contracting process in good faith and accordingly define resilience-draining aggressions, at any stage of the process, as bad faith.

Utilizing the good faith principle in this way has several advantages. The first comes from the intrinsic source of the duty rather than a reliance on the suspicious interventionist state. Additionally, emphasizing bad faith instead of state protection of certain vulnerable groups shifts the attention to those who misbehave while avoiding the stigma that sometimes unjustly follows state protections (Feingold 2022). All in all, it has the potential to ensure, with private law tools, market citizenship for all.

III. Resisting Resilience Drainage via Corporate Law

Our discussions of the private-public divide and the right to make and enforce contracts have demonstrated how resilience analysis mandates an alternative legal approach to private law to prevent resilience drainage and promote market citizenship. In certain cases, which we discuss below, it is also necessary to monitor the impact of corporate law on resilience allocation. This body of law allows business people to act and profit in the market not by themselves but via corporations, awarding them significant resilience that they sometimes misuse while harming others. A recent and significant example is the use of market powers to drain the resilience of others by imposing and projecting traditionalist views of gender, sexuality, marriage, and family planning. We use this phenomenon to show how both the principle of corporate separateness and the conventional interpretation of corporate purpose are sites of resilience drainage. We also argue that a responsive state could and should operate its corporate law to prevent such manipulation.

A. The Problem of Market Evangelism

In recent years, and particularly since the approval of same-sex marriage by the Supreme Court, conservative advocacy groups have led in courts a battle for a new right. They have argued that incorporated businesses owned by devoted Christians should be able to shape their business policies to express their owner's traditionalist beliefs—no matter the harm to others such policies inflict. Relying on the First Amendment's two prongs of free exercise of religion and free speech, businesses argued that their owners' religious beliefs justify harsh decisions. Known cases that gained Supreme Court attention and much publicity include removing contraceptives from employees' health plans in *Burwell v. Hobby Lobby* (2014), declaring refusals to serve same-sex couples in *Masterpiece Cakeshop Ltd.* v. *Colorado Civil Rights Commission* (2018), and terminating transgender employees in *Bostock v. Clayton County* (2020). In all those cases and numerous similar instances, businesses have engaged in a project that political scientist Wendy Brown called "market evangelism" (2015).

As Brown explained it, market evangelism is an integral part of the neoliberal project: it commits to imposing traditional values *within* the market to disseminate them *outside* of the market. As a business behavior with political goals, market evangelism involves "utilizing market activities (hiring, leasing, selling), market entities (corporations), and market tools (contracts) to evangelize society" (Keren 2022:935).

Before we add more, it is important to recognize that market evangelism conflicts with the private-public dichotomy. The claim that businesses owned by religious owners should somehow be allowed to express and promote beliefs through the transactional world directly refutes the myth of separated domains. Indeed, market evangelism intentionally uses private activities to achieve social results. Admittedly, as our earlier criticism of the myth of separate domains suggests, and as many business practices branded as "green" can illustrate, there is nothing wrong or unusual about such a blurring of the lines. However, in the case of market evangelism, more than a blur occurs. Rather, the insistence of some people on their liberties has a devastating impact on others.

Most directly, users of contraceptives are directly harmed when their employers deny coverage of their family planning needs. Further, as to refusals to sell goods or provide services, we have already introduced the humiliation generally caused by rejections that target people for who they are. The ideological attack on LGBTQ+ people through the market is a specific and brutal example of such market humiliation. Indeed, due to juridical victories in market evangelism cases, some businesses already make anti-LGBTQ+ offensive statements on their websites—ones that are alarmingly akin to traumatic signs used in the past against other disfavored groups (Melling 2019). For example, in one such case, an incorporated photography business now makes, with judicial permission, the following declaration:

> I cannot positively depict anything that. . . devalues marriage between one man and one woman. I also can't photograph anything that conflicts with my religious conviction that marriage is a covenant relationship before God between one man and one woman (for example, I don't photograph same-sex weddings). (*Chelsey Nelson Photography LLC v. Louisville/Jefferson County Metro Government* 2022)

With the spread of such declarations nationwide and with the Supreme Court considering allowing them more broadly (*303 Creative, LLC v. Elenis* 2022), our market has become increasingly and visibly segregated. Such segregation not only turns actual participation in the market uncertain, but it also becomes a source of what we discussed earlier: deep and ongoing humiliation followed by related health problems.

Despite those severe negative consequences to others, the present legal analysis of the issue of expressing religious objections through the market has led courts to increasingly side with religious business owners. This rising judicial approach sets aside the facts: that those owners had chosen to incorporate their businesses, and their corporations are nonhuman entities and thus unable to hold religious beliefs. Instead, courts have demonstrated a willingness to attribute to corporations their owners' beliefs. By doing so, they have legitimized a corporate behavior that intentionally harms other constituencies: from employees to clients to entire communities.

The leading case on this point is *Hobby Lobby*. In this case, the Supreme Court famously treated the religious owners of a large company with numerous employees and their company as if they were one, allowing the business entity to deprive its employees of health insurance coverage of contraceptives due to the personal beliefs of the shareholders. For example, at one point of its analysis the Court said: "protecting the free exercise rights of corporations like Hobby Lobby . . . *protects the religious liberty of the humans who own and control those companies*. . . . Corporations, 'separate and apart from' the human beings who own, run, and are employed by them, cannot do anything at all" (*Burwell v. Hobby Lobby Stores, Inc.* 2014).

Notably, the entire project of market evangelism heavily depends on resilience allocation to companies via corporate law. This is so because few to no market actors would nowadays run businesses without incorporating them, making the way the state operates its corporate law crucial. Given the magnitude of the damage inflicted by market evangelism, it is thus essential to critically review the judicial willingness to treat owners and their corporations as one and the jurisprudential assumption that market evangelism is a legitimate corporate purpose. We take these tasks one at a time to demonstrate why and how corporate law should be used to prevent religious owners from draining the resilience of those who do not adhere to the most traditionalist values.

B. A Vulnerability-Based Response

1. Corporate Separateness and Shareholder's Limited Liability

One of the fundamental principles of corporate law is the separateness of the incorporated entity from its human owners. The central derivative of this principle is the doctrine of shareholder's limited liability, which releases owners from liability for their companies' wrongdoings and debts (Model Business Corporation Act § 6.22). Jurists and economists cite many rationales for protecting shareholders by awarding them limited liability. A leading justification is a wish to support the ability to raise capital from investors who presumptively would be reluctant to join the company in return for investment if doing so entailed high risk to their personal property (Bainbridge 2001:495; Millon 2007). Accordingly, conventional analysis frames limited liability as a mechanism of transferring insolvency risks from shareholders, usually thought of as the company's owners, to its creditors (in the broadest sense) in case the company's debt exceeds the corporate assets. In this sense, limited liability functions as a subsidy for businesses designed to encourage business activity. Such business activity, it is assumed, involves more than enriching shareholders; it carries broad economic benefits to society, thus justifying social support via law.

Notably, limited liability is only made possible due to the separate personality of the corporation: since the corporation is recognized by law as a separate legal entity, its debts could be assigned to the corporation itself rather than its shareholders. By shielding shareholders from corporate misfortunes, the doctrine of limited liability creates a considerable benefit for shareholders bestowed upon them by law. Another benefit that flows from the corporations' separate existence is that the business can continue to operate, notwithstanding the disability or death of one of its owners. As currently understood, these benefits are economic in nature. In the vocabulary of vulnerability theory, however, the benefits also have a significant non-economic meaning: they are state-conferred resources of immense resilience for shareholders. For example, wealth accumulated via their separate companies can serve shareholders to pay for medical expenses others cannot afford when facing sickness.

Nevertheless, corporate separateness and limited liability are not absolute ideas and some exceptions apply. A leading albeit fairly narrow divergence from those principles is the "veil piercing" doctrine. This legal metaphor stands for the idea that in defined cases, the general separation between the corporation and its shareholders (the veil) must be ignored (pierced). By and large, veil piercing works *against* shareholders: courts assign shareholders full, not limited, liability for their corporations' wrongdoing. The rationale for this exception is to deter shareholders from misusing their incorporated entity for fraudulent or other illegal purposes that do not create the value society attributes to legitimate business activities (Macey and Mitts 2014). For that reason, veil piercing is also usually understood as enhancing efficiency. When weighing the economic benefits of limited liability against its economic costs, it sometimes "makes more economic sense" (Easterbrook and Fischel 1991:54–5) to allow creditors to puncture the corporate veil and reach the shareholders' assets.

It is this exception of veil piercing that incorporated businesses led by conservative advocacy groups now seek to utilize in their efforts to avoid coverage for contraceptives and exclude LGBTQ+ parties from the marketplace. Shielded by the veil for all other purposes and enjoying the resilience that comes with the limits on their liability, business owners now demand temporary and selective removal of the veil that separates them and their companies. They argue that courts should peek behind the veil for a brief moment only so their personal beliefs can be attributed to their incorporated business. Then, they implicitly argue, the veil can be dropped back to its normal position and continue to protect them from any other possible responsibility for their companies' acts.

This claim is highly questionable even when reviewed merely from a corporate law perspective and before examining it from a vulnerability perspective (Ackerman and Cole 2016). First, it reverses how the veil-piercing idea had been working for centuries and should operate according to corporate law theories. In the usual litigation, shareholders resist the piercing to retain their special protection. Here, however, they request disregarding the veil instead of fighting against it. Accordingly, some legal scholars have called this "insider reverse veil piercing." This designation highlights how letting shareholders ("insiders") use veil-piercing turns the doctrine on its head: from one supposed to restrain business owners to one that promotes their interests (Bainbridge 2013).

Second, as other scholars argue, what is requested is not at all veil piercing because at no moment are business owners willing to truly remove the veil. Instead, they engage in an unprecedented "veil peeking" (Pargendler 2021). Describing this aspect of the manipulation, political scientist Wendy Brown emphasized that corporate owners want "a shield for their personal assets and the capacity to extend the sweep and reach of their sword from behind that shield" (2015:185). And third, because doctrines such as limited liability and veil piercing are perceived as responding to economic concerns, some theorists insisted that extending peoples' rights to corporations has no room under any recognizable corporate law principle (Macey 2019:1208).

In what follows, we supplement these critical views of decisions like *Hobby Lobby* and *Masterpiece Cakeshop*—that ignored corporate separateness—with a resilience-based analysis. Following the general insights of vulnerability theory, we first explain how ascribing religious beliefs to corporations creates resilience drainage and then propose how corporate law should better be used to prevent such an outcome.

As a starting point, the strong association between corporate law and economic metrics should not mislead anyone, and it must be recognized that attributing human religiosity to corporations presents a social justice issue. The problem is that permitting corporations to engage in market evangelism by manipulating corporate principles leads to a highly distorted resilience allocation. On the side of religious business owners, there is a demand for *excessive* resilience. Conversely, on the side of LGBTQ+ parties, this demand causes *insufficient* resilience.

This effect on resilience must be suppressed by the state. Since the state has created corporate entities and shareholders' limited liability in support of markets, it should not allow those shareholders to accumulate additional resilience by adding to their economic protections constitutional safeguards reserved for humans, such as the right of free exercise of religion. In the words of political scientist Wendy Brown (2015), corporate owners should not be awarded "a shield for their personal assets and the capacity to extend the sweep and reach of their sword from behind that shield" (p. 185). And, from a resilience perspective, the state must most forcefully prevent such disproportionate resilience accumulation when its mere goal is to drain the resilience of others—those that business owners find objectionable and unworthy.

While the Supreme Court approved the incoherent use of the corporate veil in *Hobby Lobby* and *Masterpiece Cakeshop*, and some lower courts followed (*Telescope Media Grp. v. Lucero* 2019), vulnerability theory inspires a wholly different approach. Instead of following the Court's focus on the First Amendment, the theory calls, once again, for enhanced attention to private law, offering a normative path to market citizenship that does not solely depend on "public" law. Concretely, we argue that *corporate law itself* can and should be used to help maintain a marketplace accessible to all.

Generally, it is important to recognize that the same corporate separateness that yields benefits to shareholders and their corporations alike should prevent blending them together when it comes to fostering evangelical goals. If shareholders truly differ from the entity they own, as our corporate law principles insist, their human feelings and beliefs should not be attributed to the incorporated business they chose to run. Therefore, a central way to operationalize corporate law in a way that allocates resilience equitably is to adhere to the conventional boundaries of veil piercing, disallowing usage of the doctrine on behalf of shareholders (instead of against them) that is also applied only partially and selectively. Such an approach has the advantage of tightly aligning with existing corporate law while preventing shareholders from using their particular resilience inadequately.

Moreover, the vulnerability approach to corporate law offers a formidable reply to a concrete argument raised in *Hobby Lobby* in support of allowing corporations to engage in market evangelism. There, the claim was that religious people who use corporations should not be treated differently than those who run their businesses without incorporation (*Burwell v. Hobby Lobby, Inc.* 2014). However, vulnerability analysis illuminates a palpable difference between the groups: only people who incorporate their business enjoy the extra protection of limited liability, which in turn justifies a restraint on how they use it. On this point, it is worth remembering that we merely propose to hold business owners to their choice to run their businesses as corporations. The state does not impose incorporation; therefore, anyone interested in integrating their beliefs with their business policies can freely elect to make a living as a sole proprietor or establish a partnership. However, once the choice to incorporate was executed, the combination of corporate benefits and personal rights should be made legally unavailable.

Furthermore, by identifying the particular problem of resilience drainage, we offer another compelling reason to limit market actors that enjoy limited liability from setting aside the veil when they see fit. Highlighting the damage to others' coping resources, we maintain that the state that awards the protection of limited liability to promote business activity has a special and enhanced obligation to prevent this harmful effect. It thus must forcefully insist that enjoying the right to incorporate comes with a duty to avoid using the very legal structure that allows profitability as a tool to deprive others of their needs and dignity.

A careful application of corporate doctrines would encourage more people to express their personal religious objections outside the market while leaving the marketplace more accessible to everyone. In this way, a state operating as a responsive state would prevent resilience drainage not only by directly imposing norms of equality but also by applying its corporate law. Significantly, doing so would utilize the expressive power of law—including private law—to educate business owners that their market citizenship includes a duty to avoid harming other market citizens.

2. Corporate Purpose

Another argument utilized by religious owners of incorporated businesses ostensibly bypasses the veil-piercing problem by relying on the corporation's direct action. This argument is abstractly founded on an expanded understanding of the goals that the corporations themselves are allowed to pursue. Advocates of permitting market evangelism via corporations assert that corporations' purpose is seldom limited to profit-making on behalf of shareholders. Instead, they say, companies frequently engage in fostering non-economic values. On this point, religious owners and their supporters compare the situation to progressive corporations that promote their owners' left-leaning values, such as environmentalism or social justice (Donyets-Kedar and Sitbon 2023). Why can't religious business people, they ask, use their corporations in the same way?

This argument touches on a famous debate within corporate law, and a response to this debate calls, again, for a focus on resilience. We do this in two steps. The first introduces the debate to show why a vulnerability approach would sometimes support, or even demand, a corporate pursuit of non-economic goals. The second step, however, emphasizes that such a perspective does not lead to a blank license to pursue *any* non-economic goals. Instead, we argue, it necessitates a more nuanced approach that can distinguish between goals that can be adequately promoted and those that should not be legitimized. To fulfill this task, resilience analysis is the key.

A much-debated question regarding corporations is whether they ought to maximize shareholder value, or rather are allowed, or even required, to balance profit-maximization against additional concerns from the welfare of other stakeholders, such as employees, to various social interests, like public health and safety. The traditional answer is narrow. It requires corporate leaders to focus on profitability and, for the most part, overlook other constituencies and values (Donyets-Kedar and Sitbon 2021). This view rests on two assumptions discussed earlier in connection with the private-public divide. One is that people are, first and foremost, autonomous and self-reliant and therefore are justified in pursuing their individual interests while disregarding other concerns. The other assumption is that self-interests are best achieved through the free market, with minimal state intervention.

This narrow perspective has influenced the conventional division of labor between corporate law and public law. In this view, because they are perceived as economic tools for promoting self-interests in the market, corporations should be supervised by corporate law only as much as it helps them achieve such goals. Based on the same logic, caring for other constituencies and values must be delegated to different fields of law. Significantly, many of those legal fields—from labor and tax laws to environmental regulations—lie *outside* the realm of private law and are understood as limiting the market's operation. For those reasons, the narrow approach interprets corporate law as calling on corporate actors to prioritize profits over other concerns.

On the other side of the debate are those alarmed by the detrimental consequences of the narrow view. The focus on profits and the license to disregard others has often led corporate leaders to increase value by harmful business strategies that have harmed individuals' physical and mental well-being, the strength of communities, the state of democracies around the world, and the ecological condition of the globe. Examples are numerous. A recent one is Facebook's exploitation of user information without their consent or knowledge to support the Trump presidential campaign in the Cambridge Analytica scandal. After the testimony of whistleblower Frances Haugen, exposed by the Wall Street Journal's "Facebook Files," it became clear that Facebook was well aware of much of its wrongdoing but repeatedly preferred its profits over the privacy of its users (The Wall Street Journal 2019; Greer 2019). Overall, the negative outcomes of a narrow approach to corporate purpose reinforce structures of privilege and inequality. A corporate law that adopts this approach does not do enough to limit corporations' ability to abuse their power at the expense of human well-being (Donyets-Kedar and Sitbon 2023).

To be able to address the problem, we need to re-conceptualize some fundamental assumptions regarding the purpose of corporations and corporate law, a task for which vulnerability theory offers valuable tools. As a starting point, the theory inspires re-framing the corporation not as an isolated economic unit but rather as a socio-economic enterprise, inseparable from the broader social context within which it operates. This view leads to a need to abandon the traditional narrow approach to corporate purpose. It calls to replace a self-centered focus with a stakeholder-oriented emphasis to highlight the corporate's interrelations with a broader set of constituencies.

In general, therefore, vulnerability analysis offers a strong justification for a new corporate compass that directs corporations to destinations beyond profit-maximizing. It empowers analyzing corporate questions with an eye to their impact on "outsiders:" local communities, employees, suppliers, and even the environment. So, in the debate surrounding corporate purpose, the normative answer arising from vulnerability analysis is utterly different than the traditional one: corporations can and should be pursuing goals beyond profit maximization. Moreover, they should also be held responsible when their narrow focus on economic gains harms others around them.

But does taking this broader approach mean that religious business owners should be allowed to direct their companies to promote the most traditionalist values by, for example, refusing to serve same-sex couples and excluding contraceptives from their employees' health plans? Asked from a vulnerability perspective: are religious business owners similar—as they had alleged in *Hobby Lobby*—to business owners who direct their companies to foster environmental justice?

Here, the answer is firmly negative. Non-economic purposes are not all the same and cannot all be legitimate for corporations to pursue. The key to distinguishing desirable (or even just allowable) objectives from those that should be proscribed is, again, resilience. Vulnerability theory identifies corporations and corporate law not merely as economic devices for promoting self-interest, but rather as an important way in which the state already and always engages in resilience distribution. This focus generates a guiding principle that has immense normative value. It directs us to consider the broad implications of corporate conduct on people's actual lives (Donyets-Kedar 2017a; Rahman 2018). Accordingly, the question should be: what is the impact of any given conduct on the equitable allocation of resilience among members of society?

We argue that applying such a nuanced approach to what corporations do creates a radical change in the debate around corporate purpose. Instead of assessing corporate acts based on their alignment with profit accumulation, the attention should shift to appraising them based on their effect on levels of resilience. And this is where our current emphasis on resilience drainage becomes crucial. Corporate engagement in market evangelism should not be tolerated by a responsive state, not because corporations cannot pursue religious goals at the expense of profit. Indeed, our analysis would not yield an objection if companies like Hobby Lobby and Masterpiece Cakeshop donated to religious organizations that foster traditionalist views. The problem, we insist, comes from the severe damage to others that the kind of market evangelism deployed by those companies causes. Consequentially, the responsive state must forbid excluding LGBTQ+ clients and denying coverage of contraceptives because the companies engaged in this value-promoting conduct weaponize their resilience to deplete resources—mental and tangible—from others. All told, a truly equitable allocation of resilience demands a market open to all in which everyone can have access to what they need and want.

Of note here is a central normative advantage of the resilience perspective. The state's duty to prevent resilience drainage we have proposed allows a value-neutral approach to the corporate purpose debate. It accepts the *Hobby Lobby* claim that many corporations stray away from profit-maximizing as descriptively correct and normatively desirable *regardless* of the non-economic value adopted by the corporation. However, our approach rejects the ensuing comparison between environmental and religious goals if and when the latter are carried out while injuring others. The type of market evangelism led by corporations like Hobby Lobby and Masterpiece Cakeshop cannot be tolerated by a responsive state not because the state disrespects individuals' religious views or wishes to compel them to speak against their values but because they use their market citizenship to undermine the full market citizenship of others.

IV. Conclusion

Private law is a mechanism through which the state confers resilience. However, while bestowing privileges upon some market actors, the current state does not do enough to ensure these are not abused and do not undermine the resilience of others. We have shown that both in contract law and corporate law, the legal principles that serve as resources of resilience are susceptible to misuse. From the right to make and enforce contracts to the protection of limited liability and the ability to promote non-economic corporate purposes, those benefiting from the system may also seek to drain the resilience of others.

Using and further developing the tools of vulnerability theory, we have thus called for reforms that focus on private law as it applies to market relations. A responsive state should counter resilience drainage within the marketplace as part of its more general obligation to respond to inevitable vulnerability. As we have emphasized from the beginning, the responsive state cannot fulfill its task by merely engaging in vertical acts that confer resilience on state members and their social institutions. Equitable allocation of resilience cannot be achieved and maintained without state monitoring of *horizontal* behaviors—the way actors with an abundance of resilience impact the resilience of those with whom they interact. Such horizontal dealings fall mainly within the scope of private law, and since the state is very active in this domain, it must use this body of law to prevent unjust usage of resilience.

We have offered the term *market citizenship* to capture the horizontal dimension of the much-needed work of the responsive state. Like general citizenship, the one exercised via the market should also come with duties and not only rights. Resilience analysis clarifies that a central duty should be attached to market citizenship and demand doing no harm to the resilience of fellow market citizens.

Last, beyond making a case for state protection of market citizenship for all, we hope our analysis also demonstrated the powerfulness of vulnerability theory itself. Far from remaining abstract, the theory offers essential and concrete normative guidance for handling pressing social issues and undoing the neoliberal damage to our social fabric. Furthermore, our analysis also illuminates vulnerability theory's normative versatility. The theory does not always support solutions that can be easily branded progressive or conservative. Instead, its resilience-oriented focus sometimes supports the left-leaning approach (e.g., expanding good faith in contract law), but at other times it promotes a more conservative one (e.g., limiting veil piercing under corporate law). By providing a normative formula rather than any specific content, vulnerability theory proves itself rich and inclusive enough to offer guidelines on numerous challenging issues to come.

Reference List

Abrams, Kathryn and Hila Keren. 2013. "Legal Hopes: Enhancing Resilience Through the External Cultivation of Positive Emotions." *Northern Ireland Law Quarterly* 64:111–23. doi:10.53386/nilq.v64i1.337.

Ackerman, Robert and Lance Cole. 2016. "Making Corporate Law More Communitarian: A Proposed Response to the Roberts Court's Personification of Corporations." *Brooklyn Law Review* 81(3):895, 1014.

Bainbridge, Stephen M. 2001. "Abolishing Veil Piercing." *Journal of Corporation Law* 26(3):479–535.

———. 2013. "Using Reverse Veil Piercing to Vindicate the Free Exercise Rights of Incorporated Employers." *Green Bag* 16(3):235–49.

Barak, Aharon. 1996. "Constitutional Human Rights and Private Law." *Yale Law School Faculty Scholarship Review of Constitutional Studies* 3(2):218–81.

Bostock v. Clayton County, 590 U.S. (2020).

Brown, Wendy. 2015. *Undoing the Demos: Neoliberalism's Stealth Revolution.* Princeton, NJ: Princeton University Press.

Burwell v. Hobby Lobby Stores, Inc., 573 U.S. 682 (2014).

Chelsey Nelson Photography LLC v. Louisville/Jefferson County Metro Government, 479 F.Supp.3d 543 (W.D. Ky. 2022).

Chen, Zhansheng, Kipling D. Williams, Julie Fitness, and Nicola C. Newton. 2008. "When Hurt Will Not Heal: Exploring the Capacity to Relive Social and Physical Pain." *Psychological Science* 19(8):789–95. doi:10.1111/j.1467-9280.2008.02158.

303 Creative, LLC v Elenis, 142 S.Ct. 1106 (2022) (Mem).

Cummings v. Premier Rehab Keller, PLLC, 142 S. Ct. 1562 (2022).

Donyets-Kedar, Ronit. 2017a. "Challenging Corporate Personhood Theory: Reclaiming the Public." *Law and Ethics of Human Rights* 11(1):61–88.

———. 2017b. "Rethinking Responsibility in Private Law." Pp. 34–60 in *Privatization, Vulnerability and Social Responsibility*, edited by Martha Fineman, Titti Mattsson, and Ulrika Andersson. London: Routledge-Taylor & Francis.

Donyets-Kedar, Ronit and Ofer Sitbon. 2021. "Beyond Neoliberalism: Allocating Resilience through Corporate Law." *Vulnerability Theory Symposium*, September 13. Law and Political Economy Project (https://lpeproject.org/blog/beyond-neoliberalism-allocating-resilience-through-corporate-law).

———. 2023. "Hiding in Plain Sight: Corporate Legal Responsibility." *Southwestern Journal of International Law* 29.

Easterbrook, Frank and Daniel R. Fischel. 1991. *The Economic Structure of Corporate Form*. Cambridge, MA: Harvard University Press.

Eisenberg, Melvin Aron. 2000. "The Emergence of Dynamic Contract Law." *California Law Review* 88(6):1743–814. doi:10.2307/3481209.

Farnsworth, Edgar A. 1987. "Precontractual Liability and Preliminary Agreements: Fair Dealing and Failed Negotiations." *Columbia Law Review* 87(2):217–84. doi:10.2307/1122561.

Feingold, Jonathan. 2022. "Civil Right Catch 22s." *Cardozo Law Review* 43(5): 1855–921.

Fineman, Martha Albertson. 2000. "Cracking the Foundational Myths: Independence, Autonomy, and Self-Sufficiency." *American University Journal of Gender, Social Policy & the Law* 8(1):13–29.

———. 2008. "The Vulnerable Subject: Anchoring Equality in the Human Condition." *Yale Journal of Law and Feminism* 20:1–23.

———. 2010. "The Vulnerable Subject and the Responsive State." *Emory Law Journal* 60:251–75.

———. 2017. "Vulnerability and Inevitable Inequality." *Oslo Law Review* 4:133–49.

———. 2020. "Beyond Equality and Discrimination." *SMU Law Review Forum* 73:51–62. doi:10.25172/slrf.73.1.7.

François, Aderson B. 2021. "A Lost World: Sallie Robinson, The Civil Rights Cases, and Missing Narratives of Slavery in the Supreme Court's Reconstruction Jurisprudence." *Georgetown Law Journal* 109:1015–79.

Greer, Evan. 2019. "Mark Zuckerberg has to go. Here are 25 reasons why." *The Guardian*, May 8 (www.theguardian.com/commentisfree/2019/may/08/mark-zuckerberg-has-to-go).

Jogdand, Yashpal, Sammyh Khan, and Stephen Reicher. "The Context, Content, and Claims of Humiliation in Response to Collective Victimhood." Pp. 77–82 in *The Social Psychology of Collective Victimhood*, edited by Johanna Ray Vollhardt. Oxford: Oxford University Press.

Jones v. Alfred H. Mayer Co., 392 U.S. 409 (1968).

Jones v. Wal-Mart Stores, No. 4:19CV74 JCH, 2020 U.S. Dist. LEXIS 20252 (E.D. Mo. February 6, 2020).

Keren, Hila. 2005. "'We Insist! Freedom Now': Does Contract Doctrine Have Anything Constitutional to Say?" *Michigan Journal of Race and Law* 11(8):133–93.

———. 2020. "Divided & Conquered: The Neoliberal Roots and Emotional Consequences of the Arbitration Revolution." *Florida Law Review* 72(3):575–638.

———. 2021. "Resilience Draining and the Role of Private Law." *Vulnerability Theory Symposium*, September 13. Law and Political Economy Project (https://lpeproject.org/blog/beyond-neoliberalism-allocating-resilience-through-corporate-law).

———. 2022. "Separating Church and Market: The Duty to Secure Market Citizenship for All." *UC Irvine Law Review* 12(3):907–68.

———. 2023. "Market Humiliation." *Loyola of Los Angeles Law Review* 56(2).

Kessler, Friedrich and Edith Fine. 1964. "Culpa in Contrahendo, Bargaining in Good Faith, and Freedom of Contract: A Comparative Study." *Harvard Law Review* 77(3):410–49.

Klein, Donald C. 1991. "The Humiliation Dynamic: An Overview." *Journal of Primary Prevention* 12:93–121.

Leong, Nancy. 2021. "Enjoyed by White Citizens." *Georgetown Law Journal* 109:1421–72.

Macey, Jonathan and Joshua Mitts. 2014. "Finding Order in the Morass: The Three Real Justifications for Piercing the Corporate Veil." *Cornell Law Review* 100(1):99–156.

Macey, Joshua. 2019. "What Corporate Veil?" *Michigan Law Review* 117(6): 1195–214.

Markovits, Daniel. 2004. "The No-Retraction Principle and the Morality of Negotiations." *University of Pennsylvania Law Review* 152:1903–21.

Martinez v. San Diego Country Credit Union, 50 Cal. App. 5th 1048 (2020).

Masterpiece Cakeshop Ltd. v. Colorado Civil Rights Commission, 584 U.S. (2018).

Melling, Louise. 2019. "Heterosexuals Only: Signs of the Times?" Pp. 245–55 in *Religion, Freedom, LGBT Rights, and the Prospects for Common Ground*, edited by William N. Eskridge, Jr. and Robin Fretwell Wilson. Cambridge: Cambridge University Press.

Miller, Alan and Romen Perry. 2013. "Good Faith Performance." *Iowa Law Review* 98:689–745.

Millon, David K. 2007. "Piercing the Corporate Veil, Financial Responsibility and the Limits of the Limited." *Emory Law Journal* 56(5):1305–82.

Otten, Marte, Lisbeth Mann, Jos J. A. van Berkum, and Kai J. Jonas. 2017. "No Laughing Matter: How the Presence of Laughing Witnesses Changes the Perception of Insults." *Social Neuroscience* 12(2):182–93. doi:10.1080/17470919.2016.1162194.

Pargendler, Mariana. 2021. "Veil Peeking: The Corporation as a Nexus for Regulation." *University of Pennsylvania Law Review* 169:717–81.

Rahman, K. Sabeel. 2018. "Regulating Informational Infrastructure: Internet Platforms as the New Public Utilities." *Georgetown Law Technology Review* 2:234–51.

Restatement (2nd) of Contracts: Duty of Good Faith and Fair Dealing § 205 (1981).

Reynolds v. Robert Hasbany, MD PLLC, 323 Mich. App. 426 (Mich. Ct. App. 2018).

Sepper, Elizabeth. 2021. "The Original Meaning of 'Full and Equal Enjoyment' of Public Accommodations." *California Law Review Online* 11:572–92. doi:10.15779/Z38CN6Z09Q.

Summers, Robert S. 1982. "The General Duty of Good Faith—Its Recognition and Conceptualization." *Cornell Law Review* 67(4):810–40.

Telescope Media Group. v. Lucero, 936 F.3d 740 (8th Cir. 2019).

Thomas, Suja A. 2021. "The Customer Caste: Lawful Discrimination by Public Businesses." *California Law Review* 109:141–208. doi:10.15779/Z38HT2GC4S.

Torres, Walter J. and Raymond M. Bergner. 2012. "Severe Public Humiliation: Its Nature, Consequences, and Clinical Treatment." *Psychotherapy* 49(4):492–501. doi:10.1037/a0029271.

Tsesis, Alexander. 2021."Furthering American Freedom: Civil Rights & the Thirteenth Amendment." *Boston College Law Review* 45:307–91.

Uniform Commercial Code (U.C.C.): Obligation of Good Faith U.C.C. § 1–304 (2011).

United States v. Stanley, 109 U.S. 3 (1883).
U.S. Department of Justice. 2022. *Confronting Discrimination in Hotels, Bars, and Other Palaces of Public Accommodation*. Washington, DC: Civil Rights Division, U.S Department of Justice (www.justice.gov/crt/page/file/1466211/download).
Wall Street Journal. 2019. *The Facebook Files: A Wall Street Journal Investigation* (www.wsj.com/articles/the-facebook-files-11631713039).
West, Robin L. 2019. *Civil Rights: Rethinking Their Natural Foundation*. Cambridge: Cambridge University Press.
Wolff, Tobias Barrington. 2002. "The Thirteenth Amendment and Slavery in the Global Economy." *Columbia Law Review* 102:973–1050. doi:10.2307/1123649.

PART IV

The Public Nature of "Private" Property

7

HOUSING TRUSTS AND RESILIENT CITIES

Hierarchy, Resources, and Resilience

Marc L. Roark

Housing trust funds emerged in the 1970s as a vehicle to redirect city funds into affordable housing projects through dedicated revenue streams. Campaigns through the 1980s made the housing trust fund one vehicle for local governments needing to address the affordable housing gap (Kushner et al. 2011). Eventually, housing trusts became vehicles from which state and federal housing policy funneled some resources (and at times attracted resources), financing the way both cities and private actors would interact with affordable housing delivery. Housing trust funds are sources of revenue set aside by the local municipality or state to accomplish affordable housing options in the face of budgetary threats to affordable housing delivery. They serve to provide funding for homeless initiatives, repairs to tenancies, eviction relief, and other affordable housing challenges faced in American cities today. There are more than 600 local housing trust funds, 49 state housing trust funds, and a federal housing trust fund that all work to shield resources directed to low-income housing.

The Housing Trust emerged in a period in which housing has been dominated by binary approaches to the delivery of housing. On the one hand, home ownership is the primary vehicle through which the state invests in housing for individuals (Roark 2017:7). The alternative is the rental market, which produces its own set of threats to affordable housing, whether it's an unrestrained market that pushes low income people away from economic opportunity; the lack of control that low income persons have over the security of their tenure[1]; the state's ambivalence or inability to enforce housing code provisions that provide safe and sanitary places for people to live (Mulvaney and Singer 2018); or the eviction process which is laden with its own set of costs and burdens that unduly impact impoverished persons (Desmond 2012;

DOI: 10.4324/9781003323242-12

Desmond 2016; Roark 2015). Housing trust funds attempt to offset some of the burdens that low-income persons face in housing by sourcing funds that target some of the potential obstacles that may arise, including maintenance of older properties that are tenant occupied, rental assistance to avoid evictions, or even affording individuals subsidized capacities to purchase a home.

Indeed, housing and the mechanics of housing delivery are a ripe area for considering how vulnerability theory navigates collective problems involving state responses. On the one hand, housing is intimately connected to the individual, implicating the psychic and constitutional meanings of "home" with the preservation of embedded characteristics of individuals such as autonomy and identity (Fox 2007; Roark 2014). When the state allocates resources, such as financial aid or direct housing, recipients can be characterized as having caused their own financial need, through laziness, poor choices, or other failures to launch into responsible citizenry. Likewise, the state itself feels the threat these criticisms impugn, raising critiques about how the state spends collective resources, whether the state is bloated with largess, or whether the state is encouraging irresponsible citizenry.

On the other side, landlords who rent to individuals seeking affordable housing are not uninterested in the way that housing policy is carried out, including the profit they receive in rental income, the preservation of property assets, and relationships amongst neighbors who own property nearby. Landlord profit from housing comes from two distinct sources: the equity in the value of the property and the monthly rental returns for leasing the property. Property owners that rely solely on monthly rental returns as a primary source for value have incentives to reduce their costs associated with maintaining the property. Matthew Desmond's *Forced Out!* profiles the efforts of landlords to avoid paying property maintenance costs in the face of habitability standards that harm renters as a strategy to preserve monthly value (2016). In other works, I describe this sector as gap-rental housing as the market is built by the lack of other affordable housing options (Roark 2014, 2015). Section 8 landlords often rely on monthly rentals, though they are incentivized to maintain basic standards by the Section 8 criteria. The irony of Section 8 housing is that residents are often perceived as unworthy recipients of state housing vouchers, while landlords who receive up to 125% of market value are rarely viewed as receiving government handouts. Arguably, property has framed that problem so that the owner is perceived as performing a public service, while the renter is seen as morally deficient for needing housing assistance.

Housing also implicates collective needs and interests. The financial securitization of housing in the last 40 years has revealed how collective interests in housing shape the mechanisms that facilitate housing, and the rights and interests of landlords and tenants in these properties. For years, redlining restricted access to lending in certain neighborhoods, increasing the cost of housing for low-income borrowers. Neighborhoods may enforce covenants that restrict whether property may be "rented" by an owner on the theory that rental properties decrease neighborhood value or attract tenants that do not fit in the neighborhood culture (Boyack 2014). Indeed, the reduction of available supply in housing through limits on rentals, and market access, shape overall conditions of affordable housing demands that the state faces.

The state's interest in housing is also tied to other direct problems that the state is charged with addressing.[2] For example, public health outcomes have been implicitly associated with the quality and permanence of housing. Educational outcomes and economic outcomes have been directly tied to where a person lives. Housing precarity is a direct interest that costs the state more revenue each year in addressing the consequences of housing instability than it would to provide affordable stable housing.[3] For example, studies have shown that states spend more money policing and regulating homelessness due to a lack of affordable housing; spend more money on healthcare costs; on education costs; and on policing costs. As one author writes about choices of expenditures, "the complexity of city policy making and the realities of limited resources often require elected officials to make a choice in their support for different types of policies" (Basolo 2000). The point is that having housing embeds individuals with some built in resilience, such as seen in the 2020 COVID-19 lockdowns where states took extra measures to keep individuals in homes for social distancing. In the end, housing means more than just the economic interests of one person, or the social interests of another, but rather represents a fundamental need for individuals that the state either recognizes or masks to its own peril.

This Chapter unpacks how cities, states, and federal actors responded to threats from both the financial viability of affordable housing and their own financial precarity through the housing trust—positioning housing trusts as a form of resilience in the face of housing precarity experienced at the local level. To be sure, I am not arguing that housing trusts are an optimal choice for a resilience-seeking state. This is no love letter to the housing trust. Rather, what I seek is to be descriptive of the conditions that have led to the housing trust and to ask us to ruminate on the essential question of responsibility. By linking the housing trust to the legitimacy gap and the resource gap that cities faced in the 1980s, this chapter ultimately asks us to ponder the question: what is a responsive state and what should we expect of it?

Vulnerability and Affordable Housing Resilience

Fineman's vulnerability theory offers an insight into how property itself affords resilience to states even when the state is invisible within the "property problem" (2008:2). Since vulnerability is understood as an inevitable and constant characteristic of the human condition, Fineman's vulnerability theory demands that we resist the habit of defining the "vulnerability" of one in counterpoint to the presumed "invulnerability" of the other. Fineman also distinguishes between "background resilience"—accumulated over time; and the resilience that is allocated to mitigate vulnerability in moments of crisis. Her approach re-locates the underpinning source of difference between people's abilities to navigate opportunities and support and gaps and pitfalls, away from the idea that some *people* are more or less vulnerable than others, to focus on differences in people's *opportunities* to accumulate and access resilience through their interactions with social institutions. Echoing the methodological insights of wicked problem theory, vulnerability theory seeks to avoid the trap of analytical frames that prematurely narrow and constrain the problem space and limit potential solutions. Because she seeks to avoid: "inherently privileg[ing] any one outcome of political deliberation," Fineman described her approach as: "invit[ing], if anything, a high degree of epistemic humility" (Grear 2016, as cited in Fox O'Mahony and Roark 2022:218).

As vulnerability theory concerns the inherent vulnerability of humans, social institutions, including 'the state' are inherently vulnerable. Fineman argued that, like people, the societal institutions we create to mitigate our vulnerabilities: the market, the family, the welfare system, the institution of private property, the state: "are also vulnerable to things like decay, manipulation, corruption, and decline" (Fineman 2013a:88). Fineman (2008) asserts that "societal institutions themselves are not fool proof shelters, even in the short term" (p. 12). Institutions enable us to "mediate, compensate, and lessen our vulnerability" through the accumulation of assets of resilience, but these institutions are also themselves vulnerable (Fineman 2008:12). The concept of institutional vulnerability is not unfamiliar to liberal property theorists: indeed, concern for the "institution of private property" is a regular theme in liberal property theories (Fox O'Mahony and Roark 2022). The general assumption that property law decision-making must protect and uphold the institution of private property implies that, without appropriate normative direction, legal and policy decisions risk damaging this foundational institution.

For Fineman, the institutions that produce and provide resilience to mitigate our vulnerabilities are central because it is the institutional structures and relationships in which vulnerable subjects are embedded that determine each individual's particular experience of vulnerability, through the quality and quantity of resources (*resilience*) that we inherit, accumulate or are capable of accessing in any given moment (Fineman 2013b:21). She argues that: "[w]e are not born resilient; it is produced over time and within state-created institutions and in social, political, and economic relationships" (Fineman 2015:2050). Fineman highlights the central role of "the state" in creating and sustaining the economic (e.g., the market), social (e.g., the family), legal (e.g., constitutions), and political (government) institutions that produce and allocate resilience. These institutions of resilience are created, maintained and regulated through law; and through this relationship, law confers legitimacy on their operation and power over individuals (Fineman 2011:16). Fineman's aim was to bring the state back into view: looking to the state as a source of resilience, and re-imagining individuals' relationships to the state as a resilience-producing institution.

Fineman's interest in the state is primarily geared around re-conceptualizing its role as "active but non-authoritarian"—what she terms a "responsive state" (2008:19). She argues, again, that this reflects an underpinning reality—that the state is always actively shaping institutions, although: "present conceptions of the state underestimate or even ignore the many ways in which the state—through law—shapes institutions from their inception to their dissolution" (p. 19). A central concern is that, by looking away from the state—and law—as a producer of institutional resilience, we fail to pay attention to the way this resilience is allocated. By magnifying the state's responsibility for the institutions and structures it constructs and uses, Fineman advances her central normative claim: "[that] vulnerability analysis demands that the state give equal regard to the shared vulnerability of all individuals" (2008:20). The state's responsibilities thus extend both to all individuals, and to: "how the state has responded to, shaped, enabled, or curtailed its institutions" (p. 20). In her final normative move, Fineman asks:

> Has [the state] acted toward those institutions in ways that are consistent with its obligation to support the implementation and maintenance of a vital and robust equality regime—a regime in which individuals have a true opportunity to develop the range of assets they need to give them resilience in the face of their vulnerabilities?
>
> *(2008:20)*

Fineman argues that: "[t]he realities of universal and constant vulnerability argue for a responsive state that ensures equality of opportunity and meaningful, not merely formal access for individuals to society's institutions" (2015:626). This approach brings the operation and impact of the state, its institutions and structures, into focus. Fineman re-positions this "responsive state" as a means of achieving "a more nuanced sense of what constitutes equal opportunity than currently theorized—one that is more sensitive to existing inequalities and more demanding of the state" (2008:20).

Affordable Housing as an Inherent Vulnerability

Affordable housing reveals individual and institutional vulnerabilities that emerge in conflicts facing state responses to the problem. On the one hand, affordable housing is rooted in the growing costs of housing, primarily in urban areas, due in part to cities' rent-seeking in exchange for higher tax revenue. It implicates city budgets which primarily rely on the property tax system and state and federal allocations to solve local problems (at least problems that require expenditures). And it often requires cities to allocate either physical resources (land or buildings) or financial resources (vouchers or other housing allowances) to solve. Importantly, city officials live where affordable housing problems come home to roost, more so than state or federal officials, who can choose to frame away the problems of living without affordable housing to suit their own interests. the problem that the lack of affordable housing cause. Individuals in cities who believe they are paying too much in taxes to support affordable housing goals may find state or federal officials receptive to calls to limit the city's ability to collect more tax revenue when framed as a charge between property rights of owners and entitlement spending by cities.

Notably, every time a city spends money on a project or an initiative, it opens at least three lines of inquiry about the city's expenditure. First, it raises questions about the source of the revenue that is being spent: did the money come from taxes collected on property owners, from sales taxes, or from bonds issued by the city? Second, it raises questions about the relative worth of the spending: is the city spending revenue on this project to the neglect of others? How does the city choose what projects to spend money on? And how responsive should the city be to affordable housing interests? And third, it raises questions about the long-term effects of this spending: does the spending inure to the benefit of the city? Or is the spending going to harm the city over the long-term? Often these questions are asked in isolation of each other, as political talking points, or after-the-fact lamenting about projects or programs that have been framed as one problem or another.

Reductionist frames elide the complexities of problems, in ways that translate and make visible the "official," "relevant," or legible aspects of the problem, while concealing (or, in Law's terms, "Othering") aspects of the problem that sit outside the official or dominant paradigm. As well as raising justice concerns, the effects of framing can practically hinder attempts to resolve complex or wicked problems. When conflicting ideas are located within distinct and competing frames, there is a risk that problem solving collapses into rhetorical deadlock, with analyses and proposals advanced from distinct (and sometimes polarized) positions which "mostly talk past each other" (Winter 2001:748). This creates a barrier to problem-solving, and when problems seem like "lost causes," it inhibits collective action. This dilemma was articulated by Thomas Ross in his essay "The Rhetoric of Poverty: Their Immorality, Our Helplessness". Ross (1990) observed that "poverty" is typically characterized, by courts, as an unsolvable problem: "one of daunting complexity that is virtually beyond solution." By constructing poverty as a complex and daunting problem—a "wicked problem"—there is a danger that stakeholders (in Ross's analysis, judges) may abdicate responsibility to seek out solutions, because they deem themselves helpless to act (p. 1501).

Affordable housing is both a state problem as it draws on resources that are collective in nature, (Rolnik 2013:1058) and a property problem as it interacts with both housing markets and private housing arrangements through landlord tenant rights (Roark 2017). When resources are strained by demands, like caring for aging infrastructure, the problem can seem dire if not hopeless. States experience vulnerability as a human institution, just like individuals (owners/neighbors) and other institutions (markets, communities, housing systems, and private property).

State legitimacy is often tied to how the state responds to human vulnerabilities. All humans require housing as a basic human need. When we talk about affordable housing, we are talking about the ability of individuals in particular geographies to maintain adequate housing, within the constraint of their resources, that does not render them unable to attend to other needs. For example, the Department of Housing and Urban Development (HUD) defines affordable housing as one which a "household can obtain for 30 percent or less of its income" (Yglesias 2015). This definition is geographically based, as the definition of what may be affordable in Omaha Nebraska will vary greatly from what it affordable in New York City or Los Angeles, California. Since the 1950s, the U.S. has employed a process known as means testing to determine what constitutes affordable housing and who qualifies for housing assistance. For example, HUD defines low-income persons as those that make less than 80% of the median family income for a particular region; and defines extremely low-income persons as those whose incomes do not exceed 30% of the median family income. Both defining points are geography based as well, as incomes in different locations will have different medians and different low income and extremely low-income points. Yet, using these two numbers, HUD can produce a generally defined range for what constitutes an affordable housing cost—suggesting that housing is affordable if it costs less than 24% of the area median income.

But because housing is fixed in places, where markets and wage considerations dictate access, advocates have suggested looking to a different metric—the housing wage gap—for evaluating whether housing is affordable in a community. The housing wage gap considers what a person would need to earn through full-time work to afford a two-bedroom rental based on the HUD standard for an affordable home. The housing wage metric does not consider what actual wages are in a community, but rather bases the metric on the cost of housing. In short, the housing wage gap defines housing affordability by the market conditions in which housing is found. Notably, a 2022 report by the National Low Income Housing Coalition highlights the fact that two full time wage earners at the federal minimum wage would only

TABLE 7.1 Minimum Housing Wage by State

State	*Average (Annual) Income*	*(Annual) Income Required for 2 BR*	*Current Minimum Wage*	*Average Monthly Wage for Renters*	*Average Monthly Cost for 2 BR*	*Average Monthly Cost for 1 BR*
AL	$66,123	$32,110	$7.25	$496	$803	$665
AK	$92,899	$52,147	$10.19	$697	$1,304	$1,005
AZ	$72,954	$43,892	$12.00	$547	$1,097	$882
AR	$61,408	$29,514	$10.00	$461	$738	$593
CA	$90,909	$76,879	$13.00	$682	$1,922	$1,522
CO	$91,959	$55,016	$12.00	$690	$1,375	$1,103
CT	$101,816	$54,956	$11.00	$764	$1,374	$1,109
DE	$86,342	$45,669	$9.25	$648	$1,142	$940
FL	$68,669	$50,807	$8.56	$515	$1,270	$1,027
GA	$72,224	$39,758	$7.25	$542	$994	$858
HI	$97,168	$80,613	$10.10	$729	$2,015	$1,541
ID	$68,372	$34,511	$7.25	$513	$863	$680
IL	$85,252	$44,310	$10.00	$639	$1,108	$934
IN	$72,950	$33,940	$7.25	$547	$848	$685
IO	$79,229	$32,151	$7.25	$594	$847	$632
KS	$74,642	$34,185	$7.25	$560	$855	$675
KY	$66,539	$31,183	$7.25	$499	$780	$620
LA	$64,793	$36,356	$7.25	$486	$909	$756
ME	$76,811	$41,156	$12.00	$576	$1,029	$813
MD	$109,357	$58,866	$11.00	$820	$1,459	$1,223
Mass	$105,892	$73,890	$12.57	$794	$1,847	$1,498
MT	$74,703	$36,227	$9.65	$560	$906	$717
MN	$92,812	$42,705	$10.00	$696	$1,068	$847
Miss	$57,678	$30,977	$7.25	$433	$774	$641
MO	$73,483	$33,424	$9.45	$551	$836	$662
Mont	$73,104	$35,112	$8.65	$548	$878	$684
NE	$78,740	$33,838	$9.00	$591	$846	$668
NV	$72,497	$42,592	$9.00	$544	$1,065	$858
NH	$94,756	$48,726	$7.25	$711	$1,218	$948
NJ	$102,843	$61,762	$11.00	$771	$1,544	$1,263
NM	$62,865	$34,047	$9.00	$471	$851	$696
NY	$87,886	$67,653	$11.80	$659	$1,691	$1,457
NC	$71,385	$36,751	$7.25	$535	$919	$773
ND	$88,698	$33,647	$7.25	$665	$841	$666
OH	$74,544	$33,267	$8.70	$559	$832	$656
OK	$66,385	$33,132	$7.25	$498	$828	$653
OR	$78,661	$50,687	$12.00	$590	$1,267	$1,046
PA	$82,696	$39,992	$7.25	$620	$1,000	$811
RI	$87,969	$44,023	$10.50	$660	$1,101	$911
SC	$67,964	$35,984	$7.25	$510	$900	$771
SD	$76,055	$31,701	$9.30	$570	$793	$621
TE	$67,463	$35,550	$7.25	$506	$889	$734

State	*Average (Annual) Income*	*(Annual) Income Required for 2 BR*	*Current Minimum Wage*	*Average Monthly Wage for Renters*	*Average Monthly Cost for 2 BR*	*Average Monthly Cost for 1 BR*
TX	$75,592	$43,478	$7.25	$567	$1,087	$892
UT	$82,685	$41,251	$7.25	$620	$1,031	$845
VT	$78,736	$48,597	$10.96	$591	$1,215	$969
VA	$93,280	$49,167	$7.25	$700	$1,229	$1,052
WA	$93,484	$63,352	$13.50	$701	$1,584	$1,286
WV	$61,519	$31,135	$8.75	$461	$778	$640
WN	$80,442	$35,913	$7.25	$603	$898	$721
WY	$80,329	$35,663	$7.25	$602	$892	$719
DC	$126,000	$68,280	$15.00	$945	$1,707	$1,500
PR	$25,255	$19,473	$7.25	$189	$487	$419

qualify for the median two-bedroom rental on an affordable basis in three states: Mississippi, Arkansas, and West Virginia.

Affordable housing is a pressing issue for cities and local governments for several reasons. First, the "regulation of housing is a basic function of government" (Kraus 2013). Housing is a concern of the city not only because it maintains and delivers certain affordable housing stock (usually public housing and scattered site housing), but also because it regulates land controls that have a direct impact on the delivery of housing (Davidson 2017). Sometimes, cities have a Janus-like view where active efforts may be directed to making housing resources affordable through rent control and subsidies, while it continues to enforce and pass land use controls that raise the ultimate cost of housing (Metcalf 2018). Studies also show that lower income communities place a higher strain on public budgets relating to basic services (not including the provision of public housing)—including police and fire protection (Kraus 2013). The cost of policing criminal activity, the impact that schools in low-income areas have on students income trajectory (Gladwell 2016), plus the public health costs associated with poverty in low income regions suggests that affordable stable housing is a lynch-pin issue that dictates the resilience of individuals, but in turn the resilience of cities. In short, the lack of affordable housing can drastically increase costs and visible pressures that cities feel (such as blight, criminal activity, and poverty), while providing affordable housing resources can offset those issues. How responsive a state is to the types of resilience individuals have in housing can dictate how large the resilience gap is that a city faces when tackling structural problems.

A question that is at least as important as what do cities spend their resources on, is where do cities get their resources from? In general, funding from cities comes from two different types of resources—available monies collected through taxation and debt issued to either offset budget shortfalls, build and repair infrastructure, or attract business (Hackworth 2007). Debt that is used to cover budget shortfalls is typically short term and is directly related to the anticipated collection of tax revenue. Longer term debt used for infrastructure projects usually derives from general obligation bonds and revenue bonds issued for a specific purpose by the city. Lastly, cities can use tax credit financing to attract businesses to the city. Because cities are dependent on its ability to borrow funds either for its budget shortfalls or for building projects, its rating with municipal rating agencies shape city decision making. For example, in the 1970s when New York City was on the cusp of bankruptcy, the banks and rating agencies were the first to require draconian cuts to the social services and personnel as a condition to lending money to close the gap in its shortfall of resources, even before the New York Financial Control Board did the same a few years later.

Because of reductions in federal funding that could be dedicated to affordable housing, the pressure on city finances intensified. This became clear in places like Chicago, where stories relating to the reduction of staff dedicated to public housing plants became more prominent. This was captured in tales from Chicago's public housing residents as they reported about the futility they felt from reporting maintenance needs. In an exhaustive look at New York's Housing Authority success, Nicholas Bloom (2009) notes that one of the reasons for New York public housing's persistence was its maintenance staff, which regularly and professionally attended to housing complex needs not as poor places to live, but rather as places where poor people live. Still, in the 1980s, the New York City Housing Authority, like others around the country, experienced significant cuts to staff due to federal withdrawal of funding from social housing projects (Bloom 2015). As a result, maintenance issues were delayed or not performed at all. As one resident reported to Bloom, "sometimes you can 'do more with less,' but sometimes 'less is less' " (Bloom 2015:107).

These deteriorating conditions with fewer staff to maintain them also led to more physical deterioration. These also became hazards for residents in these places. As noted by one author in the 1990s a combination of low-grade materials, plus few resources for maintenance and the intensification of living conditions led to infrastructure that was increasingly cheaper to tear down than to repair and maintain (Schill 1993). The city's delivery of housing options was influenced by the resources (or lack thereof) cities had to address property deterioration and maintenance (Parikh and Zhaochen 2017). The resulting resource gap shaped the public response to affordable housing delivery, including in some instances rises in evictions due to limited resources.

During the post war consensus era, cities' capacity to address affordable housing and budget shortfalls were shaped in part by property resources.

During the 1950s and 1960s property was a public asset that could be used to solve public problems, if only the city had access to other resources to make those projects viable. The 1949 Housing Act provided cities with financial resources and capabilities to address low-income areas that had been plagued by inadequate housing. This new public housing infrastructure was built on city land with federal dollars to address housing short falls that plagued the poorest citizens. While those resources were curtailed and cut even at their inception, the infusion of cash enabled cities to construct large-scale public housing complexes to close the affordable housing gap (Schill 1993). But as public housing deteriorated in the 1970s and 1980s cities simultaneously lacked the resources to renew those spaces. In that context, the city increasingly saw its property resources as a potential way of increasing tax revenue—either by encouraging developers to create multi-use developments that lured in sales and use tax revenue or by attracting residents to mixed income housing that would spend money (as regressive tax revenue). Public property shifted from a resource to be put to physical use, to one that could be financialized for greater tax values.

Again, the Federal Government would be instrumental in shaping programs that would ultimately serve to reshape public housing and public housing delivery. One program in particular—Hope VI—paved the way for cities to demolish public housing properties that were no longer viable for service and then repurpose those properties for mixed income redevelopment. To do so, cities adopted mixed finance development where private developers received some form of tax credit (usually LIHTC) to build properties that would attract both market rate renters and low-income vulnerable populations. Notably, federal auditors in 2002 discovered evidence that grants were being awarded on the ability of the area to generate revenue for the city, rather than the actual state of the housing to be demolished. In short, a wholistic shift in the way the state perceived itself in relation to private property was underway. Absorbing a neoliberal ideology, the state moved from seeing itself as a pivotal actor in the delivery of housing services, to one whose competency was challenged in the political discourse. Visible failures in public housing in St. Louis and Chicago fostered a narrative that the state is not as well-equipped to handle social problems as the private market. The resulting shift was to turn over publicly supporting housing programs to private side investors reinforcing the view that the state's role was to manage resources for property owners, not manage property (Goetz 2013).

In the U.S., neoliberal distrust of the state emerges in two distinctive contexts: in the tendency to favor single family ownership as the principal model for housing delivery programs; and in the creation by the state of private markets for public housing provision (Hirt 2014). Both traditional Section 8 voucher programs and the creation of tax-credit financing for public housing projects (such as through HOPE VI programs and RAD Redevelopment

Programs) are built on the state encouraging private ownership to solve public problems by either subsidizing the owners of properties or by providing cheap access to capital to construct more housing (Goetz 2013).

In this way, neoliberalism provides a meta-narrative that elides complex practices of scaling, scale jumping, and hybridity amongst different levels of state governance (Starecheski 2016). Nowhere is that clearer than in the way the city views its responsibilities and how it manages the financial obligations upon which those responsibilities depend (Hackworth 2007). This has implications across different levels of the state, as they interact within their capacities and capabilities as defined by their governing structure. The housing trust provides a compartmentalized arena to see all these interactions.

The financial and ideological threats that cities faced in the context of affordable housing delivery were legion. By the 1970s a wholistic shift in not only what resources were available to the city to accomplish affordable housing programs was underway, but also the resources themselves were subject to their own limitations due to shoddy materials used in the first place. Where the city turned to in the face of financial and ideological assault was the Housing Trust Fund.

How Cities Sought Resilience in the Form of Housing Trust Funds

The current landscape of affordable housing provision can be dissected on several levels. First, the Federal Government continues to be the primary source of revenue for provision of affordable housing programs. Those funds, though, have been redirected away from state and local access and instead primarily benefit private owners—landlords and developers. The local-state's involvement with those funds has primarily become ministerial—ensuring that those who seek the funds (whether landlords or tenants) qualify under the various federal rules that may apply. These local officials on the ground often lack the discretion to direct those funds to needs that may be related to housing delivery. In short, the local state is often directed how to spend federal resources, but lacks the input to suggest how those funds can better serve the community need. This implicates limits on the powers of the municipality to address local problems (like housing), and its dependency on the federal government for resources necessary to address those same problems.

The mechanics of housing trust funds, such as the sources cities draw on to fund the trust, tell us something about what kinds of threats cities and states recognize in the affordable housing context. For example, cities will often use funds collected from uses that negatively impact affordable housing as a source of revenue for the housing trust. They also reflect the choices for the types of projects cities prioritize in affordable housing. Housing trusts emerged to earmark revenue for affordable housing challenges that federal subsidies to landlords and developers did not address. Often the sources of these earmarked funds tell us something about what types of threats the state is responding to. In some instances, the sources of the earmarked funds are based on a theory of forcing parties most directly tied to the loss of affordable housing to internalize those costs, such as when cities require developers to pay impact fees, or when the city charges a transient tax on outsiders coming into the city. In some instances, cities recognize that the rising cost around housing are tied to market impacts that cannot be attributed to any single party or class of actors. Some cities responding in this context have adopted finance tools for housing trust funds that reflect those market increases—such as tax increment financing. And in some instances, cities recognize that the loss of affordable housing may be caused by other conditions that can't be attributed to a specific process or a specific party or class of parties. In those instances, cities have either budgeted for specific budget allocations for housing trust funds or have directed "overages" from city budgets to provide a revenue base.

When cities decide to redevelop areas that it has deemed as economically distressed, or blighted, it is usually accompanied by a values-making rhetoric. The language that is used and the images portrayed are directed to the community to see the potential of economic growth and prosperity as a cure for a sick community. Words like "order" and "growth" are contrasted with diseases like "crime," "blight," and "poverty." Reforming the land is about reforming the visible contradictions of growth and harmony that the city seeks to replace. Harvey Molotch, in the late 1970s, pinpointed that the primary economic and political animation for U.S. cities was growth, or increase (Logan and Molotch 1987). Defining growth through population increase, intensified land use patterns of industry, commerce, retail, and increased levels of financial activity, his theory helped explain why, despite growth rhetoric spurring city action, many of the benefits of growth were allusive to the poorest regions of the city, its residents, or the surrounding region. Molotch's work supported the idea that city growth decisions rarely benefit everyone in the city; instead, they benefit a select few, whose ownership stake places them in the core of the growth machine.

While the theory of the urban growth machine has most directly challenged basic assumptions of urban growth decision-making's reach, it has also been used to explain how decision-making is often hostile to low-income populations. In fact, often the target areas of the growth machine are spaces where public housing units sat, affordable housing options were viable, or homeless persons lived. When new public housing developments are proposed, they are rarely in a geographic proximity that would otherwise allow those residents to participate in the growth machine's energy. For example, several recent studies have pointed to the lack of food resources in the poorest neighborhoods—a fact that remains unchanged when public housing units are torn down and rebuilt in the same geography.

Understanding that these choices are not cost-free has animated cities to create mechanisms that force developers to internalize those costs as part of the cost of doing business. Recognizing that developers and property owners that locate their economic prosperity within the city's growth trajectory that impacts low-income areas, some cities have turned to exactions and taxes as a way to recover costs that arise in the city's growth that adversely effects low-income housing. They are also related to the federal withdrawal of funding that subsidized various municipal programs that offset costs internalized by the city (Bauman and Ethier 1987). And at times, these projects may target public housing developments that are either out of service, or that are in distress. Cities have bargained with developers to transfer interests in these parcels in exchange for the provision of some affordable housing. Still, affordable housing is rarely replaced on a one-to-one basis—leaving a gap in housing provision through these developments.

Cities bolster resources they have for affordable housing delivery through direct and indirect cost recoupment. Direct cost recoupment is where cities specifically allocated resources from the budget to deal with affordable housing issues. Indirect cost recoupment occurs when the city doesn't specifically budget an amount for affordable housing, but rather allocates incomes that comes from specific sources to affordable housing. This may occur though impact fees where a development has a negative effect on affordable housing in a community; or a linkage fee where affordable housing is reduced. Another source of revenue for cities relating to affordable housing problems are indirect fees, such as taxes directed at specific problems. The short-term rental tax is one such indirect fee, where cities seek to offset the costs of transitioning traditional housing to short-term vacation rentals.

A second way cities seek to create funding for affordable housing initiatives is to look outside the traditional budget process. These allocations are built on two related rationales. First, in a period where the state is withdrawing from the provision of social programs like housing, earmarking funds outside of the budget process provides political cover in an era where housing programs are under siege. The ability to fund affordable housing programs without impacting other areas of city government is certainly a lesson learned from New York's near municipal bankruptcy, as the looming city debt resulted in basic city services like fire, police, and sanitation service withdrawal from whole sections of the city. Additionally, allocating specific revenue to affordable housing projects reduces the likelihood that advocates must petition and plead for funding, competing with other city priorities in the budget process. Cities have used two basic types of tools to allocate funding outside of direct city budgets for Housing Trusts: tax increment financing models, and budget overage allocations.

One model for allocating money outside of the regular budget cycle is tax increment financing. Tax increment financing takes advantage of future rising real estate values to allocate the increases in tax collections for specific purposes (Briffault 2010:66). Tax increment financing is typically project-based, where the municipality uses the anticipated increase in tax revenue as an "advance" for developments that fill the city's housing needs. Indeed, tax increment financing is not without controversy, as some perceive it as a way of avoiding bringing taxation requests to the voters. Luther 1987). In the late 2000s it was described as the "most widely used local government program for financing economic development in the United States" (Briffault 2010:65).

A second set of tools that cities have used to fund housing trust programs outside of general budget programs are overage allocations. Overage allocations occur when cities unexpectedly spend less money in a particular area, or obtain an unexpected win-fall by collecting additional lease revenue, or selling municipal property it had not planned to sell. Some of these programs are narrowly tailored. For example, in Los Angeles, overages received in the budget allocated for municipal utility services go to funds to provide services for the homeless. Others are broader, giving the city the discretion to direct funds into a general housing fund, rather than specifically allocated.

Scale, Resilience Gaps, and Responsibility

In this last section, I want to focus on the scale issues that have led to the emergence of the housing trust and that continue to haunt the delivery of affordable housing in cities. Scale is a concept of comparison that can be applied across a variety of relationships, from the way discourse is deployed in a particular discipline or culture; to the measurement of resources or capabilities to respond to problems; to distance or costs that make problems more challenging to solve; to hierarchies, competencies, or powers to solve problems. When we think about housing trusts, their emergence was fueled by problems that could be described implicating all of these areas. Scale is an important concept to reveal in property matters because individuals and entities with greater stores of resilience can jump scales more efficiently than those with fewer stores of resilience. The ability to choose the rhetorical, resource, or hierarchical basis for comparison (or multiple combinations thereof) gives actors more flexibility to navigate complex problems to their advantage.

As a reflection on discourse, the Housing Trust reflects the neoliberal turn in American politics and governance favored private property and privatized responses to public problems over the top-down collective approaches fueled by Keynesian economics. This rhetorical turn created legitimacy gaps throughout the 1980s as government officials and politicians' questioned spending on public housing, declaring it a failure and transitioning to a move to favor private suppliers over public holdings. This discourse also has fueled the animus against those that access public resources, elevating the claims that government spending is wasteful because those that receive the benefits are unworthy. Importantly, these critiques often frame out the private owner from view, even though the owner is the actual recipient of government subsidies that support affordable housing initiatives. As the dominant discourse adopted these narratives, cities sought ways to address affordable housing shortages that did not raise critiques about municipal spending, while empowering private developers to carry out housing delivery.

From a resource perspective, housing trusts emerge as cities competed for resources that private contractors had on offer to solve collective problems. In the absence of these resources, cities turned to instruments that enabled them to compete for developer funds, leveraging the only asset they had—available land or control over zoning conditions—to bargain for the supply of affordable housing provision. This resource gap created by federal retrenchment of resources exacerbated challenges that cities faced, possessing deteriorating infrastructure with few resources to address the problem, reinforced the rhetorical dialectic that assumed government spending was wasteful; that people who lived in such run-down places deserved what they got; and that questioned why the city invested in those places to begin with.

Perhaps the most daunting scaled problem for cities that implicated housing trusts was the hierarchical challenges of local offices to address the housing shortfall. On the one hand, municipalities found themselves impotent to deal with broad collective problems, like affordable housing. Deteriorating infrastructure along with depleting resources fueled the resource gaps and increased the affordability gaps by citizens. Developers soon began to protest municipalities use of fees to restrict certain property uses, appealing to state legislatures to constrain the municipal power that imposed these mandates. In some states, new statutes cabined the local authority by requiring dedications of property or imposing exactions on developers. The Supreme Court in the *Nollan/Dolan* decisions backed the developers and legislators, requiring a rational nexus between a land use dedication and the impact caused by the development, as well as "rough proportionality" between the dedication and the impact (Selmi 2011:606). These developments meant that if municipalities sought to use the *Euclidian* formula of "comprehensiveness" to justify its actions, it would have to pay for it as a taking, rather than merely impose that cost as a fee.

What housing trusts revealed are the failings that retrenchment from housing need in the 1970s and 1980s caused for municipalities. Left behind are the gaps as the state walked away from its responsibility to provide stable affordable housing for the community. A vulnerability approach to this problem asks the central question of what would a state which is theorized "as the legitimate governing entity," and which is "tasked with a responsibility to establish and monitor social institutions and relationships that facilitate the acquisition of individual and social resilience" do in the face of dire housing need?

Notes

1 Tenure security means not only whether a tenant should be entitled to remain in the premises during his lease, but also whether a tenant should be presumed to renew that lease after it ends. No states offer legal protections that ensure a presumptive right to renew a tenancy beyond a lease term. The Low-Income Housing Tax Credit (LIHTC) which subsidizes the development of affordable housing under a mandate that the property deliver affordable housing for a mandatory period of 15 years and a continuing period of 15 more years requires that landlords continue to preserve affordable housing, but does not guarantee access to that housing to a particular tenant.

2 In 1965 *Medical Care* editorial on Health and Housing, one author noted that "20 percent of the average American city's residential area is slums, yet 33 percent of the total population lives [there], 35 percent of the city's fires occur [there], 50 percent of the disease occurs [there] 45 percent of the major crimes occur [there], 60 percent of the tuberculosis cases originate [there] 55 percent of juvenile delinquency occurs [there] 50 percent of arrests are made [there]; they cost the taxpayer 45 percent of all city service expenditure."

3 Numerous studies have been conducted considering the economic costs of policing homelessness compared to housing provision. One such report found that providing affordable supportive housing would reduce city expenditures by two thirds what the city pays to police the homeless (Shinn 2014).

Reference List

Basolo, Victoria. 2000. "City Spending on Economic Development Versus Affordable Housing: Does Inter-City Competition or Local Politics Drive Decisions?" *Journal of Urban Affairs* 22(3):317–32. doi:10.1111/0735-2166.00059.

Bauman, Gus and William H. Ethier. 1987. "Development Exactions and Impact Fees: A Survey of American Practices Commentary." *Land Use Law & Zoning Digest* 39(7):3–11.

Bloom, Nicholas Dagen. 2009. *Public Housing That Worked: New York in the Twentieth Century*. Philadelphia: University of Pennsylvania Press.

———. 2015. "MYTH #4 High-Rise Public Housing Is Unmanageable." Pp. 91–118 in *Public Housing Myths: Perception, Reality, and Social Policy*, edited by Nicholas Dagen Bloom, Fritz Umbach, and Lawrence J. Vale. Ithaca, NY: Cornell University Press.

Boyack, Andrea J. 2014. "American Dream in Flux: The Endangered Right to Lease a Home." *Real Property, Trust and Estate Law Journal* 49(2):203–300.

Briffault, Richard. 2010. "The Most Popular Tool: Tax Increment Financing and the Political Economy of Local Government Symposium: Reassessing the State and Local Government Toolkit." *University of Chicago Law Review* 77(1):65–96.

Davidson, Nestor M. 2017. "Affordable Housing Law and Policy in an Era of Big Data." *Fordham Urban Law Journal* 44:277–300 (https://ir.lawnet.fordham.edu/ulj/vol44/iss2/2).

Desmond, Matthew. 2012. "Eviction and the Reproduction of Urban Poverty." *American Journal of Sociology* 118(1):88–133. https://doi.org/10.1086/666082.
———. 2016. "Forced Out!" *The New Yorker*, January 31 (www.newyorker.com/magazine/2016/02/08/forced-out).
Fineman, Martha Albertson. 2008. "The Vulnerable Subject: Anchoring Equality in the Human Condition." *Yale Journal of Law and Feminism* 20:1–23.
———. 2011. "Vulnerability, Equality and the Human Condition." Pp. 53–63 in *Gender, Sexualities and Law*, edited by Jackie Jones, Anna Grear, Rachel Anne Fenton, and Kim Stevenson. London: Routledge.
———. 2013a. "Afterword: Vulnerability and Resilience." *Retfærd: Nordic Journal of Law and Justice* 36(3):84–9.
———. 2013b. "Equality, Autonomy, and the Vulnerable Subkect in Law and Politics." Pp. 13–28 in *Vulnerability: Reflections on a New Ethical Foundation for Law and Politics*, edited by Martha Albertson Fineman and Anna Grear. New York, NY: Ashgate Publishing Ltd.
———. 2015. "Equality and Difference—The Restrained State." *Alabama Law Review* 66:626–45.
Fox O'Mahony, Lorna. 2007. *Conceptualising Home: Theories, Laws and Policies*. Portland, OR: Hart Publishing. doi:10.5040/9781474200554.
Fox O'Mahony, Lorna and Marc L. Roark. 2022. *Squatting and the State: Resilient Property in an Age of Crisis*. Cambridge: Cambridge University Press. doi:10.1017/9781108767873.
Gladwell, Malcolm. 2016. "Carlos Doesn't Remember." In *Revisionist History*, produced by Pushkin, podcast, 33:26 (www.pushkin.fm/podcasts/revisionist-history/carlos-doesnt-remember).
Goetz, Edward, G. 2013. *New Deal Ruins: Race, Economic Justice, and Public Housing Policy*. Ithaca, NY: Cornell University Press.
Grear, Anna. 2016. "Vulnerability, Advanced Global Capitalism, and Co-Symptomatic Injustice: Locating the Vulnerable Subject." Pp. 41–60 in *Vulnerability: Reflections on a New Ethical Foundation for Law and Politics*, edited by Martha Albertson Fineman and Anna Grear. New York, NY: Taylor & Francis.
Hackworth, Jason. 2007. *The Neoliberal City: Governance, Ideology, and Development in American Urbanism*. Ithaca, NY: Cornell University Press.
Hirt, Sonia A. 2014. *Zoned in the USA: The Origins and Implications of American Land-Use Regulation*. Ithaca, NY: Cornell University Press.
Kraus, Neil. 2013. " 'The Number One Issue'? The Struggle for Affordable Housing." Pp. 131–61 in *Majoritarian* Cities*: Policy Making and Inequality in Urban Politics*. University of Michigan Press (www.jstor.org/stable/10.3998/mpub.4773062.8).
Kushner, James A., Charles E. Daye, Peter W. Salsich, Jr., Henry W. McGee, Jr., W. Dennis Keating, Barbara L. Bezdek, Otto J. Hetzel, Daniel R. Mandelker, and Robert M. Washburn. 2011. *Housing and Community Development: Cases and Materials*. 4th ed. Durham, NC: Carolina Academic Press.
Logan, John R. and Harvey Luskin Molotch. 1987. *Urban Fortunes: The Political Economy of Place*. Berkeley, CA: University of California Press.
Luther, Joseph F. 1987. "Tax Increment Financing: Municipalities Avoiding Voter Accountability Comment." *Detroit College of Law Review* 1987:1.
Metcalf, Gabriel. 2018. "Sand Castles Before the Tide? Affordable Housing in Expensive Cities." *The Journal of Economic Perspectives* 32(1):59–80.

Mulvaney, Timothy M. and Joseph William Singer. 2018. "Move Along to Where? Property in Service of Democracy (A Tribute to André van Der Walt)." Pp. 1–20 in *Transformative Property Law: A Fetschrift in Honour of AJ van Der Walt*, edited by G. Muller and R. Brits. Johannesburg: Juta Press.

National Low Income Housing Coalition. 2022. *Out of Reach: The High Cost of Housing*. Report (PDF) (https://nlihc.org/sites/default/files/2022_OOR.pdf).

Parikh, Samir D. and Zhaochen He. 2017. "Failing Cities and the Red Queen Phenomenon." *Boston College Law Review* 58(2):599–638.

Roark, Marc L. 2014. "Homelessness at the Cathedral." *Missouri Law Review* 80(1):53–130.

———. 2015. "Human Impact Statements." *Washburn Law Journal* 54(3):649–82.

———. 2017. "Under-Propertied Persons." *Cornell Journal of Law and Public Policy* 27(1):1–64.

Rolnik, Raquel. 2013. "Late Neoliberalism: The Financialization of Homeownership and Housing Rights." *International Journal of Urban and Regional Research* 37(3):1058–66. doi:10.1111/1468-2427.12062.

Ross, Thomas. 1990. "The Rhetoric of Poverty: Their Immorality, Our Helplessness." *Georgetown Law Journal* 79(5):1499–548.

Schill, Michael H. 1993. "Distressed Public Housing: Where Do We Go from Here?" *The University of Chicago Law Review* 60(2):497–554. https://doi.org/10.2307/1600078.

Selmi, Daniel P. 2011. "The Contract Transformation in Land Use Regulation." *Stanford Law Review* 63(3):591–646.

Shinn, Gregory. 2014. "The Current Crisis and the Economic Impact of Providing Sustainable Housing Solutions." *Rethink Homelessness*, Central Florida Commission on Homelessness. Report (PDF) (https://shnny.org/uploads/Florida-Homelessness-Report-2014.pdf).

Starecheski, Amy. 2016. *Ours to Lose: When Squatters Became Homeowners in New York City*. Chicago: University of Chicago Press.

Winter, Stephen L. 2001. "The Next Century of Legal Thought." *Cardozo Law Review* 22:747–72.

Yglesias, Matthew. 2015. "Everything You Need to Know About the Affordable Housing Debate." *Vox*, May 11 (www.vox.com/2014/4/10/18076868/affordable-housing-explained).

8

VULNERABILITY, RESILIENCE, AND THE FAIR HOUSING ACT

Xiaoqian Hu

The 1968 Fair Housing Act (FHA) is the most important antidiscrimination housing legislation today. It prohibits discrimination based on race, color, religion, sex, handicap, familial status, and national origin in housing provision, transactions, financing, and related services. Prohibited actions include those that harbor a discriminatory intent and those that, regardless of intent, unjustifiably cause a segregating effect or adversely impact one of the protected groups. However, the FHA as a law in action is incapable of addressing systemic housing inequity in America. This chapter builds upon vulnerability theory to critique some of the limits and proposes a reinterpretation of the FHA to enhance its egalitarian capability. Although the chapter focuses on the FHA, much of the analysis also applies to antidiscrimination law more broadly.

I. Some Limits of the FHA

I have critiqued the FHA's equity limits in detail elsewhere (Hu 2022). Here I briefly articulate two flaws: A) excessive deference to defense, and B) an illegal immorality versus legal privilege dichotomy.

A. Excessive Deference to Defense

Outside the disability-reasonable accommodation context, FHA litigation is brought under one or both doctrines: disparate treatment and disparate impact. Disparate treatment prohibits intentional discrimination of individuals or groups based on race, color, religion, sex, handicap, familial status, and national origin. Given that direct evidence of intentional discrimination

DOI: 10.4324/9781003323242-13

is rare, most disparate treatment cases involve indirect or circumstantial evidence. The plaintiff first establishes a rebuttable prima facie case of intentional discrimination, often by demonstrating differential treatment and correlation with one of the protected statuses.[1] The burden then shifts to the defendant to present a legitimate, nondiscriminatory reason for the differential treatment. Once that is met, the burden shifts back to the plaintiff to prove that the defendant's reason is pretextual.

The three steps outlined above are standard practice in FHA adjudication. What has escaped critical attention is the second step: what constitutes a legitimate, nondiscriminatory reason? This question entails a factual question of whether the defendant has a reason and a normative question of whether the reason is legitimate and nondiscriminatory. Trial courts view this dual question as a purely factual question and delegate it to the jury, thus validating the prevailing social norms in the area where the lawsuit is being litigated and institutionalizing the locale's discriminatory status quo (Hu 2022). When the question is for the court to decide, courts rarely scrutinize defense beyond pretext, as if *any* interest can justify differential treatment of members of legally protected groups. For instance, courts have affirmed as "legitimate and nondiscriminatory" justifications for denying (the construction of) housing to members of protected groups such as "poor credit ratings," "decreased property values," rental units always "poorly maintained," promoting "family values," "transients" harmful to communities, "preserving the character of the neighborhood," etc. (Hu 2022).

Disparate impact prohibits actions that illegitimately create a discriminatory impact regardless of discriminatory intent. To establish disparate impact liability, 1) the plaintiff must establish *prime facie* disparate impact that satisfies the robust causality requirement, 2) the defendant may show evidence that the practice serves a valid interest, and 3) the plaintiff then demonstrates the existence of an alternative that serves the same interest but with a less discriminatory effect (*Texas Department of Housing and Community Affairs v. Inclusive Communities Project, Inc.* [hereinafter *Inclusive Communities*] *2015*). However, the Supreme Court does not explain what constitutes a valid interest that trumps the interest of not exacerbating racial (or other) inequality, nor does it require a weighing of competing interests to determine whether the interest served by the practice is worth the sacrifice. The Court's omission seems to indicate that any valid interest could defeat a disparate impact claim. Following *Inclusive Communities*' strong deference to the defendant, lower courts have validated many practices that had disparate impacts on protected groups.[2] For example, in a 2021 case from Arizona, a water company charged public housing residents a security deposit 3.3 times the amount it did non-public housing residents, on the ground that some past public housing tenants defaulted on water bills and the county public housing authority refused to pay for them (*Southwest Fair Housing Council, Inc.*

v. Maricopa Water District 2021). Although the Nineth Circuit affirmed that this practice robustly caused a disparate impact on African American, Native American, and single mother tenants, it held that the higher deposit was a "common-sense business practice[]. . .to stay in business" and the company did not violate the FHA (2021:974). Per this ruling, racial minorities and single mothers affected by the deposit policy are punished not only by their own financial insecurity but also by the financial insecurity of others who are as disadvantaged as them.

To mitigate excessive deference toward FHA defendants, courts use other instruments—pretext analysis in disparate treatment and means-end nexus analysis in disparate impact. However, these other instruments cannot do the work that delimiting justificatory interests is designed to do. Pretext analysis allows all defendants who have a genuine conflict of interests with a plaintiff to escape liability. Means-end nexus analysis, as Justice Kennedy points out, is designed to target "artificial, arbitrary, and unnecessary" actions that hinder housing access and services (*Inclusive Communities* 2015:540). A means-end nexus analysis may conclude that a means is reasonable if it considers the defendant's interest as the primary end. But the same analysis may well conclude that the means is artificial, arbitrary, or unnecessary if it considers the plaintiff's interest as the primary end or if it considers both parties' interests as equally important ends.

By regarding any rational interest as "valid" or "legitimate and nondiscriminatory," courts are essentially declaring one or both of two messages: 1) the plaintiff suffers no harm in being treated worse than other similarly situated persons; 2) the plaintiff's harm should be sacrificed to satisfy any rational interest of the defendant. The first message is factually false. The second is morally flawed. From a Hohfeldian perspective, when a court uncritically defers to a defendant's interest, the right to nondiscrimination is supplanted by a privilege to discriminate, and the FHA is used to authorize discrimination rather than condemn it.

B. Illegal Immorality Versus Legal Privilege

The courts' refusal to scrutinize defense beyond plaintiff-demonstrated pretext and excessive means creates a categorical dichotomy in FHA jurisprudence. In one category, the defendant has acted immorally, either by intentionally treating a plaintiff worse because of their race, religion, or another protected status or by adopting a means that artificially, arbitrarily, and unnecessarily harms members of a protected group. The defendant has committed an illegal discrimination in violation of the FHA. This is the category of illegal immorality. In the other category, the defendant pursues an otherwise legitimate self-interest and, in the process, causes a disparate harm to members of a legally protected group. The defendant is legally privileged to commit the harm 1) if the victims are known individuals, or 2) where the victims are indefinite members of a group, if the victims fail to show a better alternative than the defendant's chosen method. This is the category of default legal privilege.

A refusal to weigh and reason about competing interests forces courts to equate plaintiff redress with defendant moral deficit. Use race to illustrate. For a plaintiff to win, they must prove the defendant is a "racist" perpetrator—racist by way of intent under disparate treatment, and racist by way of consequence under disparate impact. If the plaintiff fails to prove the defendant is racist, the law denies the existence of racial harm and victimhood, and the plaintiff risks being accused of "playing the race card" and "imagining racism where none exists" (Ford 2008:340). Equating plaintiff redress with defendant immorality renders fair housing litigation a morally charged, divisive zero-sum game (Hu 2022).

A perpetrator/victim dichotomy along the lines of race, sex, religion, etc. is problematic. First, its success depends on the divisive labeling of some actors as bigoted or callous villains. The labelling nurtures defensiveness and resentment, mobilizes anti-antidiscrimination resistance (in particular, anti-antiracism), and over time corrodes the FHA's legitimacy and effectiveness (Hu 2022). Second, it obscures the fact that many social injustices are suffered by people across identity groups and hinders cross-identity coalition building to tackle these injustices (Fineman 2013:628, 635–6). Third and relatedly, it detracts from systemic scrutiny of society's "political and economic organization," which is necessary for confronting structural inequality beyond individual discrimination (Hu 2022; Fineman 2013:628).

When a defendant's challenged act is to pursue an otherwise legitimate interest, courts' refusal to scrutinize this interest beyond pretext and excessiveness gives the defendant a broad legal privilege to harm members of legally protected groups. A lack of judicial scrutiny of completing stakeholder interests then creates a small island of prohibited moral deficit surrounded by a vast ocean of legal privilege to harm.

The illegal immorality versus legal privilege distinction is justified by the "self-regarding" versus "other-regarding" acts distinction crucial to the liberal legal tradition. As Joseph Singer (1982) explains, the liberal legal tradition faces a ubiquitous conflict between one's liberty (freedom to act) and another's security (protection from harm caused by others' action). Classical liberal thinkers sought to use a meta-theory of self-regarding versus other-regarding acts to explain away this conflict. Under this meta-theory, the law allows individuals to conduct acts that concern only themselves but intervenes when individuals conduct acts that harm (or are expected to harm) others. On appearance, this theory allows the liberal legal tradition to be able to guarantee both maximum liberty and sufficient security.

Courts adjudicating FHA disputes seem to be applying (consciously or otherwise) this self- versus other-regarding distinction. In disparate treatment litigation, if a defendant intended to discriminate based on one of the seven categories, the act was other-regarding, and thus the harm should be redressed and the act prohibited. If the defendant had no intent to discriminate based on a protected category and instead was acting out of self-interest, then the act was self-regarding and the defendant had the liberty to act as such under the law. In disparate impact litigation, if a defendant was pursuing their own interest and the plaintiff cannot prove that the defendant adopted an unnecessarily excessive method to pursue that interest, then the defendant was conducting a self-regarding act and had the liberty to do so. It was only when the defendant's act was proven to be unnecessarily excessive that the exceeded portion became other-regarding, for which the defendant should be responsible.

However, as Singer has shown, the distinction between self-regarding and other-regarding acts is flawed. The law permits a large and growing number of supposedly self-regarding acts that do harm to others. These include a vast array of acts of economic competition and acts that are not tortious under strict liability or negligence. The law permits these other-harming acts not because lawmakers have a different notion on where the line between self-regarding and other-regarding should be drawn, but because in these cases the act is both self- and other-regarding and lawmakers deploy policy arguments to weight the competing interests and decide in the end to side with one's liberty and against another's security. Hence, against the wish of its proponents, a faithful implementation of the distinction would create a legal system that drastically curtails individual liberties.

The overlapping and inseparable nature of "self-regarding" and "other-regarding" acts lies at the heart of many antidiscrimination cases. Richard Thompson Ford (2008) summarizes the overlapping nature of discrimination and its complex judicial determination in the employment context (p. 213):

> Claims of intentional discrimination do not turn on a simple factual question of whether a prohibited state of mind caused a decision. They turn on more nuanced policy questions that require courts to balance the liberties of employers against the rights of employees; the interests of society in vibrant free markets against the interests of society in social justice; the value of expressive and associative liberty against the value of equal opportunity and race and sex integration.

The same overlap and conflict exist in FHA disputes. A landlord's interest in stabler and higher rent income may conflict with prospective tenants' interest in stabler and more affordable housing. A Homeowners' Association's interest in satisfying majority residents' desire for tranquility may conflict with the interest of families with small children in housing with community amenities. City council members' interest in securing voter support may conflict with the interests of racial minorities, single mothers, and people with disabilities in living in areas of opportunity, closer to their place of work, or in home-like settings. In these cases, an act in pursuit of one's own interest negatively affects the interests of others. Courts cannot wish away others' interests on the ground that the defendant was pursuing "their own" interest. As Singer criticizes, adherents of the self- versus other- regarding acts "minimized the extent to which politics and morality and law involve difficult choices and sacrifices," and self-deceivingly "made [the] system of justice appear to be far more wonderful than it could ever be" (1982:1022–3).

C. A Vulnerability Evaluation

From a vulnerability perspective, the self- versus other-regarding distinction, like the liberal legal tradition whose liberty-security conflict it sought to harmonize, takes a mechanical view toward society and a homogenizing view toward the human subject. In this mechanical view, society is comprised of largely separate spheres of human actions. I have absolute liberty to do whatever concerns only me; you have equally absolute liberty to do whatever concerns only you; it is only when my action concerns your sphere of interests that my liberty becomes suspect and may need curtailment. When human actions do meet, the dynamics between them are like the dynamics between discrete moving parts of a machine, operating with simple, clearly traceable and quantifiable cause and effect. This mechanical view underlies not only the illegal immorality versus legal privilege distinction in FHA jurisprudence, but also its individualist approach to discrimination-harm causation. Per this approach, undesirable inequality is caused by a specific perpetrator, whose specific act causes harm to a specific victim in isolation from other actors and social conditions, and whose harm-causing act is morally blameworthy and legally unexcused (Freeman 1978; Barns 2020).

One cannot help but exclaim the irony of courts' adoption of a mechanical outlook on social interaction, as Emile Durkheim posited 130 years ago that the increasing differences, interactions, and interdependence between individuals had led modern society away from mechanical solidarity to organic solidarity (1933). Whether one agrees or not with Durkheim's thesis, the human world is not a machine. The different physical conditions that we each initially inhabit (born white versus black, rich versus poor, with disability versus without, etc.) beget subsequent differences in our physical and social conditions (Fineman 2012:60–1). These different conditions then interact with each other and differentially produce individually particular vulnerabilities and resilience assets. The effect can be concurrent or sequential, cumulative or countervailing (Fineman 2012:1757). In this organically moving world, human actions and external conditions (institutions in particular) are "intertwined, symbiotic, and interdependent with each other and also with the state and its apparatus" (Fineman 2012:1760). A mechanical view toward society is wrong not only because people's interests conflict much more frequently than the liberal model is willing to admit (as Singer and others have rightly pointed out), but also because people's interests (and their choices and perceptions of them) and avenues to pursue them are physically and socially constituted in dynamic, complex ways. It is wishful thinking that undesirable inequities can all be traced mechanically to singular wrongs committed by morally blameworthy perpetrators.

Relatedly, the distinction between self-regarding and other-regarding acts, and the liberal legal tradition at large, achieve formal equality by "shearing subjects of all distinguishing embodiment or particularity" and turning them into "purely theoretical subjects, outside of any substantive context" (Halewood 1996:1340). For these abstract subjects, housing equity only requires equal entry to society's economic life—All individuals, regardless of their status or physio-social condition, should enjoy formal equality as participants in the housing sphere; and all housing actors should ignore, unsee, or in other ways treat as irrelevant their own as well as others' identities such as race, religion, and sex. Once formal entry is given, participants' homogeneity and autonomy, viz., socio-physical transcendence, will lead to sufficiently equal outcomes.

However, human subjects are not homogenized, transcendental beings. Our physical embodiment makes us susceptible to harm, and the physio-social conditions which we inhabit as individuals and as members of social groups build or drain our resilience against harm in differential ways (Fineman 2015; Keren and Dnoyets-Kedar 2023). We can escape neither our physio-social conditions nor the personally particular experiences of vulnerability and resilience shaped by these conditions (Fineman 2015). In the same vein, the seven protected identities are physically embodied and socially embedded. People can tell I am Asian by looking at my face, and being Asian entails concrete and at times dangerous social and political consequences. In the housing sphere, houses with photos of Black families are repeatedly appraised at lower values than houses with photos of White families (Endale 2021). Our identity and selfhood are inextricably bound to the internal conditions of society's economic life, which are a key cause of material inequality.

While equal entry is important, it leaves economic life's internal inequality-producing conditions intact. Despite the FHA's textual prohibition, courts' uncritical deference to defendant interests gives housing actors broad liberty to deploy society's unequal economic conditions to harm and disadvantage legally protected groups. Thanks to this "equality=equal entry" understanding, wealth discrimination is legal (*U.S. v. City of Birmingham* 1984); referenda to limit provision of low-and moderate-income housing are constitutional (*James v. Valtierra* 1971); and the government has no affirmative duty to provide housing of any quality for anyone (*Lindsey v. Normet*

1972). A refusal to confront society's internal economic conditions builds a pro-status quo and anti-redistribution bias into the FHA as a law in action. Confronting this bias and truly realizing housing equity requires the law to re-embody and re-embed the human subject and legally recognized identities in the physio-social ecology. It requires policies of economic allocation and distribution. At the very least, it requires courts and enforcers of the FHA to scrutinize defendant interests and explain when and why defendants' interests should come out ahead. We explore these issues in Section II.

II. Reinterpreting the FHA Through Vulnerability Theory

The previous section critiques problematic practices in courts' adjudication of FHA cases that lack direct evidence of intentional discrimination. On the one hand, courts equate plaintiff remedy with defendant immorality; punish mechanically traceable individual discrimination; turn FHA litigation into a morally charged, divisive zero-sum game; and mobilize anti-antidiscrimination sentiment. On the other hand, when the disputed act is in pursuit of otherwise legitimate interests, courts show excessive deference to these interests; grant defendants a broad legal privilege to harm legally protected but socioeconomically disadvantaged groups; and in this way condone systemic inequality.

In this section, I explain how reinterpreting the FHA through vulnerability theory can facilitate changes to address these problems on micro and broader levels. The micro level focuses on FHA adjudication. The broader levels concern more systemic actions by government actors.

A. A Social-Situational View of Harm and Discrimination

Vulnerability theory locates the roots of vulnerability in the fact that all human beings, regardless of our specific identities, are physically embodied and socially embedded. The condition of vulnerability is universal: it transcends identity divisions; is not caused by individuals' immorality or incompetence; and does not rely on naming, blaming, or shaming to justify purposive remedial action (Fineman 2012:1752–63). While vulnerability is universal, manifested harms and individuals' resilience against them are socially and situationally constituted. As people are in "different stages and manifestations of embodiment" and are "differently embedded in social relationships and with societal institutions," the more important analysis is examining how vulnerability is experienced as "particular, varied, and unique at the individual level" (Fineman 2015:613, 618). As I explain below, this social-situational view toward harm and discrimination could aid FHA adjudication in addressing divisive moralism and anti-egalitarian bias.

Ford inspirationally calls on us to "[s]uppose we reserved the moral condemnation that typically accompanies the word 'racism' for clear cases of bigotry, and we thought of the more complex and nuanced problems in the way we think of, say, air pollution, rather than in the way we think of rape or murder" (Ford 2008:213). A social-situational approach to harm and discrimination could help us make that transformation. It could redirect litigants' and judges' attention away from emotionally charged accusations of bigotry and moral extortion and toward pragmatic assessment of social-situational causes of harms, and ultimately toward reasoned arguments about redress. More specifically, litigants and judges may:

1) Investigate the nature and magnitude of all stakeholders' concrete manifestations of vulnerability, including the plaintiff's harm, the defendant's burden to avoid harm, and, if relevant, the broader harm or burden to society.
2) Assess the necessity and proportionality of remedy for each party's manifested vulnerabilities, that is, to or not to engage in the alleged discriminatory action, or some other alternative.
3) Interpret the FHA through moral, ethical, and/or pragmatic discursive arguments.
4) Apply the discursive reasoning to analyze harm, burden, and remedy and explain why the plaintiff should shoulder the harm caused by the defendant's act or why the defendant should bear the burden of not harming the plaintiff.

The factual inquiries are to interrogate harm, discrimination, and the availability and choices of solutions by embodying and embedding the abstracted individuals and their identities back in the physio-social ecology. The legal-normative reasoning seeks to make the most persuasive legal intervention in complex socioeconomic life to foster fair housing.

Take the 2021 Arizona case again (*Southwest Fair Housing Council v. Mariposa Water District*). A court adopting a vulnerability approach would investigate (and litigants adopting a vulnerability lens would produce evidence on), among other issues,

1) The concrete harms the plaintiffs suffered due to the higher deposit, for example, having to compromise on food consumption or clothes for their children; heightened risks of default on water bills; and heightened risks of default on rent;
2) The impact of delinquencies by past public housing tenants on the company's financial viability;
3) The frequency and magnitude of unpaid bills by public housing residents versus non-public housing residents;
4) To what extent the company's suing of or negotiation with defaulting residents and the county public housing authority can mitigate the burden of unpaid bills;

5) Given that customer default is a market risk faced by all businesses, should the company be given stronger protection than what is given to a typical business;
6) Are there other methods to mitigate the company's burden of unpaid bills or the tenants' harm caused by higher water deposits;
7) If there are no alternative solutions to either party's manifested vulnerabilities, how should the FHA (possibly, and other relevant laws and the state and federal Constitutions) decide between the tenants' harm and the company's burden;
8) If the tenants should shoulder the harm, is a deposit 3.3 times the normal rate ($180 instead of $55) proportional to the mitigation of the company's burden?

As this long list of inquiries reveals, vulnerability theory does not provide a shortcut out of complex social problems. With certainty, a vulnerability model will require courts and litigants to do more work and expose courts' reasoning as more able to be criticized than under a traditional liberal model. After all, many discrimination questions are policy questions that require courts to go beyond the interests of the litigants, evaluate the interests of wider sections of society, and make moral and ethical judgments.

A most difficult fair housing policy question is: where there is no alternative to alleviating either party's manifested vulnerabilities, who, between the plaintiff and the defendant, should bear the costs of harm or avoiding harm? Take the following common scenario, for example. A city with an affordable housing shortage rejects a developer's rezoning application to build a multifamily apartment complex in a single-family neighborhood because of residents' concern that the development would "decrease property values" and "increase traffic, noise, and crime." For the analysis here, let us set aside the question of whether "decreas[ing] property values" and "increase[d] traffic, noise, and crime" are coded language to exclude racial minorities and nonaffluent families with children, and instead view these as genuine concerns about property values, traffic, noise, and crime.[3] Let us also assume that there is no alternative solution that would allow the complex to be built without effecting these unwelcomed changes in the community.

Then the question of who should bear the costs becomes a question of cost allocation. It is a social fact that a sizeable group of people of any race or other identity will inevitably increase traffic, noise, and risk of crime and for these reasons may negatively impact the property values in a low-density neighborhood. It is a social fact that both existing and future residents of a neighborhood are members of and contributors to local and wider society. It is also a social fact that existing residents benefit from and depend upon not only their own contributions to society, but also contributions of others—including people who cannot afford a single-family home in their neighborhood (think of grocery workers, nurses, teachers, janitors, auto shop employees, etc.). The costs of traffic, noise, risk of crime, and a myriad of other forms of pollution and harm are byproducts of societal functioning and individual living, and hence are collective costs of society. Should some members of society be allowed to take a high percentage of social goods and shoulder a low percentage of social "bads" simply because they can afford to pay more or arrived in a better-endowed neighborhood first? Conversely, should some members of society be forced to take a low percentage of social goods and shoulder a high percentage of social bads simply because they are poorer or have been historically excluded from better-endowed neighborhoods? For those who take a high percentage of goods and low percentage of bads, should their privileged position be protected by the law or political power, or should others be allowed to use market and nonmarket forces to make social conditions less unequal? Alternatively, should those who take a high percentage of goods and low percentage of bads pay for their privilege by compensating the disadvantaged for the latter's disproportionate shouldering of bads?

These questions cannot be resolved by resorting to abstract concepts of property rights and personal liberty. They require a combination of 1) universal, often abstract moral ideals about equality and justice, often recognized in foundational legal texts; 2) pluralist, often contested ethical values, explicated in legislation and precedent, about the meanings of social membership and fairness given the semi-autonomy and inter-dependence of societal members; and lastly, 3) pragmatic, factually grounded analysis of costs, benefits, and efficiency or expediency (Habermas 1998). Hermeneutically, these inquiries require a richer and more realistic understanding of the human subject as embodied and embedded and of society as enveloping, constituting, and conditioning the lives and life choices of human subjects. Operationally, they require juridical argumentation to shed the status of a formalist, paternalist monolog proclaiming ultimate truth and assume the status of a mixed-method, intersubjective dialog seeking to persuade and open for criticism (1998). This change is necessary, if "we are no longer dealing with disembodied, omniscient beings who exist beyond the empirical realm and are capable of context-free action," and instead, "are concerned with finite, embodied actors who are socialized in concrete forms of life, situated in historical time and social space, and caught up in networks of communicative action" (Haberman 1998:324).

There are two immediate concerns for a vulnerability-informed FHA as delineated above. First, compelling courts to weigh competing interests and remedies might result in courts micromanaging and second-guessing private and public actors in their daily actions. Such micromanaging and second-guessing would infringe upon at least the defendant's autonomy or authority and might produce wrong or costly results and even undermine judicial legitimacy. While a poor application of a vulnerability approach might indeed create these problems, a thoughtful application would facilitate private and public actors in making equity-inducing decisions. A thoughtful court could lay down the major interests that a given type of actors should consider, provide general but principled reasoning as to how to weigh these interests and corresponding remedies, and delineate procedural steps that actors could follow to comply with the FHA. In fact, courts routinely conduct this type of investigation, weighing, and reasoning in property, contract, tort, and constitutional lawsuits, without micromanaging the lives of individuals or activities of enterprises.

A second concern is that, since a vulnerability lens requires social-situational analyses of all stakeholders in an FHA lawsuit, this "individualism ad infinitum" approach would bypass group categories such as race, religion, and sex and render these identities irrelevant. This label and concern are misconceived. For one, some FHA cases involve direct evidence of intentional discrimination. The current juridical logic is well-equipped to address these cases. For another, identities such as race and sex are not only (and not even primarily) physical differences, but social institutions that shape and differentiate individuals' experiences of vulnerability and resilience. As such, these identities are among the very subject matters of a vulnerability inquiry. Finally, a vulnerability analysis is not to be conflated with a class analysis. A class analysis focuses primarily on society's material-economic conditions, while a vulnerability lens inquires not only the material-economic, but also the cultural-symbolic, and is keenly aware of the intersectional nature (to borrow from intersectionality theory) between the material and the cultural.

B. A Reconceptualized State for Systemic Action

While judicial weighing of private and societal harm of discrimination against private and societal burden to not cause discriminatory harm can enhance the FHA's egalitarian capability, it is a rather limited step. Courts may weigh harm and burden and conclude that no remedy is due; most instances of housing inequity are not litigated; and litigation is an individuated, ex post facto reaction to problems. True housing equity requires holistic, structural, and proactive action to reform the social conditions and deter inequities from arising in the first place.

Yet, a holistic solution requires a richer and more constructive conceptualization of the state than the one provided by the liberal legal tradition. The liberal tradition views the state as deriving from a tacit social contract (or forced agreement, per Richard Epstein) wherein individuals surrender some of their liberty and property in exchange for security (Locke 1823:149–58; Epstein 2014:20). As Singer (1982) explains, "since liberal citizens are motivated by self-interest, the only way to achieve security is to give power to the state to limit freedom of action. The contradiction between freedom of action and security therefore translates into the contradiction between individual rights and state powers" (p. 980). Because state power is innately and inescapably coercive, it must be vigilantly restrained (Epstein 2014).

Integral to this conception of the minimal state is the conception that liberty and security can help individuals obtain all resilience assets needed for human surviving and thriving; that they are "Mother assets" or "Creator assets" which beget all other assets. As Habermas puts it:

> Liberal argumentation aims its salvos against the potential for disruption posed by an administrative power that hinders the spontaneous social commerce of private persons. The liberal model hinges . . . on the constitutional framework for an economic society that is supposed to guarantee an essentially nonpolitical common good by satisfying personal life plans and private expectations of happiness.
>
> *(1998: 298)*

In order for this "spontaneous social commerce of private persons" to satisfy the "personal life plans and private expectations of happiness," the liberal model has to assume that individuals are similarly situated in this economic society such that after the liberty-security exchange with the state, everyone is left in possession of roughly the same amount of Creator assets. This initial equality will ensure continued equality in one's ability to procure resilience assets. The liberal human condition is linear, starting with liberty and security and culminating with full human emancipation.

Vulnerability theory offers a pluralist conceptualization of the human condition. The human subject needs a variety of assets that come in different forms from different sources—physical (e.g., housing), human (e.g., education), social (i.e., family networks), ecological (i.e., a healthy environment), and existential (i.e., spiritual belonging) (Fineman 2015:618). This pluralist understanding views liberty and security as important resilience assets, but on their own insufficient to generate all assets for human survival and flourishing. This pluralist view of human resilience is accompanied by a pluralist view of the state. The necessity for and legitimacy of the state lie in its ability to provide or help individuals obtain all resilience assets to cope with human vulnerability (Fineman 2019:368). An analysis of the state must focus on its resilience performance: is it providing individuals with or depriving them of resilience assets, and to what degree? Is it enabling or disabling individuals as they seek resilience assets themselves, and to what degree? Put in Lockean terms, resilience provision is the social compact between the individuals and the state.

A resilience conceptualization neither glorifies nor demonizes the state. It neither fetishizes nor despises regulation. Rather, it requires ceaseless evaluation of how legal structures and political relationships constitute the state and its operations, and how concrete state actions (or lack thereof) confer privilege and disadvantage on individuals and groups either in isolation or, more likely, in connection with other institutions and relationships (Fineman 2012:1758). It compels all stakeholders to methodically examine the differences and their institutional causes (Fineman 2013:638). In the resilience university there is no "end of history" for institutional scrutiny and reimagination.

In the fair housing context, this ceaseless scrutiny of socially produced differences requires the state to recognize the various harms and burdens; interrogate their causes; make pragmatic, ethical, and moral judgments; and innovate institutional solutions. It requires the state to reflect on its own socially embedded yet singularly most (though far from fully) autonomous nature, re-examine the conventional public/private distinction, and re-invent institutions to make social conditions equitable. This is the kind of holistic, systemic, proactive, and reactive action that is needed for combating undesirable inequality.

There are two immediate concerns with holistic action by a resilience state. First, an organic view of human interaction is paralyzing, because if all things are related, to fix one we must fix all, and as a result we can only throw up our hands in despair. This is a misunderstanding. An organic view is not a totalizing view. Within a system or society, there are micro, mezzo, and macro systems and ecologies of cause and effect, as well as localized pressure points that affect a wider environment. FHA litigation and investigation are micro systems that are in operation in innumerable places at a given time. A city council deciding the siting and construction of various types of housing, infrastructure, and other amenities exemplifies a mezzo system that affects a larger population. A reconceptualized state reexamining its antidiscrimination law is an example of a macro system redesign. Lastly, regarding localized pressure points, minimum lot size requirements may be an overlooked bottleneck for equitable housing in an otherwise amenable city. All these system levels and bottlenecks are appropriate points of entry for equity-enhancing initiatives.

A second concern is that a reimagined, systemically active state might abolish all private spheres, and society under such a state would be "paternalism/maternalism all the way down." This concern, again misconstrued, requires a longer response than can comfortably fit in this chapter. Below is a brief summary of a longer analysis.[4] First, privacy and self-authorship are crucial components of human resilience, the preservation of which is part of state responsibility. Second, a vulnerability conceptualization of the human subject and the state is complemented by a discourse-theoretic conception of law and democracy. The state in this conception abides by democratic deliberative processes of lawmaking, administration, and law application through undistorted, iterative formal and informal communication entailing moral, ethical, and pragmatic discourses as well as strategic compromises (Habermas 1998). Rather than an authoritarian pater/mater, the state is an institutionalized space where citizens become at once authors and subjects of law and administrative action (Habermas 1998). Third, this deliberative democracy sets no limits on subjects of deliberation, and citizens can and should debate and thematize what is desirably personal and what is necessarily social. This deliberative accessibility and thematization is categorically distinct from interference with rights, which requires reallocation of powers and responsibilities of concerned actors. It is only when public deliberation leads to lawmaking that reallocates public and private powers, liberties, and responsibilities that one may say the state has disrupted the private sphere (Habermas 1998). Yet, this disruption is not a unilateral imposition but a bottom-up democratic legal change.

Lastly, there are good reasons for citizens to debate and for lawmakers to reconsider the traditional liberal public/private distinction. The liberal tradition envisions a restrained state and an expansive society of maximally unconstrained individuals. In this vision, all non-state actors are presumptively private individuals and all rules and institutions created by non-state actors are presumptively within the private sphere. This view ignores the fact that many non-state actors are created, their contours shaped, or their activities licensed by state law (Kennedy 1991; Fineman 2019:365–6). It also is increasingly anachronistic today with the rise of mega-corporations, foundations, and associational players wielding far-reaching influence on public life. Vulnerability theory takes to heart that concrete social conditions which shape individual experiences of vulnerability and resilience are created by not only the state, but also powerful corporate and associational actors. These are strong reasons for renewed public debate and legislative examination of the traditional public/private distinction.

III. Conclusion

Reinterpreting the FHA through a vulnerability lens has the potential to substantially advance housing equity. First, a vulnerability-informed FHA will take a social-situational rather than moral-individual view toward harm and discrimination. In cases that lack direct evidence of intentional discrimination and that involve a genuine conflict of interests, this view will allow courts to shift attention away from finding flaws in the moral character of the litigants and avoid fanning anti-antidiscrimination sentiment. More importantly, it will allow courts to weigh competing interests, scrutinize the (un)desirability of inequalities produced by existing economic conditions, and make reasoned arguments for or against such inequalities. This juridical practice will enable courts to overcome their uncritical deference to defense and mitigate the FHA's anti-redistribution bias.

Second, vulnerability theory can help us escape the one-dimensional conceptualization of the state as the paramount (albeit necessary) oppressor and adopt a richer and multi-pronged conceptualization of the state as the paramount resilience guarantor. We will assess and critique state action by investigating whether and how much the state builds resilience for, or drains resilience from, differently situated individuals. This new conceptualization creates space for the state with all its functionaries to take holistic, systematic, proactive and reactive actions to address housing and other forms of inequity.

Lastly, a reconceptualization of the state does not mean dismantling all existing laws, institutions, and political structures. As my reinterpretation of the FHA has hopefully shown, much progress can be made by repurposing rather than abolishing existing legal infrastructure. The advancement of equity will benefit from a variety of strategies, not all of which require total destruction and rebuilding.

Notes

1 McDonnell Douglas Corp. v. Green, 411 U.S. 792 (1973); Asbury v. Brougham, 866 F.2d 1276, 1279 (10th Cir. 1989, citing *McDonnell Douglas*). If the defendant is a government actor, some courts apply the standard set in Village of Arlington Heights v. Metropolitan Housing Development Corp., 429 U.S. 252, 265–268 (1977), which requires, among others, that intentional discrimination is a motivating factor in the defendant's action and that the action has a disparate impact on one of the legally protected groups.
2 For a detailed analysis of uncritical judicial deference to disparate impact defense, *see* Hu 2022.
3 For analyses on when and why these reasons are racial code words, *see* Hu 2023b; Pfeiffer and Hu 2023.
4 A more detailed response is in Hu 2023a.

Reference List

Barnes, Kristen. 2020. "The Pieces of Housing Integration." *Case Western Reserve Law Review* 70:717–48.

Durkheim, Emile. 1933. *The Division of Labor in Society*. Translated by George Simpson. Glencoe, IL: Free Press (original book published in 1893).

Endale, Brook. 2021. "Home Appraisal Increased by Almost $100,000 After Black Family Hid Their Race." *USA Today*, September 13 (www.usatoday.com/story/money/nation-now/2021/09/13/home-appraisal-grew-almost-100-000-after-black-family-hid-their-race/8316884002/).

Epstein, Richard A. 2014. *The Classical Liberal Constitution: The Uncertain Quest for Limited Government*. Cambridge and London: Harvard University Press.

Fineman, Martha Albertson. 2012. "Beyond Identities: The Limits of an Antidiscrimination Approach to Equality." *Boston University Law Review* 92:1713–70.

———. 2013. "Feminism, Masculinities, and Multiple Identities." *Nevada Law Journal* 13:619–39.

———. 2015. "Equality and Difference—The Restrained State." *Alabama Law Review* 66:609–26.

———. 2019. "Vulnerability and Social Justice." *Valparaiso University Law Review* 53:341–69.

Ford, Richard Thompson. 2008. *The Race Card: How Bluffing About Bias Makes Race Relations Worse*. New York: Farrar, Status and Giroux.

Freeman, Alan David. 1978. "Legitimizing Racial Discrimination Through Antidiscrimination Law: A Critical Review of Supreme Court Doctrine." *Minnesota Law Review* 62:1049–119.

Habermas, Jürgen. 1998. *Between Facts and Norms: Contributions to a Discourse Theory of Law and Democracy*. Translated by William Rehg. New Baskerville: MIT Press.

Halewood, Peter. 1996. "Law's Bodies: Disembodiment and the Structure of Liberal Property Rights." *Iowa Law Review* 81:1331–93.

Hu, Xiaoqian. 2022. "A Right to Nondiscrimination and a Duty of Reasonable Accommodation." Unpublished manuscript.

———. 2023a. "Social Property." Unpublished manuscript.

———. 2023b. "Euclidean Racism." Unpublished manuscript.

James v. Valtierra, 402 U.S. 137 (1971).

Kennedy, Duncan. 1991. "The Stakes of Law, or Hale and Foucault!" *Legal Studies Forum* 15(4):327–65.

Keren, Hila and Ronit Donyets-Kedar. 2023. "Market Citizenship, Resilience Drainage, and the Role of Private Law." In *Law, Vulnerability, and the Responsive State: Beyond Equality and Liberty*, edited by M. Fineman and L. Spitz. London: Routledge-Taylor & Francis.

Lindsey v. Normet, 405 U.S. 56, 92 S.Ct. 862, 31 L.Ed.2d. 36 (1972).

Locke, John. 1823. "Two Treatises of Government." (https://www.yorku.ca/comninel/courses/3025pdf/Locke.pdf).

Pfeiffer, Deirdre and Xiaoqian Hu. 2023. "Racial Code Words: A Technical of Racism and Racialization." Unpublished manuscript.

Singer, Joseph William. 1982. "The Legal Rights Debate in Analytical Jurisprudence from Bentham to Hohfeld." *Wisconsin Law Review* 1982:975–1059.

Southwest Fair Housing Council, Inc. v. Maricopa Domestic Water Improvement District, 17 F.4th 950 (2021).

Texas Department of Housing and Community Affairs v. Inclusive Communities Project, Inc., 576 U.S. 519 (2015).

U.S. v. City of Birmingham, Mich., 538 F. Supp. 819, 830 (E.D. Mich.1982), *aff'd as modified*, 727 F.2d 560 (6th Cir. 1984).

PART V

The Ultimate "Private" Space—The Construction of the Family

9

THE ELDER CATCH

Engineering the Future of Caregiving

Jessica Dixon Weaver

How can I take care of both my parents and my children at the same time? This is the dilemma facing the adult children of baby boomers, the second largest generation born in the United States during the mid-twentieth century. By 2030, this generation will be aged 66 to 84 years-old and will number 61 million people. Their projected life expectancy is 15 to 20 years longer than the generation before them. While they are living longer, many of them are not living healthier. Medical technology enables elders to live with health ailments due to aging, including arthritis, Alzheimer's, bone replacements, and heart disease. Eventually these boomers will need assistance with daily living tasks at a time when their adult children are still working and caring for their own children, typically helping them prepare for college or gain independence as a young adult. This phenomenon is the "Elder Catch," a term that defines the caregiving dilemma faced by adults who are simultaneously working, tending to the daily needs of elder relatives, and in many cases, raising children (Weaver 2021:59).

Most elders assume that their adult children will care for them when they can no longer care for themselves, while others have planned to remain in their own residence or move into assisted living facilities to retain some independence. However, 25 percent of older citizens do not have any retirement, and 38 percent do not have enough savings, insurance, or investments for a nurse aid to assist with basic daily activities. There are also not enough facilities to house the number of elders who will need them, nor enough staff at these facilities to meet the demands of their clients. Finally, many close relatives have not accounted for the time and money it will cost them to support and help their elder loved one with daily caregiving needs while simultaneously caring for their own younger dependents.

DOI: 10.4324/9781003323242-15

Why is this so important? The gap between the percentage of people over the age of eighty-five in need of living assistance and the number of people available to care for them will eventually become a care crisis. In 2050, there will be 84 million elders in America, and there are not enough nurses and long-term care workers to provide elder care. More importantly, the U.S. government has not created an infrastructure to support the family members who care for 70 percent of elders at home. The future of caregiving is at a critical stage not only in America, but across the world, where there are similar uneven ratios between the number of elders in need of care and the number of relatives and caregivers available to care for them.

Prior to the global novel coronavirus (COVID-19) pandemic, many American families were caught in the Elder Catch. Almost one-quarter of adults ages 45 to 64 care for an aging adult. There are over 40 million unpaid caregivers of adults ages 65 and older in the United States. Six-in-ten caregivers are employed and half of them work full-time. Studies show that burnout from caregiving responsibilities costs companies $13.4 billion in health care expenses, and employees who care for aging parents are more likely to be less productive, take more time off, and arrive late to work on a regular basis. The Elder Catch has a steep price.

The state has always expected that the traditional family framework would operate to care for vulnerable members. The traditional caregiving model is centered on a woman providing uncompensated care for children, elders, or anyone ill or disabled within the family. Throughout the history of the U.S., the normative status quo of private family care has been resilient in the face of challenges and governmental denial of meaningful support. However, the conflation of work, caregiving demands, and financial limitations has stretched female caregivers to the brink, and this was never clearer than during the COVID-19 pandemic. Since February 2020, nearly two million women dropped out of the workforce in what has been named the "She-session." When the world shut down and many employees were forced to work from home during the same time their children were in virtual school, women reduced their hours or quit to ensure that their children were properly cared for and educated. Two years later, approximately one million women are missing from the labor force, which is a full percentage point lower participation than it was before the pandemic. This chapter expands the discussion about caregiving by analyzing the Elder Catch within vulnerability theory.

Vulnerability theory is used to define the concept that human fragility creates dependency and a moral obligation to help those in need or at risk of harm. The paradigm within vulnerability theory posits that there is a responsive state motivated to prevent harm to the human or vulnerable subject. Because humans are bound to be vulnerable to injury at some point in life, the state is responsible for assisting people when families are unable to materially provide for one another. The existence of our system of governance is therefore justified by the fact that the institutions created by it are for the purpose of constructing a just society. The idea or nature of the responsive state is examined by the introduction of a new term within the taxonomy of vulnerability theory, resistant assets (Weaver 2021:84). Resistant assets are frameworks or social constructs used by the state to reinforce the status quo and maintain a posture of nonintervention to prevent or reduce harm to the vulnerable subject. Regarding the Elder Catch, the private family and the traditional societal role of women are resistant assets.

This chapter examines the market and government response to the caregiving crisis that American families face by wrestling with the "resistant assets" that work against efforts to expand the caregiving safety net in America. It explores flailing federal efforts by the Biden administration to "Build Back Better" the U.S. social contract and queries whether corporations are best suited to help employees survive the caregiving predicament exacerbated by the COVID-19 pandemic. At the heart of determining the architecture of caregiving is the breakdown of the private family. If there were no resistant assets, would corporate and non-profit organizations force state responsiveness to address the vulnerability all aging humans will face?

This chapter proceeds in three parts. Part I examines vulnerability theory by exploring and expanding the taxonomy of the concept. It sets forth the relationship between vulnerability and dependency and defines the terms and types of institutional assets used to explain the relationship of the state, the market, and individuals to vulnerability. In discussing how institutions address inevitable harm within society, it introduces a new term, resistant assets, and examines who controls them.

Part II examines how the family is a resistant asset and explores the ways in which caregivers prioritize family over work, even if their behavior affects their work productivity. It examines whether the impact of caregiving on corporate revenues will prompt the government to find ways to incentivize an increased market response to this private action that has typically fallen on women. It reviews the way gender impacts family economics, highlighting how women's historical numbers in the workplace have caused a distinct shift in how businesses and families thrive or fail. While female family members bear the brunt of caretaking within the family, this section explores whether the market has in fact been more responsive than the state.

Finally, Part III concludes by asserting that the Elder Catch requires a fundamental change in how the state supports caregivers within the home and the market. Currently the state is dependent on the market to force it to be truly responsive to the needs of the family. Much of the fundamental parts of the latest federal legislation designed to support family caregiving was cut from the spending package. Though women compose less than 30 percent of Congress, they make up almost 50 percent of the U.S. workforce. Part III contemplates the role of women's influence in the workplace to change their situation within the entities where they have a larger voice. Part III argues that the state must alter its reliance on resistant assets to improve the situation for caregivers and the people for whom they care. Because the state uses the resistant asset of free informal caregiving to avoid expanding the safety net for families, major social reform may require an interest convergence of market and state needs to provide a unified approach to intergenerational caregiving. If this is true, landmark federal legislation may only pass if corporations can show the state that taking care of families is good for business. This chapter illustrates how vulnerability theory must account for the ways that a shared concept of interdependency within society requires broad financial incentive.

I. Vulnerability Theory and Resistant Assets[1]

Vulnerability theory is a concept that sets up an ideal paradigm for crafting a purposefully interdependent society with a universal human subject. Rather than focusing on individual human rights, vulnerability theory is institutionally focused, and the law is intended to be central to the establishment of the state, or system of governance, and the reproduction of society. A key factor in vulnerability theory is that it embraces the potential of the state to be "a unique mechanism for the construction of a just society" (Fineman 2021). It imagines a unified, comprehensive legal subject (the human being), incorporating all variations of human development, as well as human capacities, characteristics, and abilities.

Using the traditional definition of the term "vulnerable," elders, children, and caretakers are all at some point vulnerable groups within the family. The word vulnerability is derived from the Latin word *vulnus*, which means "wound." The concept of vulnerability is used in various contexts to identify "a state of high exposure to certain risks and uncertainties, in combination with a reduced ability to protect or defend oneself against those risks and uncertainties and cope with their negative consequences" (Kirby 2006:4–5). The U.N. Department of Economic and Social Affairs identifies groups that are especially vulnerable, including the elderly and the young, and further sets forth that vulnerability can affect any group in society because "all groups face vulnerabilities that are largely the outcome of economic, social and cultural barriers restricting opportunities for and impeding the social integration and participation . . . of the groups" (U.N. Department of Economic and Social Affairs 2003:8–9).

This aspect of vulnerability was illustrated clearly during the COVID-19 pandemic. While the virus has affected all groups of people, it disproportionately affected people who were already marginalized within society. People over the age of 65 had preexisting conditions that accelerated the illnesses caused by COVID-19, causing them to die at faster rates. Elders typically have some body ailments and are more susceptible to mental decline such as dementia and Alzheimer's disease. In addition to the health danger that COVID-19 presents, social isolation from family and friends also posed a grave danger to elders in long-term care facilities. The nurses and staff members at these facilities were also vulnerable because of historical and present-day socioeconomic legal factors caused by structural sexism and racism. For those elders being cared for at home with two other generations, they faced higher risks by interacting with grandchildren who were attending school and family members who continued to work outside the home.

COVID-19 created the perfect storm for examining how the state responds to a host of competing human groups. The pandemic illustrated how everyone's health depended on the health of others. Vulnerability theory highlights that *to be human is to be vulnerable*, and that the state should seek to assist the all-encompassing person who is both a child and an elder, a young hourly paid health care worker and a middle-aged working parent, caught in the Elder Catch.

"The fundamental realization of vulnerability theory is that the individuals and groups [labelled] as 'vulnerable populations' should *not* be labelled vulnerable, nor should they be sequestered in discreet categories for the purposes of law and policy" (Fineman 2021:5). Their situation posits them as having a shared fragility of human wellbeing, and their harm is communal in a way that the state has a collective responsibility to develop a universal social-justice project that considers state action for injury or harm conceived as general and structural, not individual- or group-based.

A. The Taxonomy of Vulnerability Theory

The terminology of vulnerability theory can be expanded by recognizing a missing piece in the puzzle of human interdependence and government response. Peeling back the layers of vulnerability allows greater examination of how society is shaped and who shapes it. This is key because the framework of society is not inherently equal. In reality, society's framework begins with the creation and regulation of assets in various forms. These assets intersect and support one another to benefit those who control the institutions and created them in the first place. Assets form different layers of resilience, which is the counterpoint to vulnerability. Vulnerability theory posits that inequality of resilience is the core argument for a responsive state.

A variety of assets or resources that societal organizations and institutions provide to individuals enable them to be resilient in the face of common vulnerability. These assets interlock and overlap, creating layered opportunities and support for individuals, but they also contain gaps and potential pitfalls. Understanding the state's relationship to asset-conferring institutions provides a vocabulary in arguing for state accountability to ensure equality in response to individual and institutional vulnerability (Fineman 2010). Different asset categories, including asset-conferring, asset-preserving, and asset-enhancing systems impact how organizations and institutions work together to enable individuals and groups to recuperate and advance in the face of obstacles. On the flip side, these same systems can disable individuals and groups from recovering after a setback and propel them backwards and cause more harm or deterioration.

The term "assets" is utilized because of the World Bank's use of the term in its 2000–2001 World Development Report about poverty (Kirby 2006:18, 55). Assets are descriptors of elements needed to measure a household's exposure to vulnerability. Former international politics professor Peadar Kirby sets forth four different types of assets: (1) physical, (2) human, (3) social, and (4) environmental. Physical assets are described as institutions that impart physical or material goods through distribution of wealth and property. They essentially determine the quality of life and accumulation of resources. The Internal Revenue Service (IRS), U.S. Congress and state congresses are physical assets because they set forth tax and inheritance laws, banking rules and regulations, and credit policies. Corporations would also be included as an institution impacting physical assets. Residential property is the single biggest asset class, accounting for 40–60 percent of total household wealth in Europe and about 30 percent in the U.S.

Human assets are innate or developed abilities to make the most of a situation. They provide for the accumulation of human capability. Health and education are chief among human assets, making institutions governing these two important to evaluate with respect to a vulnerability analysis. Employers, corporations, and small businesses would also be key players in considering how institutions allow participation in the market (particularly for women) and facilitate the accumulation of material resources that help bolster individuals' resilience in the face of vulnerability.

Social assets are networks of relationships from which we gain support and strength, including family and other cultural groupings and associations. Social assets are also accumulated through political collectives in which individuals bolster their resilience by joining together to address vulnerabilities generated by the market—trade unions, political parties, welfare state, and insurance. They are also a "means through which the state or the market offer forms of social protection against risks" (Kirby 2006:64). The emergence of the welfare state and forms of insurance offered by the market became widespread instruments through which people protected themselves against risk. "It is . . . through social assets that people's entitlement, enfranchisement and empowerment . . . are primarily achieved" (Kirby 2006:64).

Environmental assets are those things upon which human life depends such as soil, water, air, and species. These assets tend to be taken for granted and treated as "externalities" by neoclassical economists, who prioritize monetary value (Kirby 2006:69). For example, Human activity has resulted in climate change that has affected access to clean water for billions of people, and land degradation has caused the disruption of the ecosystem and the extinction of many species. Environmental assets can also include the neighborhood park that builds community among residents. They are also "[e]cological resources [that] can be conferred through our position in relation to the physical or natural environments in which we find ourselves" (Fineman 2010:271).

The number of assets has been extended by feminist legal theory scholar Martha A. Fineman to five, incorporating existential assets to include a person's religion or belief system as a way to address vulnerability. These systems can also include culture, art, and politics. Existential assets help people find their place in the world and allow people to see meaning and beauty in their existence (Fineman 2010). Existential assets can be a rallying point that leads people to advocate for certain causes like civil rights or the right to life. They can also prompt people to pursue a life passion to create institutions like non-profit organizations designed to increase resilience for the vulnerable subject.

Because assets are conferred by institutions that are created and legally exist due to state mechanisms, there is some state responsibility for ensuring that the distribution of assets is equitable and fair. Fineman has also used vulnerability theory as a "powerful theoretical lens for reconfiguring legal and political approaches to inequality and disadvantage" (Mackenzie 2014:5). The concept of vulnerability and its analysis is complicated by current social and cultural norms, like racism and sexism, which are perpetrated through institutions and organizations. Eliminating discrimination based on race and gender throughout society has been elusive even with formal laws that declare the practice illegal. If the focus of vulnerability theory is the institutional creation of a just society, there must be a reparative accounting for the existing inequities caused by past harms. This essentially means that the state must address intergenerational inequalities of resilience, and by so doing it would provide more resources to individuals, families, or groups in the form of physical, human, environmental, and social assets. Resilience inequality could also be addressed by removing certain legal, political, and/or market restrictions that inhibit institutions and organizations from conferring, enhancing, or preserving assets to vulnerable subjects.

The economic ties of the family, caregiving, and the workplace are heavily entrenched with ideas of motherhood, the market, and economic efficiency. These concepts are part and parcel of social, human, physical and environmental assets within vulnerability theory. In contemplating how and to whom assets are distributed, or perhaps how assets are acquired, it is important to consider who owns various assets. The government must promulgate physical assets, which are those created by institutions or systems. The government also has direct or indirect control over many social assets such as health and education. Changes in asset distribution and political rules are relevant to changing the norms and preferences associated with economic development.

When families are stretched thin due to internal caregiving and external market stressors, one major life issue, such as a car breakdown or negative health diagnosis, can catapult them into a mountain of debt or threaten their residential security. "Family failure is an institutional, not merely a cultural problem" (Folbre 1994:119). The institutions that are responsible for distribution of the physical, social, environmental, and assets are not necessarily guided by an ideal sense of morality or justice; but rather, they are often motivated by self-preservation and rooted in selfishness. The state and its institutions are run by people. As such, the touchstones of the pillars of government and its correlative institutions must be examined within vulnerability theory.

B. Resistant Assets and the Non-Responsive State

It is vital to critique the state and how it uses institutions to support a defense to the argument of expansion of the social safety net. The concept of "resistant assets" highlights the duality of resilience for vulnerable subjects, and it can apply to individuals or institutions alike. Resistant assets are those structures or social constructs used by the state to reinforce the status quo or resist change that would positively address vulnerability. Regarding caregiving, they are usually laws or public policies that support the normative family structure and can include social mores that rely upon racial and gender stereotypes. Resistant assets can work in concert with certain resilience factors to negate state responsibility for vulnerability. This chapter asserts that unpaid family caregiving is a resistant asset of the state, and it queries what would justify additional state support of elder care for poor and middle-class families.

The term "resistant assets" tracks the taxonomy used by vulnerability theorists to describe the institutional resources or capital that exists because of laws and public policy to combat or shield groups from vulnerability. It is perhaps a difficult term to encapsulate the idea of both a positive and negative. Once broken down, the concept magnifies the two-sided nature of state structures as social network frameworks. Resistant or resistance means anti, resilience, or opposition. It also means unaffected by or impervious to something. Assets are possessions, properties, or resources. The idea is that the state has built-in mechanisms for pushing back against any argument grounded in vulnerability because of the normative institutional structures that exist in society that provide resilience to groups experiencing injury.

For example, arguments in support of grandparent caregivers or support for multigenerational families experiencing economic hardships are often negatively impacted by resilient social assets of the family that buffer vulnerable groups from injury, such as the kinship care system in the African American community or multigenerational living among immigrant families. The term resilient does not embody how this type of asset works *against* families needing assistance, typically poorer families struggling to hang on to the small bit of physical assets they possess. When families bound by love and biological ties provide the support necessary for survival, they are resilient; however, this resilience acts as a resistant asset of the state in that it provides a reason for the government *not* to enter into the private place of families to offer vital support. The word resistant brings to mind the notion of the state as a negative arbiter of resources, controlling them in ways that are usually most advantageous for groups that are in fact rarely ever vulnerable, or at least are most likely to have the highest number of physical and human assets to rebound from calamity to a stable place. While the society and state want to encourage families and communities to support one another, there are specific times when families are caught between the safety net of welfare and adequate assistance from family—times when there is no amount of altruism that will save them.

Families have been responsible for a large part of economic activity in all societies because they have produced much of the consumption, education, health, and other human capital of their members. Therefore, altruism is of primary importance in economic life in part because it dominates family behavior. Altruistic families are the foundation and safety net for all human beings and thus are considered social assets under Kirby's vulnerability theory. The market and the state are fully aware of this norm and continue to push it as a necessary part of the entire capitalist system, but without rendering value to the family members who sacrifice the most (usually women) for their time and efforts. In this way, the family is a resistant asset for the state—there is no need for the state to provide any welfare or basic social services for families when there is an intrinsic hierarchy that dictates altruistic behavior as the norm.

In a neoliberal society, resistant assets support continued arguments for freedom and independence from government intrusion on individual autonomy. For example, the descriptions of part-time workers as those who work 40 hours or less in the workforce have a damaging effect primarily on women who are caregivers. Though the Department of Labor does not provide a definitive number of hours designated as part-time work, each state provides a government code that quantifies the number of work hours that qualify state employees as part-time workers. State codes have a direct influence on private employers, and most corporations define part time work in the same way as the state. The label enables employers to offer less in compensation for the same work, no promotion opportunities, and few, if any, benefits like access to retirement funds, healthcare, family medical leave, and vacation time. Part-time workers are also frequently subjected to abusive scheduling practices. The majority (62 percent) of part-time workers choose part-time or freelance work for "non-economic reasons," with a quarter of them citing caregiving obligations (Cummins 2016). A recent study found that almost half of those seeking part-time work cite work-life balance as their first priority. In many cases, the hostility towards part-timers drives talented workers out of the workplace entirely and into entrepreneurship. The single biggest motivator for U.S. women to start their own business is a desire for more flexible work hours because they desire better work-life balance.

The analysis of whether part-time work is financially beneficial for those who need the time to spend on running a household and caregiving is clear. The average cost of day care is $12,000 annually, and the estimated cost of household help to replace a traditional at-home mom is about $96,261. Add to this number the cost of taking care of an elderly family member, and you have a salary over $150,000. The benefits of part-time work often do not outweigh the costs of a substitute caregiver.

Other examples of resistant assets include federal and state child support enforcement laws that use economic contributions as the only measure of a father's contribution toward support of his child; federal and state tax policies that favor single earner married couples (who only comprise 20% of the population); and state family laws that favor kinship care in child protection cases, but do not provide adequate state subsidies for these relatives' free child care. How do resistant assets affect caregiving? These assets continue to place the burden of caregiving on women, limit the state's obligation to provide family support for caregivers, and ultimately increase inequalities of resilience among those elders, children, and caregivers who do not have other physical and social assets to fall back on during hard times.

II. The Family as a Resistant Asset

The business of caregiving is growing rapidly because of the increased number of baby boomers who are living longer across the planet. Amid the 2020 COVID-19 crisis, the global market for health caregiving in the United States was estimated at $111.2 billion, and it is projected to more than double in size to reach $234.6 billion by 2027. Caregiving is a fundamental function of the private family, primarily performed by women. More than 51 million Americans need caregiving. Most of this caregiving is uncompensated, but technically amounts to approximately $470 billion.

In the past, the traditional expectation that families have primary responsibility for eldercare was feasible because adult children lived close to their parents, parents did not live as long, and more women stayed at home. It was assumed that familial care was given somewhat freely, but the truth is that caregiving has always cost something, and women throughout the ages have paid the costs. The difference now is that families often live far apart from one another, and whereas before siblings lived near their adult parents, now they all live in various cities, or only one adult child lives close to the parents and bears the brunt of the caretaking responsibilities. Furthermore, contemporary families may feel that they must sacrifice their life savings and life plans to take care of their elderly family members, even though this may not be feasible or desirable for them. Finally, the majority of women are in the workplace, so the number of "free" available caregivers within the family has been significantly reduced.

"Rethinking care involves dismantling the dichotomies that have delimited care: private versus public, love versus money, and altruism versus self-interest" (Glenn 2010:10). Perhaps our economic model or base assumption about the relationship of families to the public sphere is incorrect. Currently the state and the market value efficiency, lower costs, and limited state intrusion. Even the term "safety net" plainly indicates that the structures and institutions surrounding the family are insufficient to keep a good proportion of families in a safe place. Approximately 25 per cent of families with school-aged children are food insecure. Further, 30 per cent of households nation-wide spend more than a third of their income on housing. This cycle of poverty continues where lack of familial and state support for women results in their inability to gain traction in the workplace. In vulnerability terms, this is the equivalent of a lack of physical, human, and social assets.

Should caregiving and the work of women and families be the core part of the economy? How would this change the ownership and distribution of assets within vulnerability theory? The institutions and organizations that confer, preserve, and enhance assets would be forced to consider the intergenerational effects on people with the least accumulation of assets. A responsive state would have to determine how to redistribute or create more assets to achieve a just society. This inevitably could mean that the fundamental nature of many institutions and organizations focused on self-preservation would have to pivot and find ways to generate more assets, promote more sharing of assets, and encourage more interdependency among individuals and groups to balance out inequalities of resilience. If vulnerability theory is applied to the problem of the Elder Catch, the law should adjust to build an equitable and responsive state such that our social institutions, i.e., families, schools, and caregiving facilities, could maintain themselves and the relationships upon which they rely.

III. State and Market Response to the Elder Catch

Even though families have been struggling for decades to juggle care work with market work, there has not been a large political demand for state solutions to this problem until the COVID-19 pandemic. American families have demonstrated little inclination for translating their private care problems into political demands for social policy reform. The traditional belief in family responsibility for the social welfare of others persists even in the face of well-documented unmet needs and government policies that exacerbate these difficulties. Existing social policies shape the political imagination, and in many cases the law reinforces longstanding values about family responsibility, which subverts grievances grounded in notions of social responsibility.

There are some examples of joint federal and state efforts to compensate family members for their time caring for their elder parent. Benefits, coverage, eligibility, and rules vary from state to state, and this is part of the problem. Similar to the variance with fifty different approaches to COVID-19, the lack of a national response to the overwhelming needs of most families today results in inconsistences and inequality across states. Most states allow adult children caregivers to be paid via Medicaid through a Cash and Counseling program. The elderly relative must be eligible for this program, and the cash can be used to pay a caregiver. Special state programs may be available for people not eligible for Medicaid, and there are some veterans benefit programs that allow payment of family and friends. California, Nebraska, New Jersey, Washington, Oregon, and Hawaii are a few of the states that offer some form of compensation, benefits, or support to family caregivers.

The market sprang into action during the pandemic to assist employees responsible for elder care. Homethrive, a company that provides information, referrals to elder care workers, and support for employees, experienced a threefold increase in the number of companies signing up for eldercare benefits. The two primary types of eldercare benefits offered by employers are 1) dependent care assistance plans and 2) respite care. According to Forbes, 41 percent of employers offer dependent care assistance plans. These plans deduct a certain portion of an employee's paycheck (gross amount before taxes) to pay for eldercare costs. Respite care is only offered by 7 percent of companies, and it offers short term care to family members when an employee needs to rest, take time off, or go into work. Large employers are beginning to offer adult day care centers onsite, similar to childcare centers, and many allowed for continued flexibility regarding working from home and scheduling time off. Employers are benefitted by providing eldercare benefits because caregiving reduces employee work productivity by close to twenty percent, and it also increases the likelihood that employees will leave the workplace. If one in six Americans are providing care to an elderly family member, relative or friend, and half of this group reports that they do not feel as though they have a choice about taking on these responsibilities, it is likely that half or most of these workers are women. Employers are concerned about losing a good percentage of their workforce, and more than three-quarters of employers report that caregiving will be an increasingly important issue for their employees over the next five years.

President Joe Biden's infrastructure and economic recovery bill is the first time since President Franklin D. Roosevelt's New Deal that a U.S. President has sought to pass such a comprehensive social contract with Congress. This legislation aimed to increase in-home and community-based services for eldercare under Medicaid by $150 billion. The idea was to increase the availability of in-home care to low-income and disabled Americans because it historically has been too expensive and required long waitlists to obtain. It would help states build up their infrastructure to be able to serve more people and support the direct care workforce by increasing wages to chronically underpaid staff. These staff are predominately comprised of women from various minority groups. Thus, this bill served to increase physical, human, and social assets for individuals and groups that have historically experienced inequalities of resilience. The coronavirus relief bill raised federal funding for in-home eldercare for the first time since the Affordable Care Act passed eleven years ago, but the increase only lasted for a year.

President Biden's agenda was fully supported by the progressive members of the House, but centrists like Congressman Joe Manchin and Congresswoman Kyrsten Sinema withheld their approval to determine the possible hidden costs of the recovery bill. During this period of reconciliation in Congress, there were some advocates, mostly females, outside at the Capital making their voices known on this issue. However, there were not throngs of people there to make their case. While the plan was aimed at providing more access to social and human assets for low-income and minority workers, many of them are relegated to their local spaces and could only watch from afar as the country's leaders hashed out their future.

The COVID-19 crisis has illustrated how the state can and does acknowledge how children and their families' vulnerabilities are tied together, and when forced, it can expend large amounts of funding to prevent catastrophic outcomes. A more salient question arises when things return back to "normal." The reality for many poor working adult caregivers is that things were already desperate before coronavirus turned the world on its axis. Will the state be willing to mandate and support paid family medical leave to all employees after the pandemic is over? Will unemployment benefits be increased to adjust for inflation and the cost of living in most U.S. cities? Does there have to be a public health crisis for lawmakers to notice the plight of family caregivers?

The plain answer to these questions is directly tied to the economic well-being of the U.S. Vulnerability theory must account for the fact that the state is reticent to expend the capital necessary to support vulnerable families and would rather support institutions that enable it to function with less investment. A prime example is the reduction of the child tax credit that was increased during the first year of COVID-19. In addition to significantly increasing the amount paid to families with children, the government paid families monthly, it also eliminated a loophole that prevented one-third of the nation's children and half of all African American and Latino children from fully benefiting from the credit. Even though these policy changes decreased child poverty in the U.S. by 30 percent in six months, Congress did not extend this tax credit to low-income families that still needed it to pay for basic needs like food, rent, clothing, and school supplies. It would have cost an additional one billion dollars to maintain the changes to the tax credit. The federal government was only willing to support families on a short-term basis, perhaps to avoid an internal humanitarian catastrophe on the world stage.

It was only because of the pandemic that paid family medical leave became a reality in 2020, unemployment benefits were extended, and adult eligible taxpayers received three economic impact or stimulus payments, with additional money paid per minor child. However, family medical leave was not included in the final bill passed into law. The U.S. Congress was unable to pass President Biden's Build Back Better entire spending package. This particular benefit was removed from the reconciliation bill because it did not garner any bi-partisan support and two democrats raised objections to the social safety net bill. The United States is a global outlier, "one of just six countries without any form of national paid leave and one of eight without a national maternity leave" (Finn 2021).

During the COVID-19 healthcare crisis, the government appeared to be either recklessly or intentionally ineffective, which had a disparately detrimental impact on many groups, such as African Americans, Latinos, Native Americans, and women. Many have argued that the pandemic highlighted the ways in which the government is designed to perpetuate a state of inequality for some citizens with intersections of vulnerability. Food insecurity and housing instability are two major social determinants of health that drove racial disparities pre-COVID-19 and were exacerbated during the pandemic (Cannon 2020). Other social determinants, like unequal access to healthcare and education, have contributed to high rates of chronic diseases in communities of color and put these communities at increased risk for complications and death related to COVID-19. Systemic racial valuation (the inherent value of a person or group based on race) influenced who obtained empathy, care, and concern during the pandemic. (Sirleaf 2021:1830). The distribution of material conditions in health are informed by ideas of race which preserve and reinforce existing hierarchies (Sirleaf 2021). Systemic inequities revealed the stark racial disparities experienced by African American, Latino, and Indigenous populations who contracted COVID-19 were hospitalized and died in greater numbers (Benfer et al. 2020).

Ultimately the institutions and organizations responsible for the creation of a just society are run by individuals who are part of families and larger groups or people. Determining how to change the hearts and minds of the small percentage of people in power is the challenge of our times. The pandemic revealed that the state is dependent on the market to force it to be truly responsive to the needs of the family. One way to change hearts and minds may be through pressure and advocacy within the market. Women compose less than 30 percent of Congress, but they make up almost 50 percent of the U.S. workforce. Women can utilize their influence within the workplace to focus efforts to change their situation by changing the asset distribution of the entities where they have more influence and larger representation. Even if the state uses the resistant asset of free informal caregiving to avoid expanding the safety net for families, major social reform may require an interest convergence of market and state needs to provide a unified approach to intergenerational caregiving. If this is true, landmark federal legislation may only pass if corporations can show the state that taking care of families is good for business.

A shared concept of interdependency within society requires broad financial incentive. Female workers as well as supportive male workers can argue that benefits such as paid family medical leave, flexible work arrangements, and elder care resources (like an on-site elder care facility and respite care) can improve a corporation's ability to attract and retain top talent. If a company can predict an increase in productivity and a decrease in employee losses, this would motivate it to invest in building a broader safety net for the workforce. Ultimately, revenue should increase with the retention of skilled and trained employees who have the care support necessary to work full days and weeks. Beyond the economic reasons, employees' sense of security and peace regarding better home life stability would bring greater work satisfaction. The mutual benefits to both market entities and individuals could ideally lead to advocacy for state and federal laws and public policies that support increased pay and benefits for professional care workers and greater healthcare coverage for elders. Resistant assets can be used to address inequalities of resilience if female caregivers who remain in the workplace build coalitions and demonstrate how an improved social safety net increases business revenue. This chapter illustrates how creative expansion of vulnerability theory can help to conceive a multilayered solution to the Elder Catch.

Note

1 Large parts of this section of the book chapter are taken from my article, *The Perfect Storm: Coronavirus and the Elder Catch* with permission by Tulane Law Review.

Reference List

Benfer, Emily, Seema Mohapatra, Lindsay Wiley, and Ruqaiijah Yearby. 2020. "Health Justice Strategies to Combat the Pandemic: Eliminating Discrimination,

Poverty, and Health Disparities During and After COVID-19." *Yale Journal of Health Policy and Ethics* 19:122–71.

Cannon, Yael. 2020. "Injustice Is an Underlying Condition." *University of Pennsylvania Journal of Law and Public Affairs* 6:201–66.

Cummins, Denise. 2016. "Column: Working Parents Have Two Jobs—and Both are Important to the Economy." *PBS Newshour*, June 28 (www.pbs.org/newshour/making-sense/column-working-parents-have-two-jobs-and-both-are-important-to-the-economy/#.V3QnFf_3zbA.email).

Fineman, Martha Albertson. 2010. "The Vulnerable Subject and the Responsive State." *Emory Law Journal* 60:251–75.

———. 2021. "Universality, Vulnerability, and Collective Responsibility." *Les ateliers de l'ethique/The Ethics Forum* 16:1–14.

Finn, Teaganne. 2021. "Supporters of Paid Family Leave 'Disappointed' After Democrats Slash It from Biden's Plan." *NBC News*, October 27 (www.nbcnews.com/politics/congress/supporters-paid-family-leave-disappointed-after-democrats-slash-it-biden-n1282636).

Folbre, Nancy. 1994. *Who Pays for the Kids? Gender and the Structures of Constraint.* Cambridge: Harvard University Press.

Glenn, Evelyn Nakano. 2010. *Forced to Care: Coercion and Caregiving in America.* Cambridge: Harvard University Press.

Kirby, Peadar. 2006. *Vulnerability and Violence: The Impact of Globalisation.* London: Pluto Press.

Mackenzie, Catriona, Wendy Rogers, and Susan Dodds. 2014. "Introduction: What Is Vulnerability, and Why Does It Matter for Moral Theory?" Pp. 1–30 in *Vulnerability: New Essays in Ethics and Feminist Philosophy*, edited by Catriona Mackenzie, Wendy Rogers, and Susan Dodds. New York: Oxford University Press.

Sirleaf, Matiangai. 2021. "Racial Valuation of Diseases." *UCLA Law Review* 67:1820–59.

United Nations. 2003. *Report on the World Social Situation, 2003: Social Vulnerability: Sources and Challenges.* New York: United Nations Department of Economic and Social Affairs.

Weaver, Jessica Dixon. 2021. "The Perfect Storm: Coronavirus and the Elder Catch." *Tulane Law Review* 96:59–129.

10

VULNERABILITY THEORY AND THE CONCEPTION OF TIME

June Carbone and Naomi Cahn

Central to vulnerability theory is a conception of time, a conception tied to the recognition that vulnerability is an inevitable part of the life course. This temporal conception was once built into the relationship between employers and unionized workers receiving a "male family wage" and it once influenced the structure for corresponding government benefits that addressed old age, disability, and the needs of dependent children. This chapter will use the response to the COVID-19 pandemic to focus a spotlight on how the response to childcare needs reflects the compression of time built into modern capitalism through the combination of shareholder primacy and evisceration of worker protections. The chapter concludes that only a structural approach, rather than equal protection analysis, can ensure the full participation of caregivers in the wage labor economy and adequate investment in the human capital that strengthens society.

Vulnerability theory, in focusing attention on how vulnerability is universal and inevitable, acknowledges the dependency that arises from youth, old age, illness, and other naturally occurring conditions built into the human life cycle (Fineman 2008:9). Addressing this "inevitable" dependency in turn recognizes that investments—or the lack of investment—in one time period have consequences in others. "An inadequate education," for example, as Martha Fineman explains, "will impair the ability to secure employment and accumulate material goods, which will also affect well-being later in the life course, in the context of health, family formation, and prospects in old age" (Gelles and Yaffee-Bellany 2019). Yet, consequences that take place over time may not be immediately apparent and they do not show up in the balance sheets that dominate "quarterly capitalism" (Gelles and Yaffee-Bellany 2019). Instead, as Martha Fineman has explained, "[t]he liberal subject stands not

DOI: 10.4324/9781003323242-16

only outside of the passage of time, but also outside of human experience. The construction of the adult liberal subject captures only one possible developmental stage—the least vulnerable—from among the many possible stages an actual individual might pass through if s/he lives a "normal" lifespan" (Fineman 2008:11–12).

In the same vein, vulnerability theory focuses attention on the "derivative dependency" of caretakers (Fineman 2008:9). The dependency that comes from providing that care imposes what may be lifetime costs on the caregivers and vulnerability theory makes the institutional arrangements for such care and their camouflaged consequences a more visible subject of social critique (Fineman 2008:11). It makes clear that shortchanging those who provide care for the dependent is unjust and failing to invest in the infrastructure that allows individuals to be productive over the life course impoverishes not just the affected individuals but the larger society (Fineman 2019:359–60). Accordingly, addressing vulnerability "must also include a sense of collective or social justice entailing unequal allocations of responsibility and appropriate limitations on the individual." The pandemic illustrates the increasing inequality that accompanies the failure to think in broader temporal terms.

The COVID-19 pandemic focused a spotlight on these temporal failures. While the movement of mothers into the workplace has occurred on a wholesale basis, the construction of a system of early childcare support is at best a rickety and incomplete structure, whose weaknesses and inequities the pandemic brought into sharp relief. The pandemic illustrated the way that women continue to provide the bulk of care work; their workforce participation accordingly depends on their ability to access childcare services. Yet, as the United States has never adopted a comprehensive approach to early childhood needs, women's access to childcare services shapes women's relationship to paid labor, increasing the divide between those with access to the "good" jobs in the new economy that provide flexibility, paid family leave, and a measure of job security and more transient and less flexible positions that encourage the working class to cycle in and out of the labor market with little hope of advancement. The result systematically marginalizes caregivers and makes the relationship to care work a structural factor in racial and class-based inequality.

Part I discusses the varying experiences during the pandemic to show how the failure to invest in comprehensive support for investment in early childhood segments played out by race and class. The privatized system of dependent care more deeply entrenches class and race-based inequality. The upper middle class has embraced a new family system, which we have labeled "blue" (Cahn and Carbone 2010), that emphasizes investment in men and women's earning capacity. Those who follow the new model complete school, acquire skills, and secure flexible jobs before forming families.

These workers are most likely to enjoy paid family leave, flexible (if not necessarily short) hours, and the ability to work from home during the pandemic. Their labor force participation rates remained higher than those of working-class women and their employment rates rebounded more quickly to pre-pandemic levels. Instead, the costs to these women of assuming disproportionate childcare obligations take place in the hard to measure realm of limiting career advancement. Workers who have not been able to acquire desired education and skills, in contrast, have become more likely to cycle in and out of dead-end jobs in response to family needs. These workers suffered the greatest jobs losses during the pandemic and have been the slowest to return to full employment thereafter. While women continue to bear the primary responsibility for childcare and bore the largest additional burdens during the pandemic, the structural relationship between skills, jobs, and childcare determined much of the response. Black, Indigenous, and people of color faced higher childcare fees than did white people. With the COVID-19 dislocations, Black women also were most likely to fall behind on student debt or credit cards (GQR 2022). Female working-class jobs in the United States are highly concentrated in unstable, marginalized service sector employment. These jobs, which under the best of circumstances, offer neither security nor pathways to advancement, suffered the highest layoff rates during the pandemic. Moreover, as hiring resumed as the pandemic waned, these jobs offered neither paid leave nor family flexible arrangements. The responses to the pandemic thus fell along the same lines as the pre-pandemic childcare provisions: women in the marginalized jobs of the new economy cycled in and out of the workplace as their domestic responsibilities interfered with workforce participation. Both employer and employee decisions reflect immediate transactional concerns rather than longer term investment in human capital acquisition.

Part II provides a structural critique, addressing the political forces that have stalled collective responsibility. The failure to do so involves a pincer movement. On the one hand, the move toward shareholder primacy and financialization makes it difficult for individual employers to provide more generous benefits for employees beyond the elite. While corporations at the height of the industrial era invested in long-term employee tenure (and a "male family wage"), modern employers focus on bottom line reductionist metrics such as quarterly earnings. The easiest way to produce increased earnings is to cut back on labor expenses, including not only reductions in the number of employees, but fewer training programs and greater reliance on independent contractors who can be expanded or contracted in accordance with corporate needs and whose employees will be entitled to fewer benefits. This result simultaneously undermines employee security and increases the value of skilled employees—given corporate failure to invest in the training and retention programs that boost employee skills.

On the other hand, the forces of neoliberalism have undermined the possibility of a comprehensive public response. These forces defeated public action to comprehensively address early childhood needs in the seventies, derailed the subsidized childcare provisions in TANF, and undermined public mandates requiring employers to provide more comprehensive family leave. Indeed, with the pandemic, both Trump and Biden favored more generous direct payment to families and states, but Mitch McConnell blocked the Trump efforts. With Democratic majorities in Congress, the American Rescue plan modeled the type of direct payments that could stabilize family-well-being, but Senator Joe Manchin joined with Senate Republicans to block proposals to make the child allowances permanent and the Democrats lacked the votes to enact Biden's ambitious social spending bill, Build Back Better, that treated comprehensive support for early childhood as a needed part of the infrastructure of a modern economy. Some of the rhetoric (Shivaram 2021) echoed long standing canards that the recipients were undeserving.

The result aggravates societal inequalities. Employers with skilled workers they do not want to lose provide greater benefits, tying workers dependent on such benefits to their employers at the expense of greater career opportunities. Service-sector employers who employ easily replaced and inexpensive workers simply increase the employee churn. In both cases, women experience the disproportionate burden.

Part III shows how vulnerability theory leads to a collective rethinking of these unequal burdens. Such a rethinking needs to acknowledge the collective interest in providing for early childcare, the longer-term perspective that more accurately reflects the value of childcare investments, and the need to recognize the limits of private responsibility. The pandemic illustrates how a privatized system shortchanges the future and disproportionately subjects women not only to market limitations, but to the increased dangers that come from greater dependence on unreliable and potentially violent partners (Jackson and Ahmed 2022).

Part I: The Pandemic

While women disproportionately left the workforce during the pandemic, the pandemic story is as much a story of class as it is one of gender: women with less education decreased their workforce participation at almost twice the level of college graduate women (Goldin 2022:10). Moreover, the workforce participation rates of women with no more than a high school education fell at a rate more than three times higher than that for comparable men, while women with more education fared equivalently with similarly educated men, and women with a college degree saw a larger percentage increase in employment than men in either group from 2019–2021 (Fry 2022). While the initial story was that childcare responsibilities disproportionately affected women, the more nuanced account is that, because women are overrepresented in lower-paying jobs and various service sector positions that precluded them from working at home, they were more likely to exit the workforce (Fry 2022). The percentage decrease in the employment of women with less than a bachelor's degree was more severe than for any other group (Athreya and Latham 2022).

In addition to the childcare challenges, remaining employed during the pandemic posed greater risks to poor women. In January 2022, 24% of women compared to 16% of men reported that they were "very concerned" about exposure to the coronavirus at work (Parker, Mesasce, and Minkin 2022). Black people were the most concerned, with 42% of Black people, compared to 14% of white people, stating that they were "very concerned," with Hispanics in between (Parker et al. 2022). These differences reflect, in part, the fact that low-income women are more likely than other workers to be employed in positions with public contact. Black and Latinx women, for example, constituted about half of the workers in health care and nursing homes; they could not stay home and keep their jobs, and, when they remained employed, their work exposure to the COVID-19 virus made their homes sites of potential transmission (Ahmed and Jackson 2021:65).

The childcare labor force, which suffers from low pay and greater public contact, has rebounded at much slower rates than the overall labor force; (Gascon and Werner 2022) it has not yet returned to pre-pandemic levels—even as child care itself has become more expensive (Athreya and Latham 2022).

Women remain more likely than men to work less and provide the care that is needed for both children and aging relatives. Indeed, the majority of the gendered pay gap is due to the fact that, in response to increased domestic obligations, women often step back from employment into the household while the men in their lives step forward into work ("Women, Career and Family" 2021). While these forces affect all women, they play out differently by class. Better educated women, who have invested more in their careers, are more likely to stay employed but cut back on paid hours worked. Less educated women responded to pandemic demands the same way they did to domestic responsibilities before the pandemic: they cycle in and out of paid employment in accordance with family needs. Both strategies marginalize women within workplaces; for the less educated, they contribute to greater income and family instability and insecurity.

Part II: Secure Versus Precarious Family Regimes

The dominant political view over the last several decades has been a neoliberal one, in which the state's primary goal has been to support "the free market, rather than promote economic or social justice" (Eichner 2017:218).

This neoliberal philosophy is similar to the laissez-faire beliefs that generated wholesale opposition to labor market regulation during the *Lochner* era, and, as Maxine Eichner notes, neoliberalism "resuscitates much of classical liberal economics that supports laissez-faire regulation of the market" (Eichner 2017:218 n. 21). It has similarly inspired entrenched opposition today to the Affordable Care Act's premise that the government should ensure universal access to health care, with opposition to need-based programs such as Medicaid and Medicaid expansion reflecting a "long history of under-implementation or even full-out resistance to social programs that are motivated by racism or prejudice against the poor." Gluck and Scott-Railton 2020:558). Within this view, individuals are responsible for their own well-being (Romiser 2021) and employment, marriage, and a gendered allocation of child care are treated as the universally available private mechanisms for securing family sustainability (Fineman 2008:11).

Free-market capitalism by itself, however, never made such a system available to the majority of the population. Instead, both in the early industrial era and today, the system entrenches income inequality, locking families into class-based strategies addressing income insecurity. The upper middle class has embraced a new family strategy, which we term "blue," that marshals the resources for long term human capital investment by achieving a measure of stability and security before family formation. The working class, in contrast, which lacks the resources to achieve stability and security, manages childrearing in the context of contingent family and employment relationships that make it impossible to provide the investment needed to thrive in today's volatile society. The result lowers social mobility and shortchanges society as a whole.

Nineteenth century industrialization illustrated the consequences of free-market capitalism. It introduced an intrinsically insecure wage labor system with little job stability, high rates of death and injury (Guyton 1999:108).[1] and wages so low that families depended not only on wives' income but child labor; indeed, one of the distinguishing features of the early industrialization class system was the dependence of urban working classes on child labor (Ryan 1981:184–5). The middle class benefits of the new system, which encouraged greater investment in children, became available to a majority of the white working class only when, at the height of the industrial age, the United States forged a new social compact that addressed vulnerability by promoting long term employment that paid a "male family wage" (Cahn and Carbone 2021). The new social compact had two critical components: a shift in industrial employers' temporal frames from immediate needs to longer term investment in workers and the New Deal's systemization of the new model by promoting unionization and social insurance. Both components addressed vulnerability through the combination of long-term secure employment, complemented by state subsidized social insurance, and a gendered division of family roles.

The male family wage system, although long a focal point of union efforts, originated with industrial employers' needs for a secure labor force; Henry Ford made the first major commitment to the family wage system in 1914, when he responded to employee turnover of 370% in a single year, by introducing wages of $5 a day, double the norm for the era (Raff and Summers 1987:S63). Higher wages allowed him to be pickier; he largely restricted the higher wages to married men whose wives did not work outside the home (Hoffman 2001:530). Over time, he also limited managers' ability to fire workers, (Stone 2001:532) invested more in training, (Stone 2001:535, 538) and, with seniority-based benefits, commanded loyalty that paid off in terms of greater productivity (Raff and Summers 1987:S57). His system thought of the ideal worker as one embedded in a family system; he explained that "the man does the work in the shop, but his wife does the work in the home. The shop must pay them both" (Widiss 2012:737). By the middle of the twentieth century, the good jobs of the industrial era were "characterized by job ladders, limited ports of entry, and implicit contracts for long-term job security" (Stone 2001:535). These terms effectively provided for dependents through the gendered division of family responsibilities and employment terms that carried workers through from youthful inexperience through retirement.

The New Deal constructed a social insurance system that complemented the family wage ideal for "worthy" families (Skocpol 1992; McCluskey 2003:799; Roberts 1993; Hammond 2020:369). The rhetoric of the system placed responsibility on individuals to assume their appropriate role within a free market, (Fineman 2008:254) while disguising the role of government in extending the benefits of the system. Social insurance accomplished this by building subsidies into long-term employment. Old age provision was tied to payroll taxes that treated the benefits as the product of employee contributions, and the United States, unlike most other developed countries, largely provided health insurance through government subsidized employer plans. (Joint Committee on Taxation 2015:28–42 tbl.1; Gamage 2012:681). The social insurance approach, together with employer-based seniority systems, treated long-term employment as a comprehensive system addressing a variety of human needs. It also excluded transient parts of the workforce, particularly domestic and agricultural workers, who were more likely to be women, minorities, or both; while "the social insurance state" afforded "an important degree of security to a substantial segment of the working class . . . with relatively dignified and secure employment and favorable working conditions and compensation," it left out "a relatively unorganized sector, with relatively low status, irregular work, and unfavorable working conditions and compensation" (Simon 1986:1442–3).

Both the public and private portions of the family wage system relied on the corporation as "time machine," (Stout 2015) that is, they treated the corporation "as a means of transferring wealth forward and sometimes backward through time, for the benefit of present and future generations" (Stout 2015:685). Social security provides a classic case of the concept; payroll taxes paid by younger workers today fund payouts to retired workers whose own contributions may be insufficient to cover current obligations (Simon 1986:1479–80). Similarly, the combination of higher initial wages to attract workers, together with greater investment in worker training and retention, made financial sense only in a system of long term employment in which corporations could be expected to reap the benefits of such investments as employees became more productive over time (Stone 2001:535, 538). Attention to family responsibilities also created win-win consequences; employers viewed male heads of households as more responsible workers, willing to work longer hours than single men. They also found that family oriented educational and recreational activities contributed to workers' families' identification with employers, cementing worker loyalty to the company (Land 1980:64; Stone 2007:453). The family emphasis also helped channel greater investment into children, with payoffs over time for the larger society.

This system, dependent on long-term time horizons, could have easily been adjusted to accommodate women's growing workforce participation. After all, as is true for the Pregnancy Discrimination Act, pregnancy is often treated as a temporary disability akin to the kind of injuries employers have long accommodated. And women are often more productive than men over the entire life course; their peak productive years just occur at different times (Raff and Summers 1987:S70). Women, however, entered the workforce in growing numbers just as the family wage system—and the commitment to long term employment—was being dismantled, as unions diminished in strength and as political forces were succeeding in stopping the movement (slow and halting) towards a Great Society.

Consider what happened at GE, founded by Thomas Edison in the late nineteenth century. In the 1920s, GE's top executive preached "welfare capitalism" to provide health benefits and other resources to its employees (Gelles 2022b:22–3). In 1968, more than two-thirds of the American public agreed that "business tries to strike a fair balance between profits and the interests of the public" (Gelles 2022b:26). And then, Jack Welch came in.

Welch aimed with laser like focus on the long-term employment contracts that had characterized American capitalism. Within his first few years as GE's CEO, Welch's fired more than 100,000 people in a series of mass layoffs and factory closures (Davies 2022). "Up until this point, people who had a job at a company like GE or IBM basically figured that they had a job for life. But he explicitly said that this notion was going to be a thing of the past under his watch," New York Times reporter David Gelles observed (Davies 2022). Instead of focusing on long term company health, CEOs in the Welch era emphasized quarterly earnings. Welch consistently beat earnings expectations every quarter for nearly twenty years, and Wall Street rewarded his efforts by boosting the company's share price. During Welch's tenure, GE's revenue grew 385 percent, while the company's stock market value rose 4,000 percent (Ritzholtz 2017). As executive bonuses became increasingly tied to share price, companies prized the ability to cut costs—and the easiest way to do so was by laying off workers, closing plants, cutting training programs, and outsourcing operations like janitorial services to independent contractors with higher turnover and fewer benefits (Dallas 2012:279; Cahn and Carbone 2021:38). These companies also adopted short-term measures designed to increase share price, such as "reducing discretionary expenses aggressively to improve margins." Yet, these measures went to things such as cutting employee-training expenses, or terminating experienced (and relatively expensive) workers, measures likely to reduce company productivity over time (Dallas 2012:279). Welch's initiatives, as he was toasted "the manager of the century," (Gelles 2022a) helped redesign corporate America and to dismantle corporations as platforms that had once made corporate entities "vehicles for transferring wealth between generations" (Stout 2015:705).

At the same time, a neoliberal movement took hold that blocked public investment that might have compensated for the corporate cutbacks. As early as the 1970s, Congress recognized the need to address investment in children as a national priority. Richard Nixon had run for President in 1968 promising "a national commitment to providing all American children an opportunity for a healthful and stimulating development during the first five years of life," and in 1971, Congress passed the Comprehensive Child Development Act (CCDA) on a bipartisan basis (Cahn, Carbone, and Levit 2023). The bill proposed the creation of a national network of childcare centers, with fee scales designed to make the center accessible to all. Yet, Nixon vetoed it, decrying the "fiscal irresponsibility, administrative unworkability, and family-weakening implications of the system it envisions" and stating his opposition to "communal approaches to child rearing over the family-centered approach" (Nixon 1971). Nixon's veto memo gave voice to free market ideals that would become the rallying cry of the American right for the next fifty years, as conservatives reflexively opposed the expansion of any government action, whether in the form of direct expenditures on childcare, early childhood education, or employer mandates to provide paid family leave (Mahdawi 2021). The conservative movement effectively blocked such proposals as fiscally irresponsible or as government interference into business operations (Levine 2015). Welfare reform in the nineties acknowledged that poor mothers of young children could not effectively participate in the labor market without subsidized childcare, but the Personal Responsibility and Work Opportunity Reconciliation Act never kept up with its promises to provide effective subsidies; while older welfare programs had required states to guarantee that childcare benefits would be available for welfare recipients, the 1996 PRWORA legislation "consolidated federal spending on child care into the Child Care and Development Block Grant" without requiring the states to provide aid to all of those eligible (Hammond 2017:1735). Instead, the primary focus seemed to be moving recipients off welfare (Boushey 2002).

The result of both corporate and public disinvestment in families replicates the class-based inequalities of nineteenth and early twentieth century capitalism. The defining element of the new upper middle class family model, which we have termed "blue" (Cahn and Carbone 2010) because of its association with the liberal and economically prosperous areas of the country, emphasizes greater investment in adult "employability," (Stone 2001:570) that is, the ability to manage the employment adjustments needed to weather the assumption of family responsibilities, economic downturns, technological changes that create new opportunities or make once sought after skills outmoded—and, yes, global pandemics (Lundberg, Pollak, and Stearns 2016:93). Economists attribute the class-based differences in family formation to the "diverging incentives to make intensive investments in children" (Lundberg et al. 2016:98). Well-off couples delay marriage, jointly accumulate resources, premise relationship commitments on a degree of reciprocity and trust and invest in the family's collective human capital; this new system rewards those who can manage the requisite human capital investments necessary to develop "labor market nimbleness and family relationships based on flexibility, reciprocity, and trust" (Cahn and Carbone 2021:27).

Employers, in turn, provide greater protections to more skilled workers. Consider, for example, paid family leave. Those in the top-earning quartile of workers are at least twice as likely as those in the bottom quartile to hold jobs that provide paid family leave for a serious health condition, pregnancy, or new baby care. In addition, paid sick leave, which often includes time off to take children to their medical appointments is nearly universally for the top earning 25 percent of workers while barely half of workers in the lowest quartile had access to such leave (Cahn and McClain 2020:14–15). Partly as a result, well-off pregnant workers are substantially more likely to remain employed through a pregnancy and a period of newborn care (Shinall 2018:787–9).

Poorer families have no cushion. They are less likely to be in stable relationships, with financial instability increasing relationship instability; "[f]inancial organization and management can serve as proxies for long-term investments in the relationship or indicate a degree of individuality or distrust that could reduce relationship quality" (Addo and Zhang 2020:406, 408). They are less likely to have savings; a Federal Reserve Study found that 40% of American households would have difficulty paying an unexpected $400 bill (Federal Reserve Board 2019:2, 24). Poorer Americans suffer from more variable income; "low-income families experience the most frequent and largest negative income shocks," with one study finding that: "about 70 percent of low-income families experienced income instability over the 20-month observation period, defined by an arc percentage change reduction of 25 percent or more in a given month from the average of the prior 3 months" (Ha et al. 2020:130, 158). And poorer women may also be more likely to quit or be fired than better off women when they become pregnant (Strauss 2018; Shulman 2020). While better educated women are more likely to be on leave in the first few months after giving birth, nine months after the birth of a child, better educated women are more likely than less educated mothers to be employed (Han et al. 2008).

These patterns reflect in part the changing nature of employment. The new economy has created more "good jobs" with high pay and benefits and more "bad jobs" with neither (Cooke 2018:242). Women are disproportionately concentrated in low paying service sector (Bateman and Ross 2020; White House 2021) and retail jobs that offer low pay, few benefits, and limited flexibility about hours or working conditions (Perry-Jenkins and Gerstel 2020; McCleskey 2018:638). They thus have fewer resources to invest in children in absolute terms and fewer resources available to manage emergencies such as pandemics.

These patterns reflect the privatization of dependency and the shrinking of corporate time horizons. The accumulation of the resources necessary to invest in the human capital acquisition of the next generation and to provide a cushion that assists in the management of unexpected events has become more of a private matter than it was at the height of the public-private concordat that existed in the middle of the twentieth century. The key to worker advancement in the new era instead involves "employability" rather than employment. The ambitious switch jobs, cities, and relationships securing the skills that employers prize. The less fortunate cycle in and out of dead-end jobs that provide neither security nor stability. The average worker will change jobs at least twelve times; the average college graduate will do so four times in their twenties (U.S. Bureau of Labor Statistics 2020). The well-off postpone family formation until they obtain the skills, maturity, committed relationships and financial cushions necessary to thrive, while the benefits of the system move beyond the reach of the majority of the population, who see no way to marshal the resources that might provide for a more secure future. The result involves a shortchanging of their children and the larger society.

Pandemic relief provided a rare, temporary collective respite that treated family needs as a shared responsibility, with the federal government supplementing state unemployment benefits, assisting renters who might otherwise face eviction, and providing relief checks (Eichner 2022:2511). Yet the solid wall of Republican opposition, with the assistance of a few Democrats, blocked making those measures permanent.

Part III: Vulnerability Theory

An alternative vision maintains that family security and stability come from a societal design that complements the principal form of economic organization and that addresses the inevitable instability that arises from the economic system itself. (Kelton 2020:65; Fineman 1995).

This requires the creation of a new system designed to address vulnerability within the context of the information age economy. Creation of such a system requires that we rethink the relationship between citizen and state and between present and future. The old system saw the prerequisites for full citizenship and full participation in the economic system as dependent on at least a modicum of shared public and private investment: education (particularly free secondary education), employment (with a "full employment" economy and an adequate minimum wage key objectives in the industrial economy), and marriage as necessary to responsible family formation. It assumed that each citizen who sought to do so could meet these prerequisites.

The new system must reimagine education in terms of the need to acquire new skills, security in terms of the ability to ride out changes over the life course (minimum income in addition to a minimum wage), the provision of meaningful work in an era of automation (a job guarantee), and benefits that do not depend on either employment or marriage (universal health care).

In short, the system requires a new social compact between citizens and a more responsive state that provides a secure and stable foundation addressing the vulnerabilities built into the life course (Fineman 2019) and allowing for the development of the education, skills, health, and experience that promote employability and full participation in American life. A re-envisioned "state is responsible for creating and supporting structures and avenues of resilience—i.e. those resources that allow individuals to confront, adapt to, ameliorate the consequences of, compensate for, or contain the universal human condition" (Yuille 2019:468). This chapter argues that government must assume a new role, taking on responsibilities comparable to free public education and social security. Like the rise of the New Deal, implementation of such a vision will require a new political coalition capable of producing the political will to enact the necessary legislation to overcome the New Lochnerism that will inevitably stand in the way (Hammond 2020:433).

Vulnerability theory contributes to the envisioning of this system. This theory challenges the concept of the autonomous liberal subject, arguing instead that vulnerability and need are part of the basic human condition, regardless of identity characteristics. (Fineman 2010:269–75, 2012:1752–3, 2020:54; Filho 2021:1101). Accordingly, the role of the state is to be "responsive," rather than "restrained," (Fineman 2020). and to build resilience. Central to these insights is the temporal dimension: recognition that human life involves inevitable vulnerabilities that occur over the life course requires conceiving of solutions that recognize that investments in one period may pay off much later, that the investments in children, for example, that may affect not only those children's adulthoods, but the well-being of their children and grandchildren.

Building resilience requires developing a responsive state that treats investment in early childhood and inevitable points of human vulnerability as infrastructure investment. It also requires reconsidering the existing gendered allocation of responsibility, which simultaneously continues to treat women as primary caregivers and penalizes them for failure to devote their primary attention to the paid workplace. Appropriate reforms will need to acknowledge that, just as the industrial era provided worker stability and security through integrated public and private measures, today's reforms will also need to proceed along two distinct fronts. The first is transforming the winner-take-all business structure to build back in the flexibility needed to address changes over the life course; the second involves recasting the state role to complement the changing nature of employment in ensuring stability and security for all families (Bridges 2019:473; Hammond 2018:1537). In exploring how the relationship between individual and state might be reconceptualized, this article offers guidance on the first jurisprudential steps towards a redesign of the state-citizen compact that rethinks the temporal dimension underlying families, work, and society.

Note

1 "[I]n 1913 alone, more than 25,000 employees were killed in work related accidents and about 700,000 were seriously injured." Guyton 1999:108.

References

Addo, Fenaba R. and Xing Zhang. 2020. "Debt Concordance and Relationship Quality: A Couple-Level Analysis." *Journal of Family and Economic Issues* 41:405–23. doi:10.1007/s10834-020-09687-8.

Ahmed, Aziza and Jason Jackson. 2021. "Race, Risk, and Personal Responsibility in the Response to Covid-19." *Columbia Law Review Forum* 121:47–70.

Athreya, Kartik B. and Sierra Latham. 2022. "The Pandemic, Child Care and Women's Labor Force Participation." *Federal Reserve Bank of Richmond* (www.richmondfed.org/publications/research/economic_brief/2022/eb_22-16).

Bateman, Nicole and Martha Ross. 2020. "Why Has COVID-19 Been Especially Harmful for Working Women?" *The Brookings Institution* (www.brookings.edu/essay/why-has-covid-19-been-especially-harmful-for-working-women/).

Boushey, Heather. 2002. "The Effects of the Personal Responsibility and Work Opportunity Reconciliation Act on Working Families—Viewpoints." *Economic Policy Institute*, March 4 (www.epi.org/publication/webfeatures_viewpoints_tanf_testimony).

Bridges, Khiara M. 2019. "White Privilege and White Disadvantage." *Virginia Law Review* 105:449–82.

Cahn, Naomi and June Carbone. 2010: *Red Families v. Blue Families: Legal Polarization and the Creation of Culture*. New York: Oxford University Press.

———. 2021. "Uncoupling." *Arizona State Law Journal* 53:1–63.

Cahn, Naomi, June Carbone, and Nancy Levit. 2023. "Gender, Covid & Care." In *The Gender of Covid*, edited by A. Ahmed and L. McClain.

Cahn, Naomi R. and Linda C. McClain. 2020. "Gendered Complications of Covid-19: Towards A Feminist Recovery Plan." *Georgetown Journal of Gender and the Law* 22:1–57.

Cooke, Lynn Prince. 2018. "The Pathology of Patriarchy and Family Inequality." In *Unequal Family Lives: Causes and Consequences in Europe and the Americas*, edited by N. R. Cahn, J. Carbone, L. F. DeRose, and W. Bradford Wilcox. Cambridge: Cambridge University Press.

Dallas, Lynne L. 2012. "Short-Termism, the Financial Crisis, and Corporate Governance." *Journal of Corporation Law* 37:265–364.

Davies, Dave. 2022. "Short-Term Profits and Long-Term Consequences—Did Jack Welch Break Capitalism?" *Fresh Air*, June 1, produced by NPR, podcast, 35:44 (www.wbur.org/npr/1101505691/short-term-profits-and-long-term-consequences-did-jack-welch-break-capitalism).

Eichner, Maxine. 2017. "The Privatized American Family." *Notre Dame Law Review* 93:213–66.

———. 2022. "Covid-19 & the Perils of Free Market Parenting." *Fordham Law Review* 90(6):2509–28.

Federal Reserve Board. 2019. "Report on the Economic Well-Being of U.S. Households in 2018 (www.federalreserve.gov/publications/files/2018-report-economic-well-being-ushouseholds-201905.pdf).

Filho, Luciano Bottini. 2021. "Covid-19 Through Brazilian Courts: The Deserving and the Undeserving Vulnerable." *German Law Journal* 22(6):1098–114. doi:10.1017/glj.2021.55.

Fineman, Martha Albertson. 1995. *The Neutered Mother, the Sexual Family and Other Twentieth Century Tragedies*. New York and London: Routledge.

———. 2008. "The Vulnerable Subject: Anchoring Equality in the Human Condition." *Yale Journal of Law and Feminism* 20:1–23.

———. 2010. "The Vulnerable Subject and the Responsive State." *Emory Law Journal* 60:251–75.

———. 2012. "Beyond Identities: The Limits of an Antidiscrimination Approach to Equality." *Boston University Law Review* 92:1713–70.

———. 2019. "Vulnerability and Social Justice." *Valparaiso University Law Review* 53(2):341–69.

———. 2020. "Beyond Equality and Discrimination." *SMU Law Review Forum* 73:51–62. doi:10.25172/slrf.73.1.7.

Fry, Richard. 2022. "Some Gender Disparities Widened in the U.S. Workforce During the Pandemic." *Pew Research Center* (www.pewresearch.org/fact-tank/2022/01/14/some-gender-disparities-widened-in-the-u-s-workforce-during-the-pandemic/).

Gamage, David. 2012. "Perverse Incentives Arising from the Tax Provisions of Healthcare Reform: Why Further Reforms Are Needed to Prevent Avoidable Costs to Low- and Moderate-Income Workers." *Tax Law Review* 65:669–722.

Gascon, Charles S. and Devin Werner. 2022. "Pandemic, Rising Costs Challenge Child Care Industry." *Federal Reserve Bank of St. Louis*, January 13 (www.stlouisfed.org/publications/regional-economist/2022/jan/pandemic-rising-costs-challenge-child-care-industry).

Gelles, David. 2022a. "How Jack Welch's Reign at G.E. Gave Us Elon Musk's Twitter Feed." *The New York. Times*, May 21 (www.nytimes.com/2022/05/21/business/jack-welch-ge-ceo-behavior.html).

———. 2022b. *The Man Who Broke Capitalism: How Jack Welch Gutted the Heartland and Crushed the soul of Corporate American—and How to Undo His Legacy*. New York: Simon & Schuster.

Gelles, David, and David Yaffee-Bellany. 2019. "Shareholder Value Is No Longer Everything, Top CEOs Say." *The New York Times*, August 19 (www.nytimes.com/2019/08/19/business/business-roundtable-ceos-corporations.html).

Gluck, Abbe R. and Thomas Scott-Railton. 2020. "Affordable Care Act Entrenchment." *Georgetown Law Journal* 108(3):495–578.

Goldin, Claudia. 2022. "Understanding the Economic Impact of COVID-19 on Women." *Brookings Papers on Economic Activity* Spring 2022:65–139. doi:10.1353/eca.2022.0019.

GQR. 2022. "Women and work two years into the pandemic." *National Women's Law Center*, March 2 (https://nwlc.org/wp-content/uploads/2022/03/FINAL-GQR-NWLC-survey-slides-3.29.22.pdf).

Guyton, G. P. 1999. "A Brief History of Workers' Compensation." *Iowa Orthopaedic Journal* 19:106–10.

Ha, Yoonsook, Margaret M. C. Thomas, Thomas Byrne, and Daniel P. Miller. 2020. "Patterns of Multiple Instability Among Low-Income Families with Children." *Social Service Review* 94:129–68. doi:10.1086/708180.

Hammond, Andrew. 2017. "Welfare and Federalism's Peril." *Washington Law Review* 92:1721.

———. 2018. "Pleading Poverty in Federal Court." *Yale Law Journal* 128(6):1478–565.

———. 2020. "Litigating Welfare Rights: Medicaid, Snap, and the Legacy of the New Property." *Northwestern University Law Review* 115:361–436.

Han, Wen-Jui, Christopher J. Ruhm, Jane Waldfogel, and Elizabeth Wasbrook. 2008. "The Timing of Mothers' Employment After Childbirth." *Monthly Labor Review* 131(6):15–27.

Hoffman, Sharona. 2001. "Preplacement Examinations and Job-Relatedness: How to Enhance Privacy and Diminish Discrimination in the Workplace." *University of Kansas Law Review* 49:517–92.

Jackson, Jason and Aziza Ahmed. 2022. "The Public/Private Distinction in Public Health: The Case of COVID-19." *Fordham Law Review* 90(6):2541–59.

Joint Committee on Taxation. 2015. "Estimates of Federal Tax Expenditures for Fiscal Years 2015–2019" (JCX-141R-15) (www.jct.gov/publications.html?func=startdown&id=4857).

Kelton, Stephanie. 2020. *The Deficit Myth: Modern Monetary Theory and the Birth of the People's Economy*. New York: The Hachette Book Group.

Land, Hilary. 1980. "The Family Wage." *Feminist Review* 6:55–77. doi:10.1057/fr.1980.19.

Levine, Marianne. 2015. "Paul Ryan Prizes Family Time, Opposes Family Leave." *Politico* October 21 (www.politico.com/story/2015/10/paul-ryan-family-leave-speaker-house-215034).

Lundberg, Shelly, Robert A. Pollak, and Jenna Stearns. 2016. "Family Inequality: Diverging Patterns in Marriage, Cohabitation, and Childbearing." *Journal of Economic Perspectives* 30(2):79–102. doi:10.1257/jep.30.2.79.

Mahdawi, Arwa. 2021. "Why Are Republicans So Threatened by Universal Daycare?" *The Guardian*, May 1 (www.theguardian.com/commentisfree/2021/may/01/republicans-threatened-biden-universal-daycare-week-in-patriarchy).

McCluskey, Martha T. 2003. "Efficiency and Social Citizenship: Challenging the Neoliberal Attack on the Welfare State." *Indiana Law Journal* 78(2):783–876.

———. 2018. "Are We Economic Engines Too? Precarity, Productivity, and Gender." *University of Toledo Law Review* 49:631–55.

Nixon, Richard. 1971. "Excerpts from Nixon's Veto Message." *The New York Times Archives*, December 10:20 (www.nytimes.com/1971/12/10/archives/excerpts-from-nixons-veto-message.html).

Parker, Kim, Juliana Mesasce Horowitz, and Rachel Minkin. 2022. "COVID-19 Pandemic Continues to Reshape Work in America." *Pew Research Center*, February 16 (www.pewresearch.org/social-trends/2022/02/16/covid-19-pandemic-continues-to-reshape-work-in-america/).

Perry-Jenkins, Maureen and Naomi Gerstel. 2020. "Work and Family in the Second Decade of the 21st Century." *Journal of Marriage & Family* 82:420–53. doi:10.1111/jomf.12636.

Raff, Daniel M. G. and Lawrence H. Summers. 1987. "Did Henry Ford Pay Efficiency Wages?" *Journal of Labor Economics* 5(4):57–86.

Ritzholtz, Barry. 2017. "Judging GE's Jeff Immelt Versus Jack Welch." *Bloomberg*, June 12 (www.bloomberg.com/view/articles/2017-06-12/judging-ge-s-jeff-immelt-versus-jack-welch).

Roberts, Dorothy E. 1993. "Motherhood and Crime." *Iowa Law Review* 79:95–141.

Romiser, James. 2021. "Federal Government Asks Court to Scrap Challenge to Medicaid Work Requirements." *SCOTUSblog*, February 22 (www.scotusblog.com/2021/02/federal-government-asks-court-to-scrap-challenge-to-medicaid-work-requirements/).

Ryan, Mary P. 1981. *Cradle of the Middle Class: The Family in Oneida County, New York, 1790–1865*. Cambridge, New York and Melbourne: Cambridge University Press.

Shinall, Jennifer Bennett. 2018. "The Pregnancy Penalty." *Minnesota Law Review* 103:749–842.

Shivaram, Deepa. 2021. "The Expanded Child Tax Credit Expires Friday After Congress Failed to Renew It." *NPR*, December 30 (www.npr.org/2021/12/30/1069143123/expanded-child-tax-credit-expires-friday-congress).

Shulman, Robin. 2020. "If You're Pregnant and Working, Know Your Rights." *The New York Times*, April 18 (www.nytimes.com/article/pregnancy-discrimination-work.html).

Simon, William H. 1986. "Rights and Redistribution in the Welfare System." *Stanford Law Review* 38:1431–516.

Skocpol, Theda. 1992. *Protecting Soldiers and Mothers: The Political Origins of Social Policy in the United States*. Cambridge, MA: Harvard University Press.

Smith, Stacey Vanek and Claudia Goldin. 2021. "Women, Career and Family: A Conversation with Claudia Goldin." In *The Indicator from Planet Money*, November 30, produced by NPR, podcast, 09:39 (www.npr.org/2021/11/30/1060229250/women-career-and-family-a-conversation-with-claudia-goldin).

Stone, Katherine V. W. 2001. "The New Psychological Contract: Implications of the Changing Workplace for Labor and Employment Law." *University of California Los Angeles Law Review* 48:519–661.

———. 2007. "A Fatal Mismatch: Employer-Centric Benefits in a Boundaryless World." *Lewis & Clark Law Review* 11(2):451–80.

Stout, Lynn A. 2015. "The Corporation as Time Machine: Intergenerational Equity, Intergenerational Efficiency, and the Corporate Form." *Seattle University Law Review* 38:685–723.

Strauss, Elissa. 2018. "Fired for Being Pregnant: Another Kind of Discrimination Women Face at Work." *CNN*, February 1 (www.cnn.com/2018/02/01/health/fired-pregnant-parenting-strauss/index.html).

U.S. Bureau of Labor Statistics. 2020. "Number of Jobs, Labor Market Experience, and Earnings Growth: Results from a National Longitudinal Survey" (USDL-21–1567). October 20 (www.bls.gov/news.release/pdf/nlsoy.pdf).

White House. 2021. "How the Build Back Better Framework Will Support Women's Employment and Strengthen Family Economic Security." July 15 (www.whitehouse.gov/briefing-room/statements-releases/2021/07/15/fact-sheet-how-the-build-back-better-framework-will-support-womens-employment-and-strengthen-family-economic-security/).

Widiss, Deborah A. 2012. "Changing the Marriage Equation." *Washington University Law Review* 89(4):721–94.

Yuille, Lua Kamál. 2019. "Manufacturing Resilience on the Margins: Street Gangs, Property, & Vulnerability Theory." *Pennsylvania State Law Review* 123(2):463–98.

PART VI

Dimensions of Public and Private in Health Care

11

A VULNERABILITY APPROACH TO THE "RIGHT TO HEALTH CARE"

Addressing Epistemic Vulnerability

Matthew B. Lawrence

Introduction

Vulnerability theory abhors a silo. Focusing on vulnerable subjects who are unavoidably dependent on others puts relationships at the center of the way we conceive of the world (Fineman 2019:367). The subject so understood cannot be viewed in full if we look at them "alone," cut off from relationships of dependence (on family, friends, institutions, society, and so on) or, for that matter, obligations of support and positions of power that they may have as to others (children, students, and so on). Thus, from the very start, vulnerability theory pushes us to consider not just the person, but, as Fineman puts it, the "web of economic, social, cultural, and institutional relationships" in which she is embedded (Fineman 2015:622). This *relational* point of view forced by vulnerability theory is in marked contrast to the *individual* point of view forced by classical liberalism's autonomous individual. For him relationships and connections between persons are either purely optional "transactions" or unwelcome, foreign intrusions. Legal systems premised on the autonomous individual are thus especially susceptible to fragmentation (Satz 2015).

This chapter leverages vulnerability theory's relational focus to develop a new site of contestation for advancing the popular and powerful—but difficult to put into practice—concept of a "right to health care." The leading approach to giving content to the popular notion of a "right to health care" is to think of it as an individual entitlement. This approach focuses on the "downstream" perspective of an individual in need of care, ignoring key upstream choices about the allocation of resources across society and investment in infrastructure on which availability of and access to quality health

DOI: 10.4324/9781003323242-18

care depends. The vulnerability perspective shifts focus from the individual's entitlement to care to the state's obligation to provide it, and this shift from entitlement to obligation brings the "right to health care" upstream to intervene in these choices and the state's systems for making them.

To problematize the entitlement approach to the "right to health care" and illustrate the advantages of the vulnerability approach, the Chapter confronts the challenge of epistemic vulnerability. Epistemic vulnerability refers to the inevitable imperfection of systems for developing and ascertaining knowledge and, with it, the dependence of the mechanisms (including the budgeting process and cost-benefit analysis) that the U.S. federal government uses to make tradeoffs on the actors and institutions who control them. Epistemic vulnerability works far upstream from individual health care choices, making it invisible from the entitlement approach to the right to health care. Indeed, advocates and scholars can be reluctant to engage in these or other systems for making tradeoffs between prevention and rescue, health and education, or other potential targets of state support for fear they may be biased or unresponsive. The vulnerability approach to the right to health care, on the other hand, readily intervenes in these systems, highlighting failures to prioritize resilience investments as inconsistent with the right to health care. The vulnerability approach also points to avenues for improving such systems to better fulfill the state's obligations. The Chapter concludes by illustrating this point through two possible upstream reforms to advance the right to health care, "gross domestic burden" (or GDB) and care work impact statements.

A. The "Right to Health Care" and the Challenges of an Entitlement Approach

1. The Popular "Right to Health Care"

In popular opinion surveys, Americans overwhelmingly support the view that "all Americans should have a right to health care regardless of ability to pay" (The Commonwealth Fund 2019). This base of public support for a "right" to health care is influential. The Trump Administration was unable to repeal the Affordable Care Act because it was unable to find a way to do so while preserving the law's prohibition of discrimination against people with pre-existing conditions. Similarly, open calls to ration health care are believed to be politically impossible, a check that played a significant role in curbing the rise of health maintenance organizations in the 1990s. And when stories about people kicked out of the hospital without care quickly go viral, there is tremendous pressure on embarrassed hospitals.

2. Operationalizing the "Right to Health Care": The Role of Theory

While Americans say they support a "right to health care," the United States does not have a "right to health care" in the constitutional sense (Fuse Brown 2013).

Moreover, it is not clear that people have something specific in mind when they say they support a "right to health care." Yet, this concept requires elaboration to be applied to specific situations. Is access to branded drugs when an equivalent generic is available protected by the "right to health care"? Does a requirement that a person pay a $5,000 deductible out of pocket before insurance benefits kick in violate the "right"?

This Chapter takes a particular approach to the relationship between theory and the "right to health care" that focuses on what Merton (1968) calls "the middle range." It goes without saying that Americans who profess support for a "right to health care" do not have in mind some grand, fully-elaborated philosophical theory of rights, let alone the same such theory as others who support this concept. But the fact that the "right to health care" that Americans broadly support is not a completely defined concept does not mean that either the concept or the fact of its broad popular support should be tossed aside as pointless. Nor does it necessarily mean that we must get to work educating and engaging the public so that all come to agree about the same grand theory—though that might be nice.

Scholarship on the relationship between constitutional principles and social movements offers guidance on the relationship between particular legal or philosophical theories and popular conceptions (including the conception of the "right to health care"). In her study of the relationship between advocacy for the Equal Rights Amendment and its influence on courts' adoption of intermediate scrutiny, Professor Reva Siegel (2006) explained that, by delineating the scope of a "right" and framing contestation about its content, a constitutional theory can influence the formation and collaboration of social groups who, in turn, influence constitutional change. Professor Jack Balkin (2011) has traced a similar, recursive interaction between constitutional categories, social movement formation, and constitutional change in a variety of contexts.

In short, to say that the popular conception of a "right to health care" does not reflect any particular legal, normative, or philosophical view does not mean that this popular conception cannot be guided by theory, or does not need to look to theory to lend it coherence, legitimacy, and content. Nor does it mean that theory cannot be informed or refined by its engagement with the popular conception of the right to health care. Instead, what is needed is a theoretical approach that fits with, gives content to, and energizes the partially-defined, popular notion of a "right to health care." The focus of this chapter is the development of such a theoretical approach for operationalizing the popular "right to health care."

3. Entitlement Approach and Its Limitations

Professor Scheffler (2021) takes a middle-range approach to giving content to the "right to health care," deconstructing the right in *Equality and*

Sufficiency in Health Care Reform. In his careful and insightful analysis, Scheffler "distinguish[es] between two distinct conceptions of the right to health care: one which focuses on sufficient access to health care . . . and a second which focuses on equality to access to health care" (2021:144). He explains that these two different approaches to understanding the right to health care yield different results in application to particular health policy questions, and develops an insightful chart comparing their theoretical implications for the questions of utilization review, cost sharing, and privatization. For example, if the "right to health care" requires only a certain minimum of access to care (what he calls the sufficiency approach), cost sharing (such as deductibles) are permitted (p. 144, Table 7.1). If, on the other hand, the right requires equality of access (the equality approach) then it does not (because cost sharing may not impede access altogether but does produce disparities in access).

Both approaches disaggregated by Scheffler—the equality approach and the access approach—conceive of the "right to health care" as essentially an individual entitlement to particular health care goods or services in particular contexts. On the sufficiency approach, this is an entitlement to sufficient health care for the individual, and on the equality approach this is an entitlement to equal access for the individual. This is entirely consistent with other scholarship on the "right to health care," which also employs the individual entitlement approach (Fuse Brown 2013; Earnest and Bowen Matthew 2008).

The entitlement approach to the right to health care has benefits, but it also has significant flaws. In particular, the entitlement approach faces three key problems.

- First, the problem of subject: by operationalizing the right to health care around the goods and services particular people receive, the entitlement approach builds on, and therefore further entrenches the individualized conception of regulation. Coronavirus has exploited the myopia of this individualized perspective on health care, as a health care system structured around serving individual needs failed repeatedly to respond to a collective problem (Wiley 2021).
- Second, the problem of focus: by emphasizing the delivery of health care goods and services to people who need care, the entitlement approach to the right to health care obscures the role of upstream investments in resilience or prevention, including investments in education, the environment, and social services (the social determinants of health). Again, this builds on and re-enforces the problematic focus on rescue supports to the exclusion of broader investments that makes the American health care system more expensive, less effective, and more susceptible to dramatic health disparities than that of other nations (Bradley and Taylor 2013).

- Third, the problem of prioritization: Aduhelm is a recently-developed Alzheimer's drug that carries questionable effectiveness; it costs $56,000 a year, per patient. It is an extreme example of the necessity of tradeoffs. It is probably not possible for any country to afford the cost of providing every resident with every potentially-beneficial health care good or service, at least not without sacrificing investments in other areas of need. Whatever the benefit of Aduhelm, $56,000 a year might be much better spent on other goods and services—especially from the standpoint of elderly beneficiaries who have Medicare but cannot afford food, or housing. The entitlement approach to the right to health care struggles to intervene in prioritization choices, and potentially leaves them to courts who have little competence to make them.

The entitlement approach to operationalizing the right to health care has limits because it is premised on the autonomous individual. That perspective drives it to intervene in health care choices at a point (the provision of care to a person who needs it) at which crucial upstream choices about societal resource allocation and investment in prevention have already been made. It also drives enforcement of the right to health care into courts who are institutionally incompetent either to second guess those upstream choices or to alter their results. And, on the other side of this coin, the entitlement approach to the right to health care leaves the right incapable of playing a meaningful role in upstream debates—about tax cuts, budget processes, and entitlement funding—that are often the key determinants (I have called these "fiscal determinants") of health care outcomes (Lawrence 2022).

In light of these limits of the entitlement approach, might another approach to operationalizing the popular "right to health care" be possible? The next part turns to vulnerability theory to develop an alternative.

B. Vulnerability Approach: From Entitlement to Obligation

1. *Vulnerability Replaces Individual Entitlement With Collective (or State) Obligation*

Vulnerability theory offers an alternative approach: instead of an individual entitlement to health care goods and services, vulnerability develops a collective, state obligation to provide social supports and build resilience, including not only through the provision of health care goods and services but also through investment in the underlying infrastructure of resilience (Fineman 2019). This approach readily overcomes the first two limitations of the entitlement approach: that of subject and that of focus. As to subject, vulnerability replaces the idea of an individual right with that of a collective responsibility. This conception is much better suited to tackling problems like viral pandemics and health care disparities because it is not blind to spillovers, community impacts, or collective threats (or opportunities). As to focus, vulnerability appropriately emphasizes resilience, not rescue, including the "individual's location within webs of social, economic, political, and institutional relationships that structure opportunities and options" (Fineman 2013:129).

2. What Is the Content of the State's Obligation?

This leaves the problem of content and prioritization. What is the specific content of the state's obligation to provide health care or other social services? How should scarce resources be prioritized, for example, between near term needs and long-term infrastructural investments such as education, workforce, and so on? (I focus here on tangible resources but ultimately agree with Fineman that "[r]esources can come in material, social, or economic forms, including human capital, education, wealth, and group identification, as well as relationships in entities such as the familial and other institutional arrangements" [2013:128]). Are deductibles justifiable, if the case can be made that without them health care costs would rise and crowd out education, public health, housing, or other important goals? Is there ever "enough" resilience? To what extent may society permissibly allocate resources to investments (like a hydroelectric dam) that do not promote present-day resilience but are expected to increase its access to resources, and so the ability to meet society's needs, in the future? Finally, to what extent may society permissibly allocate resources to purposes that do not plausibly promote resilience either today or in the future, like a city or state paying hundreds of millions of dollars to obtain or retain a National Football League franchise?

3. A Collective, Procedural Right to Priority

Returning to the underlying idea of a "right" points to the answer. At a basic notional level—and for purposes of constitutional tiers of scrutiny—labeling something a "right" requires that it be prioritized, given a privileged status over other non-rights in decision-making. Through a vulnerability approach, the content of the state's obligation to provide health care or other social services, and to invest in resilience infrastructure, can be conceived of in terms of process, rather than substance: the state has satisfied its obligation to support its residents when it has made decisions about how to allocate the nation's scarce resources (between the market and social supports, among social supports, and so on) in a manner that strictly prioritizes resilience over other purposes. (Just how "strict" is a question beyond this chapter's scope. It may be that the obligation would insist that allocations for purposes other than directly promoting resilience be justified, if at all, by convincing evidence that they would further resilience indirectly or in the long term.)

Conceiving of the "right to health care" as an obligation that the state prioritize resilience in deciding how to allocate scarce resources does require a group-based understanding of the "right," but understanding the right this way helpfully cuts against problematic individualized perspectives. Moreover, rights whose content are defined by process rather than substance have a long history in the United States. (Take, for example, the right to due process—a central, familiar feature of American law.)

Indeed, the concept underlying the rallying cry of "no taxation without representation" that played a key role in the early history of the United States was really one of process surrounding allocation choices—the concern in this rhetoric was not government taxation of any particular good or service but rather government taxation that resulted from a decision-making process in which the person being taxed did not have a voice. Drawing from this rallying cry, the specific procedural content of a "right to health care" and other social services on a vulnerability approach can be summed up in a catch phrase as well: "*no allocation without prioritization.*" From tax cuts to property creation to defense appropriations bills, any government action (or inaction) that allocates resources can be tested by this creed, which focuses attention on the process by which the government made choices and whether that process prioritized resilience as vulnerability demands.

Consider the Tax Cuts and Jobs Act of 2017, which allocated large sums of resources to market actors (through "tax cuts"). These resources are no longer available for allocation to social programs. The resulting lack of government revenue is the but-for and proximate cause of limitations today on government investments in social programs, but this role is ignored on an entitlement approach to the right to health care. By contrast, on a vulnerability approach that sees the obligation of the responsive state to address the vulnerability of its residents as an obligation to prioritize resilience in deciding how to allocate scarce resources, the Tax Cuts and Jobs Act of 2017 would be problematized as having failed this obligation (the process leading up to its enactment did not even purport to prioritize social supports, in the present day or in the future), and so violated the right to health care.

An advantage of this process-based conception is that it implicates and indicts key legal structures that would be ignored on an entitlement approach, even though they play an outsized role in actual policymaking in the United States. Through the vulnerability approach, the rhetorical power and intuitive appeal of the concept of a "right to health care" can be given content and application in domains that the entitlement approach does not reach. These structures include cost-benefit analysis, the federal budget process, and grant award requirements.

C. Addressing Epistemic Vulnerability

Full consideration of the content of the right to health care as understood through vulnerability theory, or of all the relative strengths and weakness of this approach to conceptualizing the right as compared to others, is not possible here. To further establish that this approach is capable of intervening in upstream, infrastructural and prioritization choices, however, this section concludes by focusing on vulnerability theory's usefulness in addressing epistemic vulnerability. Subsection 1 introduces the challenge of epistemic vulnerability in infrastructural systems like the federal budget process and cost-benefit analysis. Subsection 2 addresses the need to engage in the development and operation of such systems even when they suffer from major flaws. Subsection 3 discusses particular reforms.

1. Epistemic Vulnerability

Usually when "tradeoffs" or the challenge of "prioritization" are mentioned in the same sentence as investments in spending or social services, the two are cast as enemies. Some program sounds nice, it is said, but what program will you cut to fund it—or will you raise taxes, hurt the economy, and force deeper cuts in social programs in the future? Will you rob Peter to pay Paul? I have elsewhere described this as the "Peter/Paul question" and it is indeed influential (Lawrence 2023). For example, it recently blocked COVID-19 funding necessary to address an ongoing pandemic.

"[O]bjections based on tradeoffs are only as good as our system for making them—for deciding where to direct scarce resources" (Lawrence 2023). And important U.S. prioritization systems are flawed in ways that systematically impede health investment. In *Covid-19 Reveals the Fiscal Determinants of Health*, I surveyed scholarship on several such flaws in the federal budget process. These include "(i) ignor[ing] long-term and secondary costs and benefits in estimating the effects of policy; (ii) fragment[ing] choices into largely arbitrary but outcome-determinative fiscal categories; (iii) leav[ing] a flawed federal fiscal apparatus as the main source of essential investments; and (iv) forc[ing] fragility on public goods" (2023).

Scholars have documented further flaws, like systemic undercounting in other systems. A significant body of scholarship addresses flaws in cost-benefit analysis, and Professor McCluskey (2016) has problematized the preference for corporate tax expenditures (and barriers to individual and local tax expenditures) in U.S. tax law. Even a system that features an ostensibly-neutral decision rule (like "proceed if benefits outweigh costs") can be skewed if the means that it uses to ascertain and credit information, and make estimates, is itself skewed. Costs for industry of a new regulation, for example, are both easier to consider (because they manifest in terms of dollars) and easier to obtain information about (because industry's power and processes position it to provide data) than benefits for the public, or for marginalized groups. Thus, even a decision rule of excluding "uncertain" costs or benefits can itself be skewed due to underlying variation in the sorts of costs and benefits susceptible to ready calculation.

From the standpoint of vulnerability theory, the presence of systemic flaws in the nation's systems for making allocation choices is not surprising. Vulnerability theory teaches that institutions, like people, suffer from inevitable vulnerability and are themselves dependent on "web of economic, social, cultural, and institutional relationships." There is no reason that epistemic systems like those at the heart of cost-benefit analysis or even medicine—systems for developing knowledge—should be different.

2. Respond or Reject?

As a first cut, the vulnerability approach to the right to health care offers a basis for indicting epistemic systems, like the federal budget process or cost-benefit analysis, when they de-prioritize health investments. The right to health care requires the opposite—for the state to prioritize health care in making allocation choices—so such systems violate that right.

The question then becomes: what next? One response would be to disengage from or reject epistemic systems that violate the right to health care—to reject tradeoffs altogether and insist that the state meet its obligation to respond to sickness and build resilience *regardless* of any system of tradeoffs and any alleged necessity of making them—based on the view that any such system will inappropriately undermine rather than bolster the case for investment. Another would be to try to improve or fix such systems; the Biden Administration has ostensibly taken this approach to cost-benefit analysis by mandating consideration of distributional consequences.

I believe that rejecting prioritization altogether sells vulnerability theory short for four reasons. First, prioritization is in fact inevitable in our world of scarcity, as are systems for making choices about how to allocate scarce resources. It is not possible to eliminate vulnerability entirely, no matter how much we might wish it. Nor is it possible, in a city with a limited budget, both to invest in residents' education and build a stadium for an NFL team: states, cities, localities, and even the federal government are often forced to make such choices. Moreover, even refusing to consider tradeoffs is a choice—usually, it is a choice to award a limited resource to whoever is able to get to the decisionmaker first. If tradeoffs are happening and vulnerability theory has something to say about them, then it should say it.

Second, as Revesz and Livermore explain in their argument that environmental advocates seek to reform rather than reject cost-benefit analysis, properly calibrated systems for making tradeoffs can be affirmatively useful

(2009). When done correctly, such a system can motivate changes to the status quo that are opposed by powerful groups. Heather McGhee's exploration of the costs of underinvestment motivated by racism is an example (2021).

Third, unlike the entitlement approach to the right to health care, the vulnerability approach connects the right to health care to discussions about the design (and improvement) of epistemic systems. We can respond to epistemic vulnerability by identifying and implementing incremental reforms that improve the state's ability to meet its obligation to prioritize resilience in making tradeoffs.

Fourth, vulnerability theory helps us to sort "good" incremental improvements in epistemic systems (stepping stones) from "bad" incremental reforms (stumbling blocks) that may appear helpful but ultimately be counterproductive. This is because vulnerability theory's leaping-off point is a flaw in the broader epistemic system that is the overarching framework in which we understand how law relates to its subjects, namely, the neoliberal logic that is problematized by both vulnerability theory and the law and political economy movement. The germ of that flaw is the conception of the subject of law as an autonomous individual, and Fineman and other vulnerability theorists have described various ways that this flaw biases the outputs of any inquiry premised on it (Fineman 2019). Incremental steps that constitute improvements in one, specific epistemic system (like "cost-benefit analysis") but that re-affirm the idea of an autonomous individual subject in our broad system for understanding could on net pose a setback rather than a step forward. Incremental steps that constitute improvements in a specific system but that also challenge or combat the autonomous individual, on the other hand, could be clear steps forward. (In another context, my coauthors and I referred to such reforms that challenge fixtures impeding transformational change as "confrontational incrementalism" [Wiley et al. 2021]).

3. Separating Stepping Stones From Stumbling Blocks

Consider two interventions that would promote prioritization of resilience in particular epistemic systems but with arguably-competing implications for our broader conception of the nature and subject of regulation. First, a care giver impact statement. Individuals and their friends and family performing unpaid care work for themselves and others are usually the first line of defense for sick people in the American health care system. Health care policies often increase or decrease these informal care work burdens; for example, the mandate that insurers covering contraception saved people considering new jobs from the burden of double checking that their contraceptive medicines were covered by their potential employers' plan. Ordinary cost-benefit analysis can fail to account for such care work burdens, inadvertently or otherwise.

This leads to decisions that fail to account for these burdens (or benefits), even where they might be determinative.

In a number of contexts laws or regulations today mandate that agencies focus on particular categories of impacts when considering a rule. Environmental impact statements mandated by the National Environmental Policy Act of 1969 require agencies to assess environmental impacts of proposed projects and actions. This includes qualitative or, where possible, quantitative assessment of impacts on threatened and endangered species as well as air and water quality, among other factors. Other laws and regulations mandate assessments of fiscal impacts on state and local budgets (through "unfunded mandates"), potential adverse effects on local property rights, or impacts on small businesses. Indeed, after President Clinton rescinded a Reagan-era executive order requiring assessment of impacts on "family well-being" in rulemaking, Congress enacted a statutory such requirement (Omnibus Appropriations Bill 1998).[1] The author is unaware of a study tracking whether and how that requirement has been interpreted or enforced (agencies appear to have found it inapplicable in dozens of cases and I could find none actually finding it applicable), but it appears to be focused on an understanding of family wellbeing premised on "the marital commitment."

The vulnerability approach to the right to health care suggests that one way to advance the right would be to ensure explicit consideration of care giving burdens in rulemaking through care giving impact statements, or the like. At the very least, such statements would force agencies to engage, in the course of cost-benefit analysis, with people and entities who might have knowledge of care giving impacts, and to begin to develop evidence as to such impacts. That said, it is possible that these benefits could be outweighed by costs, if the caregiving impact statement encouraged an *ad hoc*, reform-by-reform approach to evaluating policies. Such an approach would fail to capture relationships among policies, doubling down on a siloed approach to regulation.

On the other hand, scholars and policymakers have noted that invisible caregiving burdens are like a hidden tax on caregivers. Professor Hoffman (2016) collects studies estimating the informal care giving burden associated with the nation's failure to provide for those with long-term care needs, a major gap in our health care system. By some measures, these burdens would amount to $220 billion annually counting only lost wages and costs borne by friends and family. Again, the Congressional Budget Office, Office of Management and Budget, Assistant Secretary for Planning and Evaluation, and other actors that play an accounting role in our health care system could be required to invest time and energy in developing a rigorous—but not narrow or overly cautious—estimate of care work burdens.

Mere publication of such a "Gross Domestic Burden" (GDB) could help to answer Professor Fineman's longstanding emphasis on the need for full valuation of such labor (Fineman 1995). Moreover, by its very nature, such an accounting emphasizes collective responsibility for caregiving burdens so it would confront rather than accede to the larger, problematic focus on the autonomous individual that holds back prioritization of resilience in allocation decisions through the very words and concepts we use to frame and consider such decisions. Confrontationally incremental reform to advance the right to health care could be desirable, as understood through vulnerability theory.

Note

1 5 U.S.C. § 651 (note). Omnibus Appropriations Bill 1998, Pub. L. No. 105–277, § 654 ("Before implementing policies and regulations that may affect family well-being, each agency shall assess such actions with respect to whether—(1) the action strengthens or erodes the stability or safety of the family and, particularly, the marital commitment; (2) the action strengthens or erodes the authority and rights of parents in the education, nurture, and supervision of their children; (3) the action helps the family perform its functions, or substitutes governmental activity for the function; (4) the action increases or decreases disposable income or poverty of families and children; (5) the proposed benefits of the action justify the financial impact on the family; (6) the action may be carried out by State or local government or by the family; and (7) the action establishes an implicit or explicit policy concerning the relationship between the behavior and personal responsibility of youth, and the norms of society.").

Reference List

Balkin, Jack M. 2011. *Constitutional Redemption Political Faith in an Unjust World.* Cambridge, MA: Harvard University Press.

Bradley, Elizabeth and Lauren Taylor. 2013. "The American Health Care Paradox—High Spending on Health Care and Poor Health." *QJM: An International Journal of Medicine* 110:61–5.

The Commonwealth Fund, The New York Times, and Harvard T. H. Chan School of Public Health. 2019. "Americans' Values and Beliefs About National Health Insurance Reform." Report (PDF) (https://cdn1.sph.harvard.edu/wp-content/uploads/sites/94/2019/10/CMWF-NYT-Harvard_Final-Report_Oct2019.pdf).

Earnest, Mark and Dayna Bowen Matthew. 2008. "A Property Right to Medicare Care." *Journal of Legal Medicine* 29:65–9.

Fineman, Martha Albertson. 1995. *The Neutered Mother, the Sexual Family and Other Twentieth Century Tragedies.* New York and London: Routledge.

———. 2013. " 'Elderly' as Vulnerable: Rethinking the Nature of Individual and Societal Responsibility." *Elder Law Journal* 20:71–112.

———. 2015. "Equality and Difference—The Restrained State." *Alabama Law Review* 55:609–26.

———. 2019. "Vulnerability and Social Justice." *Valparaiso University Law Review* 53:341–69.

Fuse Brown, Erin. 2013. "Developing a Durable Right to Health Care." *Minnesota Journal of Law, Science & Technology* 14:439.

Hoffman, Allison K. 2016. "Reimagining the Risk of Long Term Care." *Yale Journal of Health Policy, Law, and Ethics* 16:147.

Lawrence, Matthew B. 2023. "Covid 19 Reveals the Fiscal Determinants of Health." In *Covid-19 and the Law*. Cambridge: Cambridge University Press.

McCluskey, Martha. 2016. "Framing Middle Class Insecurity: Tax and the Ideology of Unequal Economic Growth." *Fordham Law Review* 84:2699.

McGhee, Heather C. 2021. *The Sum of Us: What Racism Costs Everyone and How We Can Prosper Together*. New York: One World.

Merton, Robert King. 1968. *Social Theory and Social Structure*. New York: The Free Press.

Omnibus Appropriations Bill, 1998, Pub. L. No. 105–277, § 654.

Satz, Ani B. 2015. "Fragmentation After Health Care Reform." *Houston Journal of Health Law & Policy* 15:173–6.

Scheffler, Gabriel. 2021. "Equality and Sufficiency in Health Care Reform." *Maryland Law Review* 81:144–204.

Siegel, Reva B. 2006. "Constitutional Culture, Social Movement Conflict and Constitutional Change: The Case of the de facto ERA." *California Law Review* 94:1323–41.

Wiley, Lindsay, Erin Fuse Brown, Matthew Lawrence, and Liz McCuskey. 2021. "Health Reform Reconstruction." *U.C. Davis Law Review* 55:657.

12

DISABILITY, VULNERABILITY, AND PUBLIC HEALTH EMERGENCIES

Ani B. Satz

Introduction

From 9/11 to Hurricane Katrina and the California wildfires to the COVID-19 pandemic, individuals with disabilities face dire outcomes during public health emergencies. During the COVID-19 pandemic, for example, individuals with intellectual and developmental disabilities died at a 2–2.5 times higher rate than any other segment of the population (Shapiro 2020b). When a disaster strikes, individuals with disabilities remain deprioritized (Friedman 2006), segregated within operations more fully devoted to others (Associated Press 2006; *Freeman v. State* 2008), or die waiting for special rescue services (CBS News 2002). At the beginning of the COVID-19 pandemic, for instance, individuals with disabilities lacked initial access to vaccines (Shapiro 2020b), were deprioritized in hospitals (Contrera 2021), and died in group homes when group home workers were not considered "essential workers" under COVID-19 relief laws (Shapiro 2020b). During the pandemic, individuals with immune-related disabilities could not, without risk to their lives, take public transportation, shop in grocery stores, or return to work or school because mask mandates were lifted by federal, state, and local governments in those environments, despite a persistent high-level viral threat (McCausland 2022).

These outcomes for individuals with disabilities starkly contrast with Department of Justice statements about nondiscrimination issued during the pandemic. For example, the Office for Civil Rights of the U.S. Department of Health and Human Services (HHS) issued several statements, including: "HHS is committed to leaving no one behind during an emergency . . .. Persons with disabilities . . . should not be put at the end of the line for health

DOI: 10.4324/9781003323242-19

services during emergencies. Our civil rights laws protect the equal dignity of every human life from ruthless utilitarianism" (OCR 2020). Additionally, the Federal Emergency Management Agency issued a statement that "[c]ivil rights laws and legal authorities remain in effect, and cannot be waived, during emergencies" (FEMA 2020).

These statements are supported by disability antidiscrimination laws, which, at the federal level, include the Americans with Disabilities Act of 1990 (ADA), the Rehabilitation Act of 1973, and the antidiscrimination disability mandates of the Patient Protection and Affordable Care Act. Read through the ADA, these statutes and parallel state statutes protect individuals with disabilities as a matter of civil right. Additionally, federal and state laws—including the Robert T. Stafford Disaster Relief and Emergency Assistance Act and the Public Health Security and Bioterrorism Preparedness and Response Act—require that disability is considered in emergency planning. In the wake of Hurricane Katrina, after individuals with disabilities died waiting for help (Friedman 2006) or were even killed (Fink 2009), additional federal legislation was passed to protect individuals with disabilities in public health emergencies. These statutes include the Pandemic and All-Hazards Preparedness Act of 2006, the Post-Katrina Emergency Management Reform Act of 2006, and the PETS Evacuation and Transportation Standards Act of 2006. Nevertheless, as the COVID-19 pandemic illustrates, discrimination persists, and outcomes remain poor over a decade later.

Employing Martha Fineman's theory of vulnerability, this chapter argues that the negative outcomes for individuals with disabilities may be the result of the very way we view disability and arrange (or fail to arrange) our legal and social institutions to support it. Part II discusses the limitations of current approaches to disability protections in the context of public health emergencies. Part III discusses vulnerability theory's approach of reasoning from the body. It then uses vulnerability theory to critique relevant disability laws. Part IV uses vulnerability theory to reconceptualize disability and to situate it within health law architecture. Notably, vulnerability theory provides a means to both reconcile conflicting regulatory health and public health law and to move past the limitations of a "vulnerable populations" approach. Part V applies vulnerability theory to hospitals and public health institutions to interrogate ableist views and highlight the need for politically isolated public health authorities. Part VI uses vulnerability theory to identify tools for resilience during public health emergencies. Part VII concludes.

I. Limits of Current Approaches

In uncovering why as a society we fail to address harm to individuals with disabilities during public health emergencies, we must begin with the assumptions behind our legal protections. The ADA and related laws (hereinafter

ADA) focus on protecting qualified individuals from discrimination, rather than protecting all individuals with disabilities from harm or supporting various forms of functioning across geographic and other heterogeneous populations. Similarly, defendants' obligations to make accommodations are assessed relative to their individual capabilities and choice, rather than according to social obligations to achieve certain outcomes for individuals with disabilities. This individual-focused approach both results in some individuals with disabilities being protected while others are not and may result in accommodations that do not best support disability or denial of accommodations altogether. A related but distinct consequence of focusing on the individual is that independence is emphasized over interdependence, and public health emergencies often require collective action to mitigate or prevent harm.

To begin, the ADA centers the individual with a disability as the focal point for potential legal remedy. The ADA begins with a threshold question—an individualized inquiry—about whether an individual is disabled, has a record of disability, or is "regarded as" disabled (ADA 1990). An individual in the first two categories is assessed based on how their physical or mental impairment substantially limits them in a major life activity, such as seeing, performing manual tasks, and thinking. The ADA does not recognize *per se* disabilities, and two individuals with the same impairment may be viewed differently under the law, with one receiving protection, while the other does not. Further, an individual with a disability must prove that they are "qualified" for protections (ADA 1990). An individual is qualified for public services, programs, or activities if they "meet[] the essential eligibility requirements" they require (ADA 1990). In employment, individuals with disabilities are qualified if they have the required "personal and professional attributes" and "with or without reasonable accommodation, [they are able to] perform the essential functions of the employment position that [they] hold[] or desire[]" (ADA 1990; Regulations to Implement the Equal Employment Provisions of the ADA 1990). As a result of these disability threshold tests, some individuals with impairments will be protected, while others will not.

If an individual is protected under the ADA, a reasonable accommodation may be required. What is considered reasonable is measured relative to an individual defendant's resources and desires. A defendant need not make an accommodation that imposes an "undue hardship," meaning it requires "significant difficulty or expense" or is "unduly costly," as measured relative to the facility and overall firm's resources and, in the employment context, other employees (ADA 1990). Similarly, public services need not be altered if they impose a "fundamental alteration" of a "service, program, or activity," and alterations to existing structures that are public accommodations must be "readily achievable" and not require "much difficulty or expense" (ADA 1990). Additionally, an accommodation may not be one an individual prefers or that allows their functionality; the choice of accommodation is up to the entity making it, and it must only be viewed as reasonable in the circumstances (ADA 1990). Further, disability access extends only to particular environments (e.g., key transportation stations), not the activities the environments support (e.g., transportation generally) (ADA 1990).

This individual-centered approach has several implications. First, it is inherently adversarial. It both pits individuals with disabilities against each other for resources and places disability accommodations in conflict with a defendant's resources. This is because accommodations are viewed as something available to only some people with impairments as well as outside and in conflict with routine firm operations. In short, responsibility for disability accommodation is not a broad, social obligation but something to be assessed within discrete situations, balancing inclusion against individual firm's financial and other interests.

Second, the individual-centered approach to disability views it as exceptional rather than as part of the human experience. Vulnerability to disability throughout the life course is not viewed as something to consider at the foundations of constructing social institutions such as workplaces, hospitals, and schools. Instead, disability is considered after legal and social structures are in place, requiring modifications.

Compounding these issues with the individual-focused antidiscrimination approach—and for good historic reason—the ADA stresses independence over interdependence. The Act states, "the Nation's proper goals regarding individuals with disabilities are to assure equality of opportunity, full participation, independent living, and economic self-sufficiency for such individuals" (ADA 1990). The ADA was a response to the exclusion of individuals with disabilities from civic and social realms due to stereotypical and discriminatory views about their abilities and worth, which led to extreme segregation, unemployment, and other marginalization. But these protections aimed at addressing animus, decreasing segregation, and furthering employment for individuals do not speak to the interdependence and collective action required for improving health outcomes for individuals with disabilities during public health emergencies. Nor do they address the dependency that may arise following natural disasters or the social supports required to respond to such disasters. In fact, the ADA casts dependency in a negative light and as associated with unproductive citizenship: "the continuing existence of unfair . . . discrimination and prejudice denies people with disabilities the opportunity to compete on an equal basis . . . and costs the United States billions of dollars in unnecessary expenses resulting from dependency and nonproductivity" (ADA 1990).

II. Reasoning From the Body

Martha Fineman's theory of vulnerability suggests that the traditional legal focus on the individual is misguided. Fineman argues that we should reason from a collective notion of the body, as the body is a universal and ontological concept (Fineman 2020, 2022a, 2022b). The body's functioning is dynamic and nonlinear. It evolves throughout the lifecycle; as children, for example, our bodies require different care than they do when we are adults. Our bodies are both resilient and subject to harm. They may experience permanent or temporary impairment through illness, accident, natural disasters, and war. They may experience loss of functioning and recover or adapt using alternative modes of functioning. At times, our bodies may require episodic or permanent support.

Fineman's view of the ontological body recognizes that vulnerability to harm and other disadvantage is universal and constant (Fineman 2020, 2022a, 2022b). Vulnerability is universal because of the different characteristics, susceptibilities, and barriers of our bodies. According to Fineman, viewing vulnerability as limited in reach or exceptional both fragments the human condition and undermines a coherent theory of state responsibility. It fragments the human condition because our vulnerability is inherent in our body and our experiences. Failing to view vulnerability as universal undermines state responsibility because institutions are built to support fictitious persons who are fully functional across a lifetime, resulting in gaps in needed social support. Vulnerability also is constant because, even with precautions, it cannot be eradicated internally or externally with respect to our bodies. Vulnerability is therefore not only situational, and social structures must contemplate it from the outset.

Because our bodies are universally and constantly vulnerable, Fineman argues that we are interdependent as well as collectively linked to social institutions for support (Fineman 2020, 2022a, 2022b). There are times—such as infancy and the end of life—when everyone's bodies will require the care of others. This care is based on what Fineman terms "inevitable dependency" (Fineman 2000). There are other times when the attributes of our bodies may require care due to biological variation or bodily harm. These periods of support are not inevitable, but they are part of the human experience.

Our bodies thus tie us all to supporting social institutions (Fineman 2020, 2022a, 2022b). This embeddedness is not viewed in a negative light but instead as the inevitable result of the human condition. By viewing ourselves as embodied beings and simultaneously recognizing the attributes and limitations of our bodies, Fineman argues that we are collectively and inescapably embedded within social institutions that provide support. These institutions include the family, workplaces, schools, and hospitals. We cannot meaningfully separate ourselves from these institutions in policy or law. These institutions, she argues, are governed by the rules of a democratic state.

Fineman's vulnerable subject thus stands in stark contrast to both the dominant Hohfeldian conception of individual rights embedded in the law (Hurd and Moore 2018) and the broader liberal ideal of the fully-functioning, rational egoist embraced by John Rawls (1982) and other liberal theorists. Vulnerability theory decenters the individual and moves away from the atomistic goals of formal equality to a collective notion of substantive equality. The vulnerable subject is aware of harm and other disadvantage and understands society must respond to universal and constant vulnerability. The vulnerable subject is embedded, interdependent, inherently reliant on social institutions, and supportive of the collective good. Fineman's goal is to construct social institutions to respond to vulnerability, rather than to address inequality by the distribution of social assets. The construction of these institutions would require a radical response: a universal social justice project that considers harm to be universal, structural, and collective (Fineman 2020, 2022a, 2022b). It would reimagine the baseline for social justice.

Thus, Fineman's vulnerability theory not only casts light on the current failures with respect to protecting individuals with disabilities during public health emergencies, it also provides a means to address them. Vulnerability theory highlights that our current legal architecture is structured around the idea of an atomistic, full-functioning individual, rather than embedded, interdependent individuals with varying attributes. When individuals need support, it is viewed as unique. It is in this context that certain targeted protections—including protections for individuals with disabilities—are enacted. These laws seek to promote equal treatment but fail to view the individual as part of a collective community with shared vulnerability to harm. As a result, social institutions lack the capacity to respond to disability as part of the human condition.

These limitations manifest in a variety of ways during and following public health emergencies. Because disability is viewed as exceptional, disability accommodation is considered after social structures are in place, rather than as part of the planning of essential emergency response and remediation mechanisms (Nick et al. 2009; NACCHO 2014, 2015). Thus, emergency and post-emergency procedures as well as material supports remain inadequate, or, at worst, fail entirely to accommodate individuals with disabilities. Indications of this are numerous. Local governments and private entities have failed to integrate information from community-based organizations and disability service providers into broad, municipal emergency planning (Nick et al. 2009). While preparedness training and drills now occur at all governmental levels, first responders lack disability education and training opportunities (Santora and Weiser 2013; DiMattei 2017; Nick et al. 2009). Emergency planning drills and exercises do not focus on the functional and access needs of populations (Santora and Weiser 2013; DiMattei 2017; Nick et al. 2009). Further, individuals with disabilities are not part of preparedness planning

(Santora and Weiser 2013; DiMattei 2017; Nick et al. 2009). Emergency planning requires a lens of greater inclusion at the onset of planning—one that assumes broad population variation in functionality and vulnerability to disability—and the construction of legal and social institutions to support it.

Further, because disability is not viewed as part of the human condition, the value placed on certain methods of functioning is skewed by metrics that value some methods over others (Satz 2006, 2020). Individuals with disabilities often are separated from the general population in emergency response, viewed as having a lower quality of life, and deprioritized in the rationing of scarce health care resources (Satz 2020). During the COVID-19 pandemic, for example, at least fifteen actions were filed with HHS's Office for Civil Rights for discriminatory hospital rationing policies.

Another consequence of reasoning from the individual rather than the body is that the need for disability protections is viewed as situational rather than constant. This is inherently part of disability antidiscrimination laws, which protect individuals only in certain public spaces, such as places of public accommodation, public transportation, and work. While disability remains constant, an individual moves in and out of protections throughout their day, fragmenting the human experience (Satz 2008, 2010, 2011, 2013). This fragmented approach means that both our social institutions and protections do not reflect the realities of the lived experience (Satz 2006, 2008, 2010, 2011, 2013). For example, funding is provided to address disasters rather than to prepare in anticipation of them, limiting the reach of social institutions. Because of this, government stockpiles and other resources are inadequate to prevent rationing scenarios. Further, disability laws provide protections only for certain aspects of emergency response. For example, they protect individuals in emergency shelters but provide at best limited transportation to those shelters.

Reasoning from the body would have profound implications for how we view and respond to disability during public health emergencies and beyond. The next several parts examine how vulnerability theory could inform emergency preparedness to improve outcomes for individuals with disabilities. Vulnerability theory helps reconcile the tension between regulatory health and public health paradigms, which could assist with restructuring health law for greater inclusivity. It also provides support for protecting health institutions and public health authorities from political and other influences. Last, it provides insights into how to improve emergency preparedness by providing communities with tools for resilience.

III. Disability, the Vulnerable Subject, and Health Law

Fineman's view of the body as discussed above embraces human variation in functioning—including disability—as part of the human condition. When reasoning from the body, disability is not exceptional, and all populations are vulnerable to disability or further disability. Many people are born with functional differences, we all likely will experience disability if we live long enough, and every person is vulnerable to disability through injury or illness, possibly as the result of a public health emergency. Vulnerability theory appreciates that some individuals may experience discrimination based on disability more acutely than others, but vulnerability to disability remains a constant and shared experience.

Reasoning from the body would require a radical shift in thinking about disability in public health architecture. While the public health field necessarily looks at populations, they often are discrete ones. Deeply entrenched in public health is the idea that some individuals have more vulnerability than others and should be protected by extra measures after public health laws and policies are established. This view understands some people—such as individuals with disabilities, pregnant women, and prisoners—to be part of "vulnerable populations." In this context, an individual with a disability is treated as exceptional and subject to special policies for disability rather than universal policies that assume disability within a population. The vulnerable populations approach historically has resulted in dire outcomes for individuals with disabilities and others during public health emergencies. For example, after 9/11 and the California wildfires, special wait-for-help policies for individuals with disabilities after other self-evacuations led to the deaths of affected individuals as well as their family members, friends, and co-workers (CBS News 2002).

In contrast to the vulnerable populations approach, vulnerability theory looks to the overall human population. Thus, a shift from thinking about vulnerable populations to universal vulnerability would require that disability is considered in the formation of all policies, and social structures required to support it are funded. To be sure, this would be a seismic change in public health, and indeed with respect to health law and policy generally, for a couple of reasons. To start, the vulnerable populations approach to disability stems from the historic position of public health authorities that disability should be eliminated rather than accommodated (Roberts 2013). Because disability was to be prevented by public health measures aimed at avoiding illness or injury, disability was not otherwise contemplated by public health laws and policies (Lollar and Cres 2003). When this approach was challenged by antidiscrimination mandates, public health measures began including individuals with disabilities in emergency preparedness plans and other public health measures (Taylor 2018). This largely did not occur until the twenty-first century, when individuals with disabilities were viewed as a "vulnerable population" and considered outside baseline emergency planning (Taylor 2018).

Additionally, the alternative paradigm within health law and policy—that of regulatory health—also fails to view disability as part of the human condition. The regulatory health model seeks to prevent departures from normal functioning through health care delivery and funding aimed at preventing or overcoming disability rather than supporting alternative methods of functioning (Satz 2020). This approach does not recognize the interconnectedness of individuals as does the traditional public health approach and is thereby more strongly centered on the individual. In fact, the regulatory health approach often conflicts with population-based public health approaches in valuing individual choice over population outcomes. When these paradigms conflict, public health outcomes may be devalued. For example, public health authorities' elimination of masking and vaccine requirements during the COVID-19 pandemic demonstrates the importation of regulatory health principles valuing individual choice into governmental public health response.

Vulnerability theory offers an alternative to both the public and regulatory health approaches—a broad population approach that integrates disability at the foundation of emergency planning. It embraces disability as part of our human functionality. It also appreciates that vulnerability is constant and not situational. This requires policies that assume variations in human functioning and the development and maintenance of institutions to support them across social and civic realms. Public health measures would center universal vulnerability (instead of individuals), preparing for and providing material resources to address public health crises across a population that assumes disability. Public health policies would aim to be universal and to account for variations in human functioning from their inception, such as HHS's emPOWER map, which shows Medicare residents reliant on electricity-dependent medical equipment and other devices to better manage power outages (2022). Public health policies also would not privilege some methods of functioning over others.

Additionally, reasoning from the body, vulnerability theory offers a way of thinking about the limitations on choice posed by public health mandates. Law is understood as the coercive means by which state authority regulates daily life (Fineman 2020, 2022a, 2022b). Law should have universal applicability and operate as the least coercive means to promote well-being. While Fineman does not discuss whether this view is premised on a consequentialist or non-consequentialist view of well-being (though she does mention an "ethics of care" in her recent lectures, which would be non-consequentialist and more closely aligned with virtue ethics), she situates individual choice within broader institutional considerations. Under her view, individual choice is respected to the greatest extent possible, but trade-offs may be required for inclusion—for example, measures to stem the flow of contagious disease could restrict choice (Fineman 2020, 2022a, 2022b).

Thus, vulnerability theory allows for the reconceptualization of interdependence in public health—a key tenant of public health interventions.

Indeed, preserving public health is one of the few areas where individual civil liberties may be constrained for the greater public good in terms of mandatory vaccines and quarantine. Public health depends on solidarity and community amongst citizens to curb the spread of disease. Vulnerability theory makes clear that public health policies must assume and respond to an interconnected population of individuals with varying levels of susceptibility to illness. Further, vulnerability theory's perspectives on interdependence help reveal that perceived trade-offs between individual choice and public health may be false conflicts. For example, some individuals who refused vaccination and masks during the COVID-19 pandemic, believing these unnecessary, may not have fully appreciated their own vulnerability to the virus. Additionally, social interdependence underscores the need to take a universal approach to functional impairments in emergency planning, rather than a narrow, vulnerable populations approach. This might mean, for example, shelters with universal design features, i.e., shelters designed to accommodate multiple and diverse methods of functioning, instead of a shelter section for individuals with disabilities (Center for Universal Design 2008). Universal design features could be applied to notification, evacuation, and post-disaster relief as well. In this manner, vulnerability theory provides a new lens to understand and reconcile individual freedom and collective responsibility.

IV. Disability and the Vulnerable Institution: Hospitals and Public Health Authorities

Fineman's vulnerability theory acknowledges that, like individuals, institutions may be vulnerable (Fineman 2010). Fineman argues that states (governments) must offer tools for resilience to vulnerable people and institutions. Otherwise, institutions may be co-opted by special interests or individuals in positions of power. The COVID-19 pandemic demonstrates that hospitals and public health authorities are vulnerable to these pressures.

During the early stages of the pandemic, hospitals were influenced by ableist views that privileged those without disabilities by using formal or informal rationing metrics for the distribution of ventilators. Individuals with disabilities were either directly deprioritized based on their perceived lower health status or subject to statistical length of life comparisons that disadvantage disability. Additionally, hospitals had no-visitor policies, depriving some individuals with disabilities of advocacy (Shapiro 2020a; Abrams 2020). Further, hospitals discontinued "elective" treatment—even cancer treatment—reducing vital health maintenance treatment for some individuals with disabilities and other patients by 18–35% (Chatterjee 2022).

Similarly, public health authorities either failed to consider individuals with disabilities or were influenced by political pressure to disregard them. At the beginning of the COVID-19 pandemic, despite knowledge of heightened risk for individuals residing in residential care facilities, local and state public health authorities did not prioritize individuals with disabilities living in group homes for vaccination; meanwhile, other dense residential populations, such as nursing homes, were prioritized (Contrera 2021). As the pandemic continued into a second year, the Centers for Disease Control and Prevention, under political pressure to change its masking guidance, suggested masking was unnecessary in most circumstances if a person was vaccinated (Netburn 2021) and then ultimately only if the community rates of transmission (measured in part by hospital admissions and the percentage of beds occupied by COVID-19 patients) were high (CDC 2022). These policy shifts resulted in an almost complete abandonment of masking practices, regardless of vaccination status or actual community infection rates (Sun, Keating, and Meckler 2022; IPSOS 2022). Suddenly, individuals with autoimmune disabilities were denied meaningful inclusion into critical spaces such as grocery stores, medical facilities, and schools (Sun et al. 2022). These shifts also may undermine the ability of public health authorities subsequently to encourage masking to mitigate the spread of more contagious or dangerous viral variants, limit infections to prevent Long COVID, and alleviate prolonged strain on hospitals and their staff.

Vulnerability theory makes clear the need to politically isolate vital health care and other social institutions. When reasoning from the body, this is, in fact, essential, given our embeddedness with social institutions. Hospitals must be given training and resources to combat ableist views, and public health authorities must enjoy political isolation and empowerment.

V. Disability and Resilience in Public Health Emergencies

Vulnerability theory thus provides insights into how to improve outcomes for individuals with disabilities during public health emergencies. These theoretical insights may be used to inform law and policy guiding emergency planning and to offer individuals and institutions tools for resilience. Applying vulnerability theory to emergency planning would give rise to several areas of change.

First, disability must be viewed as part of the human condition, and emergency preparedness approached from a whole population perspective, acknowledging people have varying functional needs. This entails fundamentally different emergency preparedness to account for disability at the beginning of planning through universal policies.

Second, emergency planning must move from a crisis-response to a preparedness-response model, where vulnerability for all—including individuals with disabilities—is viewed as constant rather than situational. Resources must be sufficient to avoid rationing situations. Emergency preparedness must include inclusive emergency protocols and training requirements, adequate stockpiles, and consistent funding mechanisms.

Third, law and policy must reflect our interdependence for health as well as the varying needs of different people. Policy and law should be more universally applicable. This will require the inclusion of disability in all aspects of planning, such as the adoption of universal design principles for emergency management (notification, evacuation, and shelter). Additionally, rules of universal applicability must establish the boundaries for limitations on personal choice during public health emergencies, which might require mandates to prevent the spread of contagious disease.

Fourth, public health institutions must be protected from political and other influence. Ableist views quickly penetrate policy and on-the-ground actions in public health emergencies. Additionally, public health authorities at all levels of government must be protected from political influence and allowed to function as neutral authorities that are empowered to guide behavior during public health emergencies.

VI. Conclusion

Vulnerability theory offers a lens to both understand and address the historic and persistent harm to individuals with disabilities during public health emergencies. It challenges current policies and laws at their foundation, questioning their assumptions about disability and inclusion. By reasoning from the body, vulnerability theory views disability as part of the human condition. Our bodies and their universal and constant vulnerability tie us collectively to supporting social institutions. Operating from these assumptions moves us past the limited reach of antidiscrimination laws and the vulnerable populations approach of public health architecture to situate disability more meaningfully into law and policy affecting public health emergencies and to move closer to inclusion.

Reference List

Abrams, Abigail. 2020. "This Is Really Life or Death. For People with Disabilities, Coronavirus Is Making It Harder Than Ever to Receive Care." *Time Magazine*, April 24 (https://time.com/5826098/coronavirus-people-with-disabilities/).

Americans With Disabilities Act of 1990, 42 U.S.C. § 12101 et seq. (1990).

Associated Press. 2006. "Katrina Victim Who Dies in Wheelchair Honored." *NBC News*, September 1 (www.nbcnews.com/id/wbna14627601).

CBS News. 2002. "Friends to the End: Co-worker Refuses to Leave Paralyzed Colleague in Trade Center Disaster." *CBS News*, January 31 (www.cbsnews.com/news/friends-to-the-end-co-worker-refuses-to-leave-paralyzed-colleague-in-trade-center-disaster/).

Center for Disease Control and Prevention (CDC). 2022. "Science Brief: Indicators for Monitoring COVID-19 Community Levels and Making Public Health Recommendations (Updated August 12)." (www.cdc.gov/coronavirus/2019-ncov/science/science-briefs/indicators-monitoring-community-levels.html).

Center for Universal Design. 2008. "The Principles of Universal Design. Digital Poster (PDF). NC State University College of Design." (https://design.ncsu.edu/wp-content/uploads/2022/11/principles-of-universal-design.pdf).

Chatterjee, Rhitu. 2022. "A 'Staggering' Number of People Couldn't Get Care During the Pandemic, Poll Finds." *NPR*, August 8. Retrieved March 1, 2023 (www.npr.org/sections/health-shots/2022/08/08/1116264151/poll-1-in-5-seriously-ill-black-americans-had-a-hard-time-getting-medical-care).

Contrera, Jessica. 2021. "People with Disabilities Desperately Need the Vaccine. But States Disagree on When They'll Get it." *The Washington Post*, January 13. Retrieved March 1, 2023 (www.washingtonpost.com/dc-md-va/2021/01/13/disabled-coronavirus-vaccine-states/).

DiMattei, Christine. 2017. "Hurricane Irma Exposes Flaws in Evacuations for Medically Vulnerable in Miami-Dade." *WLRN Public Radio and Television*, October 3 (www.wlrn.org/news/2017-10-03/hurricane-irma-exposes-flaws-in-evacuations-for-medically-vulnerable-in-miami-dade).

Federal Emergency Management Agency (FEMA). 2020. "Ensuring Civil Rights During COVID-19 Response. FEMA Civil Rights Bulletin (PDF). US. Deparment of Homeland Security." April 15 (www.fema.gov/sites/default/files/2020-07/fema_ensuring-civil-rights-during-covid-19-response.pdf).

Fineman, Martha Albertson. 2000. "Cracking the Foundational Myths: Independence, Autonomy, and Self-Sufficiency." *American University Journal of Gender, Social Policy & the Law* 8(1):13–29.

———. 2010. "The Vulnerable Subject and the Responsive State." *Emory Law Journal* 60:251–75.

———. 2020. "Reasoning from the Body: Universal Vulnerability and Social Justice." Pp. 17–34 in *A Jurisprudence of the Body*, edited by C. Dietz, M. Travis, and M. Thomson. London: Palgrave Macmillan.

———. 2022a. "Reasoning from the Body." Vulnerability, Justice, and the Human Condition Lecture 1, Trinity College, October 11 (https://vimeo.com/763436327).

———. 2022b. "Vulnerability and Social Justice." Vulnerability, Justice, and the Human Condition Lecture 2, Trinity College, November 1 (https://vimeo.com/767073762).

Fink, Sheri. 2009. "The Deadly Choices at Memorial." *ProPublica*, August 27. Retrieved March 1, 2023 (www.propublica.org/article/the-deadly-choices-at-memorial-826).

Freeman v. State, 293 Ga. App. 490 (2008).

Friedman, Lex, National Council on Disability. 2006. *The Impact of Hurricanes Katrina and Rita on People with Disabilities: A Look Back and Remaining Challenges*. National Council on Disability (https://ncd.gov/publications/2006/Aug072006).

HHS emPOWER. 2022. "Medicare Electricity-Dependent Populations by Geography." [interactive map]. U.S Department of Health and Human Services (HHS) (https://empowerprogram.hhs.gov/empowermap www.latimes.com/science/story/2021-07-27/timeline-cdc-mask-guidance-during-covid-19-pandemic).

Hurd, Heidi and Michael S. Moore. 2018. "The Hohfeldian Analysis of Rights." *The American Journal of Jurisprudence* 6392:285–354. doi:10.1093/ajj/auy015.

IPSOS. 2022. "Most Americans Not Worrying about COVID Going into 2022 Holidays." ISIN: FR0000073298 (www.ipsos.com/en-us/news-polls/axios-ipsos-coronavirus-index).

Lollar, Donald J. and John E. Cres. 2003. "Redefining the Role of Public Health in Disability." *Annual Review of Public Health* 24:195–208. doi:10.1146/annurev.publhealth.24.100901.140844.

McCausland, Phil. 2022. "Disabled and Immunocompromised People Fear Lifting Mask Mandates Will Leave Them Behind." *NBC News*, February 9. Retrieved March 1, 2023 (www.nbcnews.com/health/health-care/disabled-immunocompromised-fear-covid-lifting-mask-mandates-pandemic-rcna15568).

NACCHO. 2015. "What Local Health Departments Should Know about the Population of People with Disabilities. Fact Sheet (PDF)." (www.naccho.org/uploads/downloadable-resources/Fact-Sheet_What-LHD-Should-Know.pdf).

National Association of City and City Health Officials (NACCHO). 2014. "National Assessment of the Knowledge, Awareness, and Inclusion of People with Disabilities in Local Health Departments' Public Health Practices. Research Brief (PDF)." (www.naccho.org/uploads/downloadable-resources/researchbrief_disabilityassessment_dec2014.pdf).

Netburn, Deborah. 2021. "A Timeline of the CDC's Advice on Face Masks." *Los Angeles Times*, July 27. Retrieved March 1, 2023.

Nick, Gilbert A., Elena Savoia, Loris Elqura, M. Suzanne Crowther, Bradley Cohen, Mary Leary, Tina Wright, John Auerbach, and Howard K. Koh. 2009. "Emergency Preparedness for Vulnerable Populations: People with Special Health-Care Needs." *Public Health Reports* 124(2):338–43. doi:10.1177/003335490912400225.

Office for Civil Rights (OCR). 2020. *Bulletin: Civil Rights, HIPAA, and the Coronavirus Disease 2019 (COVID-19)*. U.S Department of Health and Human Services (www.hhs.gov/sites/default/files/ocr-bulletin-3-28-20.pdf).

Rawls, John. 1982. "Social Unity and Primary Goods." Pp. 159–86 in *Utilitarianism and Beyond*, edited by A. Sen and B. Williams. New York: Cambridge University Press. doi:10.1017/CBO9780511611964.010.

Regulations to Implement the Equal Employment Provisions of the ADA. 29 C.F.R. § 1630.2(q) (1990).

Roberts, Jessica. 2013. "Health Law as Disability Rights Law." *Minnesota Law Review* 97:1963–2035.

Santora, Marc and Benjamin Weiser. 2013. "Court Says New York Neglected Disabled in Emergencies." *The New York Times*, November 7. Retrieved March 1, 2023 (www.nytimes.com/2013/11/08/nyregion/new-yorks-emergency-plans-violate-disabilities-act-judge-says.html).

Satz, Ani B. 2006. "A Jurisprudence of Dysfunction: On the Role of Normal Species Functioning in Disability Analysis." *Yale Journal of Health Policy, Law, and Ethics* 6:221–67.

———. 2008. "Disability, Vulnerability, and the Limits of Antidiscrimination." *Washington & Lee Law Review* 83:513–68.

———. 2010. "Overcoming Fragmentation in Health and Disability Law." *Emory Law Journal* 60:277–319.

———. 2011. "Fragmented Lives: Disability Discrimination and the Role of Environment-Framing." *Washington & Lee Law Review* 68:187–252.

———. 2013. "Disability, Vulnerability, and Fragmented Protections: Accessing Education, Work, and Health Care." Pp. 265–93 in *Righting Educational Wrongs:*

Disability Studies in Law and Education, edited by A. S. Kanter and B. A. Ferri. New York: Syracuse University Press.

———. 2020. "Health Care as Eugenics in Health Care as Eugenics." Pp. 20–32 in *Disability, Health, Law, and Bioethics*, edited by I. G. Cohen, C. Shachar, A. Silvers, and M. A. Stein. Cambridge University Press. doi:10.1017/9781108622851.005.

Shapiro, Joseph. 2020a. "Hospital Visitor Bans Under Scrutiny After Disability Groups Raise Concerns Over Care." *WAMU 88.5*, May 20. Retrieved March 1, 2023 (https://wamu.org/story/20/05/20/federal-government-asked-to-tell-hospitals-modify-visit-bans/).

———. 2020b. "COVID-19 Infections and Deaths Are Higher Among Those with Intellectual Disabilities." *NPR*, June 9. Retrieved March 1, 2023 (www.npr.org/2020/06/09/872401607/covid-19-infections-and-deaths-are-higher-among-those-with-intellectual-disabili).

Sun, Lena H., Dan Keating, and Laura Meckler. 2022. "CDC's New Approach to Covid Means Most Americans Can Go Without Masks." *The Washington Post*, February 25 (www.washingtonpost.com/health/2022/02/25/cdc-mask-guidance-changed-metrics/).

Taylor, Barry. 2018. "The Development of Emergency Planning for People with Disabilities Through ADA Litigation." *The John Marshall Law Review* 51:819–38.

PART VII

Vulnerability and Sovereignty

13

USING VULNERABILITY THEORY TO RECONCEIVE THE RELATIONSHIPS BETWEEN NATIVE NATIONS, THE UNITED STATES, AND STATE GOVERNMENTS

Nazune Menka and Laura Spitz

Introduction

This chapter[1] asks what happens if we center the vulnerable subject in place of the liberal subject in the context of federal Indian law. Specifically, we use a vulnerability analysis to reexamine the doctrines of dependent sovereignty,[2] federal plenary power, and trust responsibility. Vulnerability theory starts from the premise that all human beings are universally and inescapably vulnerable (Fineman 2015). Standing in contrast to the ideal liberal legal subject—which is invariably healthy, independent, and autonomous—the vulnerable subject is a more dynamic, realistic, and complete figure to place at the heart of social policy. In the human experience, there is no position of invulnerability and no possibility of achieving invulnerability (Fineman 2020). Consequently, once we acknowledge the inevitable vulnerability of all legal subjects, the focus of law and policy becomes the unequal distribution of *resilience* and the state's role in mitigating vulnerability through the creation and oversight of laws, institutions, and other mechanisms for conferring and building resilience.

In our view, bringing a vulnerability analysis to federal Indian law does at least two things. First, it challenges the idea that sovereignty is ever anything but (inter)dependent, shifting the focus away from the federal government's construction of Indigenous people as uniquely vulnerable "domestic dependent" nations or sovereigns, towards a focus on building and restoring resilience among Indigenous people, communities, and institutions. This analysis introduces a substantive conversation about which governments—Native, federal, state, or local—are best situated and resourced to ensure a more equitable distribution of assets across society. Second, such an analysis provides

DOI: 10.4324/9781003323242-21

a theoretical basis for establishing federal responsibility to Indigenous people outside the doctrine of federal plenary (exclusive and total) power over Indian Affairs. From the perspective of reconciliation, establishing resilience-building in Indigenous peoples, communities, and Nations as an ongoing and shared responsibility of the United States, and separating that responsibility from plenary power, has both reparative and restorative dimensions.

This chapter proceeds as follows. In Part I, we explore the creation and continued use of the concept of dependent sovereignty in federal Indian law. Using vulnerability theory, we reconceptualize sovereignty and trust responsibility in ways more closely aligned with the lived history and experience of Indigenous Peoples. We suggest the responsibility of the American state to Indigenous Peoples and Native Nations is not dependent upon its plenary power *over* Indian tribes but rather a part of its state responsibility *to* Indigenous Peoples. Ultimately, we argue that a vulnerability analysis supports a poly-governance framework. In Part II, we examine a contemporary example, the Indian Child Welfare Act (1978), and suggest how it might more productively be examined through a vulnerability lens. In Part III, we summarize our observations and suggest that a vulnerability analysis supports the view that: (a) decisions about governance and state responsibility should be collaborative; (b) policymakers must approach resilience projects with the recognition that legacies of colonization and oppression will require unequal efforts to restore and construct systems of resilience in different communities (including Indigenous communities); and (c) the building and restoration of resilience conferring assets within Tribal governments should be prioritized. We conclude in Part IV.

I. (Dependent) Sovereignty

a. Background: Sovereignty and Liberalism

Contested but familiar doctrinal concepts within federal Indian law include Tribal sovereignty, self-determination, and autonomy, on the one hand, and federal plenary power, trust responsibility, and paternalism, on the other. Native Nations have continuously exerted their inherent sovereignty in ongoing struggles with what is now known as the United States. In response, American legislators, policymakers, and courts have repeatedly fallen back on a long history of law and policy announcing the federal government's plenary power over Indigenous Peoples and its concomitant trust responsibility for Indigenous Peoples, through which it deploys a mixture of resources and controls as a function of its obligation toward "dependent" nations within its borders.

This contest between inherent Tribal sovereignty and American sovereignty is mostly drawn in the language and practices of liberalism. Within the framework of liberalism, the subject of law is autonomous, independent, and fully functioning, whether it be the nation state under international law or the liberal legal subject in Anglo-American law. In both cases, independence and freedom from interference are valorized. This is not surprising, as national sovereignty—including rights to exclusive jurisdiction and territory—explicitly draws upon the concept of personal freedom and individual rights (Barker 2005; Blackhawk 2020). In the context of domestic law, this has translated into a set of rules that assume and protect personal space, personal decision-making, and individual autonomy. Similarly, international law operates on the assumption that sovereignty entitles nations to exclusive jurisdiction, territorial sovereignty, and non-intervention in domestic affairs. Native Nations and Indigenous Peoples come up against liberalism both internationally and domestically. Liberalism has operated in interlocking and mutually reinforcing ways within and across these domains to serve the interests of the settler colonial nation state. Domestically, Indigenous Peoples are often constructed as a vulnerable, "dependent" population, requiring special care and oversight. Internationally, it is legally impossible within the terms of liberalism for the United States and Native Nations to both be sovereign over the same territory.

At the same time and in some important ways, the history of colonialism and Indigenous Peoples in the United States challenges the simplicity of the liberal colonial framework. For example, federal and state governments sometimes recognize inherent Tribal sovereignty, including some aspects of territorial sovereignty. This can be seen in a variety of social, political, and legal contexts, some of which we describe below. Internationally, Indigenous claims, especially and including territorial claims, have complicated the global liberal legal order because Native Nations contemporaneously exist within the borders of other nation-states or across national borders defined by the liberal legal order.

In any case, the logic of liberalism stands in the way of meaningful Tribal sovereignty in the United States for at least two reasons. First, liberalism fundamentally embraces a single territory/single sovereign conceptualization of sovereignty. Consequently, Indigenous assertions of Tribal sovereignty that do not reflect the values of liberal sovereignty—exclusive jurisdiction, territorial sovereignty, and non-intervention in domestic affairs—are not legible to the American legal and political system.[3] Put another way, the United States only recognizes sovereignty claims that align with liberal ideals. Second, liberalism is grounded in and framed by myths about dependency and vulnerability that undermine Indigenous voices by prohibiting, as disqualifying, any admission of need, inter-dependency, or vulnerability in self- or collaborative-governance conversations with federal or state governments. In other words, within the terms of liberal legalism, it is not possible to be simultaneously sovereign and vulnerable. Consequently, under liberalism the very best

Native Nations might hope for is what the United States Supreme Court has called domestic dependent nationhood or dependent sovereignty (*Cherokee Nation v. State of Georgia* 1831). In turn, this dependency discourse provides the justificatory narrative for maintaining federal plenary power over Indian Affairs, feeding the view that Indigenous Peoples are a uniquely dependent or vulnerable population, incapable of exercising national or personal sovereignty by virtue of that dependency. Thus, within this framework, liberal legalism simultaneously inscribes and denigrates vulnerability as a specifically Indigenous quality, rather than a universal human experience that may be exacerbated or mitigated by systems of governance.

b. Domestic Dependent Nations

To better understand the field of federal Indian law and the centrality of domestic dependent sovereignty within that field, it is useful to situate it within the larger international context of settler colonialism. Settler colonial nation states sought to disappear Indigenous Peoples through strategies of elimination, displacement, and containment (Taylor Saito 2020:67–78). Colonial powers such as Britain and Spain moved throughout the world, amassing land, labor, and resources beyond their territorial homelands. But rather than attempting to extract and extradite resources and wealth back to the metropole, they mostly endeavored to stay/settle. "Staying" or "settling" required both the formation of new nation-states and the conceptual and physical disappearance of Indigenous Peoples already living in those places. This was accomplished through a combination of violence, politics, and law, including—in the United States—the relegation of Native Nations to the status of domestic dependent nations.

The various federal policy priorities for managing Indian Affairs are generally viewed in chronological "eras" that have included genocide, treatymaking, removal, assimilation, and self-determination. The era of treaty making preceded the adoption of the American Constitution. Prior to the American Revolution and the formation of the United States, several colonies engaged in diplomatic treaty making with Native Nations, primarily to establish trading relationships and gain access to land (Davis, Biber, and Kempf 2022) In addition, because European colonists sought territory in North America, Native Nations were often courted for allyship in intra-European contests. Most scholars agree that this time period was marked by hybrid legal orders (Ablavsky 2015) and nuanced multicultural jurisgenesis (or lawmaking) (Williams 2005:20–2). There is little doubt that many colonists and settlers regarded Native Nations as nations-*qua*-nations at that time. However, as colonies and then states grew in power, they became increasingly hostile to Indigenous Peoples located in what they now perceived to be their territories. Tensions between the new federal government, states, and Native Nations mounted. Newer treaties were notoriously one sided, and consistently renegotiated to force the cession of more and more land. Where Native Nations once held their ancestral lands and institutions intact, waves of settlers continued to breach boundaries, break treaty promises, and destroy trust built on once sacred treaty texts.

Amid, and in part arising from, such conflicts, early 19th century American courts created the doctrinal concepts of domestic dependent nationhood and dependent sovereignty. These concepts find their origins in what has come to be known as the Marshall trilogy, three decisions of the United States Supreme Court authored by then-Chief Justice Marshall: *Johnson v. M'Intosh* (1823), *Cherokee Nation v. State of Georgia* (1831), and *Worcester v. State of Georgia* (*1832*). In 1823, the first of the Marshall cases—*Johnson v. M'Intosh*—formally adopted the doctrine of discovery, providing that the newly formed federal government had the sole authority (vis-à-vis the states) to divest Indigenous Nations of title to land through purchase or conquest. Marshall wrote, "[t]hus, all the nations of Europe, who have acquired territory on this continent, have asserted in themselves, and have recognised [sic] in others, the exclusive right of the discoverer to appropriate the lands occupied by the Indians" (*Johnson v. M'Intosh* 1923:584). The deficiencies of both the decision and the discovery doctrine are well-documented, and beyond the scope of this Chapter (Singer 2017; Davis 2017). But notably, *Johnson v. M'Intosh* set the stage for the establishment of federal plenary power over Indigenous lands and "Indian Affairs" (Davis 2017:1765).

In 1831, Chief Justice Marshall again wrote for the majority of the Supreme Court in *Cherokee Nation v. State of Georgia*. In *Cherokee Nation*, the Court invalidated Georgia state laws that purported to exercise jurisdiction in Cherokee territory. Importantly, Chief Justice Marshall held that Congress had exclusive federal plenary power over (and to engage with) Native Nations; thus, Georgia had no jurisdiction in Cherokee territory. Justice Marshall described Native Nations as "domestic dependent nations" in language that has since been construed to establish federal trust responsibility for Native Nations and Indigenous Peoples, linking notions of trust with "dominion:"

> Their relation to the United States resembles that of a ward to his guardian. . . . They and their country are considered by foreign nations, as we as by ourselves, as being so completely under the sovereignty and dominion of the United States, that any attempt to acquire their lands, or to form a political connection with them, would be considered by all as an invasion of our territory and an act of hostility.
>
> (*Cherokee Nation v. State of Georgia* 1832:33)

The following year, in *Worcester v. State of Georgia*, a Georgia state law that attempted to "seize on the whole Cherokee country, parcel it out among the neighbouring [sic] counties of the state, extend her code over the whole country, abolish its institutions and its laws, and annihilate its political existence" (*Worcester v. State of Georgia* 1832:542) was declared unconstitutional, and the sovereignty of the Cherokee Nation was reaffirmed vis-à-vis the state of Georgia. Marshall wrote that the "treaties and laws of the United States contemplate the Indian territory as completely separated from that of the states; and provide that all intercourse with them shall be carried on exclusively by the government of the union" (p. 557). He concluded: "the Cherokee [N]ation, then, is a distinct community occupying its own territory in which the laws of Georgia can have no force" (p.561).

The Marshall trilogy was an inept solution. While the doctrines of inherent sovereignty, plenary power, and trust responsibility were each grounded in a liberal logic, the practices and relationships Justice Marshall observed among states, the federal government, and Native Nations were in fact irreconcilable within liberalism. On the one hand, the trilogy recognized Tribal sovereignty over internal affairs (the doctrine of inherent sovereignty). On the other hand, it simultaneously cabined that sovereignty through the exertion of federal plenary power over Tribes (the doctrine of plenary power) and the establishment of the federal government's trust responsibility for Native Nations (the doctrine of trust responsibility). Taken together, the trilogy established the internally incoherent notion and practice of domestic dependency, wherein the federal government exercises total and exclusive power over purportedly sovereign Native Nations, which are deemed dependent upon a federal government that holds a fiduciary duty and relationship of trust toward them.

In practice, Congress has used its plenary power to legislate according to whatever era of Indian Affairs policy it finds itself in. The removal era saw the Indian Removal Act force Native Nations to cede their ancestral lands, primarily through (non-negotiable) treaties. Congress abruptly ended the treaty making era via a Congressional rider in 1871 through an exertion of plenary power that has since been questioned by legal scholars (Moore and Steele 2022). In 1887 Congress enacted the Dawes Allotment Act designed to break up Native Nation communities by forcing individual allotment ownership and distributing unclaimed lands to settlers at little to no cost. This assimilationist principle has arguably never receded but was particularly salient during the 20th century.

For example, the Indian Reorganization Act (IRA) sought to organize Native Nations into settler colonial models of governance resulting in Native Nations adopting constitutions that used blood quantum for membership, some of which remain in effect today. In 1949 the Hoover Commission Report on Indian Affairs called for complete integration of Indians—ushering in a series of congressional acts designed to terminate the federal-tribal trust relationship and allow the several states to exert power over Native

Nations. Congress issued House Resolution 108 in 1953 declaring it to be the policy of Congress to, as rapidly as possible, make the Indians subject to the same laws applicable to other citizens. This resolution called for an eventually issued report on recommendations for legislation to terminate Native Nation treaties and laws that recognized the special relationship between the federal government and Native Nations. Laws and policies designed to assimilate and terminate Native Nations included submitting Native Nations to state criminal jurisdiction, extinguishing Native Nation land claims, and relocating Indigenous Peoples to urban areas. Additionally, as has recently received widespread attention through the Federal Indian Boarding School Initiative and subsequent Investigative Report, the federal government forcibly removed Indigenous children from their homes and sent them to government and church run schools for nearly two centuries as part of "a system designed to dissolve the Indian social structure" (Newland 2022:45).

In 1970, President Richard Nixon, responding to Native Nation and Indigenous advocacy, ushered in a new federal Indian Affairs policy of self-determination. This policy was intended to "strengthen the Indian's sense of autonomy without threatening his sense of community," and encouraged Native Nations to assume control over many of the federal programs serving their communities. (Tsosie 1996:225–6). After the treaty making, removal, termination, and assimilation eras, this shift in policy by the federal government has increased access to a collaborative lawmaking process with Congress and the Executive to create what Professor Maggie Blackhawk (2020) has called a "sanctuary [for] Native Nations and Native peoples" (pp. 1874–5).

Nonetheless, the doctrine of domestic dependent nationhood retains its force, in part because its meaning remains contested. On the one hand, it can be argued that inherent Tribal sovereignty is preserved and protected *by* federal plenary power. On the other hand, and notwithstanding a long history of activism by Native Nations to retain inherent powers, the federal government continues to assert itself as the sole sovereign over the territory within its borders and continues to exact plenary authority over the ancestral territories of Native Nations and Indian Affairs.

These complexities are obscured by naturalized conceptions of legal subjecthood within American legal and social systems which render illegible the notions that Native Nations may be sovereign over their territories and/or sovereign within the boundaries of another nation. Vulnerability theory has the potential to surface these complexities and reframe the contours of sovereignty and the trust relationship by challenging the liberal premises upon which their current constructions depend. Freed from those constraints, it is possible to engage in a meaningful conversation about state responsibility to Native Nations and Indigenous Peoples and, perhaps the most interesting and pressing question, which government or governments are best situated to confer and build resilience in Native Nations and Indigenous Peoples.

II. Using Vulnerability Theory to Reconceptualize Sovereignty and the Doctrines of Plenary Power and Trust Responsibility

a. Assertion of Tribal Sovereignty Remains a Critical Component of Inherent Indigenous Power

Some scholars and activists have described the sovereignty problem in federal Indian law as intractable. The complex history of Tribal sovereignty is beyond the scope of this chapter, but a brief description of central critiques and debates is helpful to provide important context. First, scholars and activists have argued that the single sovereign/single territory conception of sovereignty fails to capture Indigenous lived experiences, legal traditions, or lifeways. This is not surprising, of course, as sovereignty finds its ideological origins in colonial legal-religious discourse (Barker 2005). "[T]he recognition of political sovereignty was originally a projection by Europeans of their own institutional structures into the activities of another cultural tradition" (Deloria 1979:27). Moreover, Native Nations have exerted inherent authority from their first contact with European colonists. Centuries of diplomacy, advocacy and activism by Native Nations tell us that inherent authority is and always has been what jurists and scholars call inherent sovereignty.

Second, critics of liberal notions of sovereignty continue to analyze whether domestic dependent sovereignty or the federal government's "plenary power" over Indian Affairs is rooted in the text of the Constitution giving rise to questions about their doctrinal legitimacy (Skibine 2006:668–70; Fletcher 2022:204–5; Davis 2017). Constitutionality aside, many scholars also caution against the abrogation of federal plenary power over Indian affairs because Native Nation advocacy in the era of Tribal self-determination has effectively limited any such exercise of Congressional plenary power in support of Tribal sovereignty (Skibine 2006; Fletcher 2022; Carlson 2022). As a legal matter, the argument goes, federal plenary power is the mechanism by which Tribal sovereignty has been both preserved and diminished (Carlson 2022:741).

Third, because the language of (liberal) sovereignty is the language of international law, its application to the situation of Native Nations within the territory of what we now call the United States makes sense only so long as we understand the relationship between the United States and Native Nations to be nation-to-nation. In the language of international law, domestic dependent sovereignty is nonsensical. The federal government's response to the idea that domestic dependent nationhood is a theoretical impossibility has been to emphasize the unique position of Indigenous Peoples and communities within its borders. But this "uniqueness" has not inured to the benefit of Native Nations. Instead, it has been used by the United States to "cabin the scope of tribal authority or to aggrandize federal power" (Ablavsky 2019a:12).

Finally, the "ubiquity of the term sovereignty to describe Native peoples' rights to autonomy sometimes renders it a synonym for all strivings for self-governance" (Ablavsky 2019b:595). Or as Professor Barker puts it, "sovereignty has become notoriously generalized to stand in for all of the inherent rights of [I]ndigenous [P]eoples" (2005:1). This has both positive and negative dimensions. On the one hand, sovereignty is a widely recognized word in ordinary discourse, and its imprecision renders it useful for political conversations in popular media and legislative debates. Discursive strategies can be usefully built around the word's polysemic features, especially when it comes to mobilization and recognition. On the other hand, precision is probably required for effective reconciliation in practical and legal terms.

Notwithstanding the seemingly intractable problems with the term, however, sovereignty has incredible purchase in the context of Indigenous Peoples' assertions of inherent power. As Professor Joanne Barker has written and others have argued, "sovereignty matters in consequential ways to understanding the political agendas, strategies, and cultural perspectives of [I]ndigenous peoples in the Americas and the Pacific" (2005:1). After World War II, the term emerged as a "particularly valued term within [I]ndigenous discourses to signify a multiplicity of legal and social rights to political, economic, and cultural self-determination" (Barker 2005:18). As importantly, sovereignty has come to represent a "political-juridical identity refuting the dominant notion that [I]ndigenous peoples were merely one among many 'minority groups' under the administration of state social service and welfare programs" (2005 :18).

For these and other reasons, we do not argue the concept should be abandoned. Rather, we suggest that vulnerability theory has the potential to unlock current places of seeming intractability and refocus discussions of states' roles and responsibilities to Native Nations and Indigenous Peoples in productive ways. This is consistent with ideas presented by Lakota scholar Vine Deloria, Jr. in his influential 1979 article, *Self Determination and the Concept of Sovereignty*. In his view, we ought not conceive of solutions that "perpetuate isolation of individuals and institutions. . . . The direction proposed is a means of allowing human energies and understandings to converge and come together to form a more sensible picture of human life" (1979:28). This realism, coupled with an acknowledgement that we live within an embodied, embedded, and interconnected set of relationships, aligns with the principles informing vulnerability theory's central premise: the vulnerable subject is a dynamic, realistic, and complete figure that must be placed at the heart of social, legal, and economic policy (Fineman 2014).

b. Sovereignty Is Inter-Dependent

Professor Fineman has argued that "human vulnerability is understood [within Vulnerability Theory] as providing the impetus for the creation of relationships and institutions and necessitating the formation of families, communities, associations, *and even political entities and nation-states*" (Fineman 2014:104, emphasis added). Put simply, the creation and maintenance of institutions and governments is necessary and appropriate to respond to our inevitable and inherent human vulnerability. But what might this mean in the context of something as complex as the relationships between the federal government and Tribal governments in the United States? Does it matter that those relationships are simultaneously inter-governmental and intra-governmental?

As we have explained, a liberal understanding of sovereignty currently frames and limits the relationships between Native Nations, Indigenous Peoples, and the federal government. Vulnerability theorists make several observations with potential application here, including that individual autonomy and independence are mythical; that only a responsive—not restrained—state can respond effectively to human vulnerability; and that "institutions must be designed to work together in interrelated, contiguous, and sequential ways" to generate the "resources and social assets that cumulatively provide resilience" (Fineman 2020:27–29).

Vulnerability theory exposes the fallacy of individual autonomy and independence at the core of liberal sovereignty, highlighting the attendant dangers of organizing a *laissez faire* legal system around the liberal legal subject. This insight is equally applicable to families, communities, institutions, governments, and nation-states: while each can be a source of resilience, none is autonomous and independent. In the case of nation-states, these arrangements are both intra-state and inter-national. Dependency between them necessarily manifests in different ways at different times but can never be avoided altogether. If all sovereigns are dependent on social relationships and arrangements, including relationships with other sovereigns and the system(s) within which they operate, then sovereignty is both realistically and ideally inter-dependent. And if that is the case—and we believe it is—then the independent/dependent binary upon which federal plenary power rests is conceptually incoherent.

c. *Indigenous Peoples Are Not a Vulnerable Population*

Liberal conceptions of sovereignty also rest on the notion that Indigenous Peoples are a specifically vulnerable population, articulated most often through what Professor Skibine calls a "dependency paradigm" to justify plenary power and federal guardianship (Skibine 2006). Vulnerability theory challenges the idea that there are distinct vulnerable populations:

> [G]roups . . . have been designated as vulnerable populations based on various identity markers. The political and legal response to any designated category of vulnerable population is typically surveillance and regulation.

> The response can be punitive and stigmatizing—as it is with prisoners, youth at risk, or single mothers needing welfare assistance. It can also be paternalistic and stigmatizing—as are the responses to the "deserving" poor, such as the elderly, or children and individuals with disabilities. But note, what is common to these two groups of designated vulnerable populations is that stigma attaches to both. Their perceived vulnerability marks them as deviant, and thus, as falling outside of the logic of a social contract that calls for a subject capable of exercising personal responsibility and asserting autonomy.
>
> (*Fineman* 2014:108–109)

By contrast, vulnerability theory recognizes that vulnerability is a universal, inevitable, and enduring aspect of the human condition, and not unique to any particular group. Populations and institutions are not more or less vulnerable; they have more or less resilience. The human condition is one of universal and continuous vulnerability (Fineman 2017) and, as embodied beings, all (not some) humans are necessarily "dependent upon and embedded within [] social relationships and institutions throughout the life-course" (Fineman 2017:2).

Historically, Indigenous Peoples were constructed as differently or uniquely vulnerable in comparison with the ideal liberal legal subject through colonial practices of dehumanization (Spitz 2021). More recently, labeling Indigenous Peoples or Native Nations as "vulnerable" has in some cases been well-intended. But in either and all cases, it has been used to justify a long history of assimilation practice, state sanctioned violence, and systemic racism (Williams 1986). Exposing the myth of uniquely Indigenous vulnerability promises to destigmatize inevitable human and institutional vulnerability wherever found, including (but not only) in Indigenous communities. Equally as important, vulnerability theory undermines a central premise limiting Tribal sovereignty: the notion that Native Nations require federal guardianship.

d. Trust Responsibility Can and Should Be Detached From the Doctrine of Plenary Power

With these ideas in mind, it becomes clear that the trust responsibility of the federal government to Native Nations and Indigenous Peoples is not dependent upon its self-dealt plenary power *over* them. Rather, the federal government has a responsibility *to* all legal subjects. To be sure, this responsibility must incorporate the recognition that Native Nations are unevenly resourced, differently situated, and heterogeneous. This is not because Indigenous Peoples are somehow uniquely vulnerable in comparison to (mythical) invulnerable people elsewhere, but because the United States, as a settler colonial nation state, sought to explicitly dismantle Indigenous resilience-conferring institutions and communities as part of its assimilation practices. In other words, the federal responsibility to confer and build resilience in Indigenous communities will be—at least in part and depending on need—a project of resilience *restoration*.

This is consistent with Professor Fineman's observation that:

> [While no] individual or group should be considered more or less vulnerable, uniquely vulnerable, or specifically or especially vulnerable . . . [,] we can think about spaces, places, and positions or relationships as indicators of the proximity of, exposure to, or probability for vulnerability to be manifested or realized in the form of dependency. By the same token, we can think of these same spaces, places, and positions as sites for the production of resilience—these are or should be thought of as sites of state responsibility.
>
> (2021)

Native Nations may be conceived as being precisely that: both a space where the probability for vulnerability to be realized in the form of dependency is high (and in fact, that dependency has been cultivated by the federal government) and a site for the production of resilience. It follows, then, that the federal government's responsibility to Indigenous Peoples will entail the conferral of restorative, resilience-conferring assets. This should mitigate the likelihood of realized vulnerability and increase the capacity of Native Nations to produce and distribute resilience across communities.

Vine Deloria, Jr. (1985) has situated the evolution of federal policy on the basis of plenary power as one in which "Indian Tribes appear to have the same political status as [] independent states . . . yet they have little real self-governance and seem to be forever mired in a state of political and economic pupilage" (p. 30). He further posits that the status of Native Nations is "a dubious blessing, conferring some benefits but exacting a tremendous price in self-esteem and independence" (p. 31). Professor Matthew Fletcher (2022) argues that "[p]lenary power does not mean absolute power; it means the power needed to fulfill a particular purpose. That purpose is the fulfillment of the federal trust responsibility, also known as the duty of protection, to Indians and tribes. That purpose originates in the treaty relationship between Indian tribes and the United States."[4]

Yet even conceived in Fletcher's terms, plenary power as a doctrine of law does not permit a case-by-case determination of a Native Nation's ability to enhance the resilience of its members and communities. The doctrine of trust responsibility, however, might. Many Native Nations have rebuilt their legal and cultural institutions in new and dynamic ways, exhibiting a resilience that has been theirs since time immemorial—despite continued and concentrated settler colonial forces acting to the contrary. Native Nations contribute to a wide body of Tribal law, assert Tribal jurisdiction over Native and non-Native owned land, and build economies from which many states seek to benefit.

Indeed, Native Nations situated to assert Tribal sovereignty have done so to the benefit of both Tribal and non-Tribal citizens and communities through various mechanisms. For example, many Native Nations engage in compacting with states to share governance over matters from taxation to environmental conservation (Newton 2012; Johnson et al. 2009; Harvard Law Review 1999). In these instances, Native Nations are often the most responsive institutional entities at the local level in supporting individual members of the community. Vulnerability theory makes room for such responsive poly-centric governance measures by recognizing the federal government's institutional role in bolstering the resilience of its citizens. We suggest that, in order to fulfill this institutional responsibility, the federal government must necessarily cede some sovereignty, make room for Native Nation assertions of sovereignty, and assist Native Nations in rebuilding in the name of increased resilience.

III. A Contemporary Example: The Indian Child Welfare Act

The Indian Child Welfare Act (ICWA) was enacted in 1978 as remedial legislation to address previous federal and state assimilationist policies and "often unwarranted" practices of removal that resulted in "the wholesale separation of Indian children from their families" (Committee on Interior and Insular Affairs 1978:8–9) and an "alarmingly high percentage of [Indian] children [being] placed in non-Indian foster and adoptive homes and institutions" (25 U.S.C. § 1901[4]). Statistics at the time of the statute's enactment showed that upwards of 25% of all Indigenous children were in foster homes, adoptive homes and/or boarding schools against the best interests of families, Tribes, and Indian communities due to the "abusive action of local, state, federal and private agency officials" (Indian Child Welfare Program 1974:1). In passing ICWA, Congress expressly invoked both its plenary power over, and its trust responsibility to, Indigenous Peoples, extolling the "special relationship between the United States and the Indian tribes and their members" (25 U.S.C. §§ 1901[1–2]).

ICWA sought to redress state and federal child welfare practices that had systematically and expansively removed Indigenous children from their families and communities without regard for how such removals resulted from a "[failure] to recognize the essential Tribal relations of Indian people and the cultural and social standards prevailing in Indian communities and families" (25 U.S.C. § 1901[5]). It ushered in a set of reforms to "protect the best interests of Indian children and to promote the stability and security of Indian tribes and families" (25 U.S.C. § 1902). These reforms established minimum standards applying to child welfare proceedings involving Indigenous children (25 U.S.C. §§ 1902, 1911–1914), provided grants to Tribal governments for the purpose of establishing and operating child welfare services (25 U.S.C. § 1931), and created specific notice and due process requirements for families subject to involuntary placement procedures (such as the removal of a child to foster care or the termination of parental rights) (§ 1912).

Scholars, activists, and the federal government have recognized ICWA as a significant improvement over the state and federal practices and policies that preceded it. The Federal Indian Boarding School Initiative Report (Newland 2022) acknowledged the federal government's previous policy was one of "cultural assimilation that coincided with Indian territorial dispossession" and the National Indian Child Welfare Association (NICWA) has described ICWA's protections as critical in "address[ing] some of the most longstanding and egregious removal practices specifically targeting Native children" (n.d.). For their part, legal scholars have been writing in support of ICWA almost since its passage, in large measure because of the waves of litigation and constitutional challenges ICWA has regularly faced (Fletcher and Khalil 2022).

Much of the scholarly defense of ICWA has been grounded in the liberal legal discourse that underwrote the legislation itself, including notions of federal plenary power and inherent sovereignty. For legal scholars who are members of Native Nations and/or well-versed in the field of federal Indian law, constitutional challenges to ICWA must fail because Native Nations are polities with inherent sovereignty. Within the terms of this doctrine, sovereignty is not bestowed upon Native Nations by Congress, but is only subject to limitations by Congress' exercise of its plenary power or as the Supreme Court limits it through implicit divestiture (LaVelle 2006). Such arguments, incorporating conceptions of both Tribal sovereignty and federal plenary power, have successfully limited legal challenges to the Act in the past.

The most recent challenge to ICWA's constitutionality, *Brackeen v. Haaland* (2022), called into question these lines of argument. In *Brackeen*, the Supreme Court granted the petitioners' writ for certiorari review to consider a Fifth Circuit Court of Appeals decision reversing the district court's determination that ICWA was unconstitutional (*Brackeen v. Haaland* 2022). The *Brackeen* petitioners, including the States of Texas, Indiana, and Louisiana and several non-Indigenous individuals challenged ICWA on two grounds. First, they argued that ICWA's preference for placing Indigenous children who are subject to removal with Indigenous families rather than non-Indigenous families violated the Equal Protection clause because it discriminated on the basis of race. Second, they argued that ICWA's placement preference exceeds Congress' Article I authority and "invad[es] the arena of child placement," which they contended is "the 'virtually exclusive province of the States'" (Petition for A Writ of Certiorari, p. i).

In making their second argument, petitioners focused on ICWA's invocation of Article I, § 8, cl. 3, which authorizes Congress to regulate commerce with Indian Tribes, arguing that ICWA does not regulate commerce, much less commerce with Indian Tribes *per se* (pp. 27–8). Notably, the petitioners failed to mention the second half of 25 U.S.C. § 1901(1), which states that, through the Indian Commerce Clause "and other constitutional authority, Congress has plenary power over Indian Affairs." Nonetheless, even as they scrupulously avoided the phrase "plenary power," the petitioners took direct aim at the plenary power doctrine by claiming that "Congress likely lacks the 'power to control' state-court custody proceedings and 'override the significant state interest in regulating . . . what is a traditionally state matter" (Petition for A Writ of Certiorari, p. 29).

Not surprisingly, the respondents' opposing brief met the petitioners' arguments on shared liberal legal terrain. Significantly, the respondents replied with several arguments sounding in notions of domestic dependence, providing an illustrative example of the ways plenary power and trust responsibility remain tethered. First, the respondents contended that existing caselaw demonstrates that ICWA distinguishes on the basis of a political classification, not race, relying upon Supreme Court authority declaring that "Indian tribes are domestic dependent nations that exercise inherent sovereign authority" (*Michigan v. Bay Mills Indian Community* 2014:788, as cited in Brief for the Federal Respondents in Opposition). The respondents' brief cited *Worcester v. Georgia* as authority for the proposition that "[m]embers of Indian tribes are members of "distinct political communities."

Second, the respondents directed the Court to the "unbroken current of judicial decisions repeatedly reaffirm[ing]" Congress' plenary power over Indian Affairs (pp. 23–4), including a string cite of more than a dozen decisions spanning over the course of a century, including the extraordinarily racist and problematic *U.S. v. Kagama* (1886:384–5, providing that "the power of the general government over these remnants of a race once powerful, now weak and diminished in numbers, is necessary to their protection"). For the respondents, Congress' plenary power emerges from both the language and the structure of the Constitution itself and establishes in the federal government "the power and the duty of exercising a fostering care and protection over all dependent Indian communities within its borders" (*U.S v. Kagama*, as cited in *U.S. v. Sandoval* 1913:25).

The fight in *Brackeen* was thus drawn in terms that would have been immediately recognizable to John Marshall's Supreme Court. Indeed, the case may usefully be conceived as an attempt to relitigate the Marshall trilogy's doctrines of Tribal sovereignty, domestic dependency, states' rights, plenary power, and the trust responsibility. The majority opinion declared ICWA a constitutional exercise of Congressional power over Indian Affairs under the Indian Commerce Clause, citing various legal doctrines including the trust responsibility (*Haaland v. Brackeen* 2023:9–12). Because the majority opinion is founded on existing doctrine, especially plenary power and trust responsibility, it does not engage in a substantive analysis of ICWA's merits as social policy (*Haaland v. Brackeen* 2023).[5] This was a missed opportunity.

Viewed through the lens of vulnerability theory, ICWA may be understood as an ambitious effort to create a more responsive system of governance by expressly addressing the interdependent nature of state and Tribal sovereignty. For example, ICWA expressly authorizes state and Tribal governments to enter into cooperative agreements for the purpose of determining exclusive or concurrent jurisdiction over child welfare proceedings (25 U.S.C. § 1919). It also establishes presumptive jurisdictional rules to ensure that Tribal governments may exercise control over, or engage in meaningful participation in, child custody proceedings brought in state courts in the first instance (§ 1911). ICWA also recognizes the limits of existing federal and state capacities to decide the best interests of Indigenous children; its implementing regulations require the use of qualified expert witnesses in removal proceedings to ensure the tribunal's informed consideration of "the prevailing social and cultural standards of the Indian child's tribe" (25 C.F.R. § 23.122). ICWA also authorizes direct grants to Native Nations to assist in the development and operation of Tribal child welfare systems, an essential component toward the improvement of community-based systems of resilience (25 U.S.C. § 1931).

Thus, while ICWA's enactment was grounded in Congress' assertion of plenary power, exercised in service of a liberal legal conception of the domestic dependency of Indigenous Peoples, we anticipate additional challenges to the Act and suggest the best argument for its continued viability may lie in a rejection of these concepts in favor of claims emphasizing interdependent sovereignty and responsive governance. While it is reasonable to question whether courts are ready to entertain such claims, the manifestly fragile status of ICWA, despite its inarguably firm grounding in the doctrines of plenary power and the trust responsibility, suggests a new approach is urgently needed.

IV. Conclusion: Vulnerability Theory, Tribal Sovereignty and Federal Responsibility

The principal legal doctrines and rules governing the relationships between Indigenous Peoples and the United States—including state and local governments—are built on and around the liberal legal subject. Unsurprisingly, assertions of Tribal sovereignty are mostly fought on the same terrain. We suggest vulnerability theory provides an opportunity to rethink about the adequacy and effectiveness of existing legal strategies of Native Nations and

Indigenous Peoples in asserting Tribal sovereignty by focusing attention on the shared responsibility of the United States and Tribal governments to build the resilience necessary for our collective communities.

We have argued that vulnerability theory challenges the view that the sovereignty problem in federal Indian law is intractable. Indigenous assertions of sovereignty that fail to adhere to liberal norms are not always legible to liberal international and Anglo-American legal systems. Instead, they are described as unrealistic or unreasonable. But that strikes us as a failure of the United States' reliance on the liberal legal order and its strictures on sovereignty. The view that nations cannot share territory or exist within the boundaries of another nation, for example, only makes sense because certain values have been naturalized in American legal and social systems. By removing the liberal legal order from the ideation of sovereignty and introducing vulnerability, resilience building, and resilience restoration in its place, a more robust conversation about the relationship by and between Native Nations and governments can occur.

Vulnerability theory also shifts the conversation away from the dangerous and stigmatizing rhetoric of liberalism toward a conversation about shared state or institutional responsibility to provide responsive "infrastructure" (Fineman 2020), or "landscapes of responsiveness" (Abrams forthcoming), across Native, federal, and state governments. The use of vulnerability theory challenges the idea that sovereignty is ever anything but interdependent, shifting the focus away from the federal government's construction of Indigenous people as domestic dependent nations towards a focus on building and restoring resilience, and opening up a substantive conversation about which governments—Native, federal, state, local—are best situated and resourced to ensure a more equitable distribution of assets and privilege across society. We also suggest that restoration of resilience-conferring assets to Native Nations should be prioritized, given the historical and intentional dismantling of resilience that gave rise to the domestic dependency of Native Nations.

Lastly, governance and state responsibility should be collaborative by and between Native Nations and the federal government to increase institutional responsiveness and resilience for all. Indeed, the early relationships by and between the federal government and Native Nations were based on the multicultural jurisgensis of diplomatic treaty making that was initially collaborative and pluralistic. A contemporary re-envisioning of these relationships might produce a more robust conception of sovereignty: where the trust relationship is separated from federal plenary power; where resilience-conferring assets are provided by the federal government to Native Nations in support of achieving whatever amount of Tribal sovereignty a Native Nation is comfortable and/or capable of asserting; and where collaborative governance by and between Native Nations and the federal and several states governments is supported.

Notes

1 We are grateful to Logan Stokes (J.D. Candidate, University of New Mexico School of Law) for excellent research assistance and to Seth Davis, Gerald Torres, and Yvonne Zylan for reading earlier drafts and providing invaluable comments.
2 Dependent sovereignty is a familiar concept in federal Indian law—and consequently an important and relevant concept for examination—but we recognize the concept of dependence in this context is highly contested. The boundaries and practices of Indigenous and federal sovereignties are made even more complex by the constitutional division of American sovereignty between federal and state governments. As Professor Gerald Torres aptly observed in reviewing this chapter, the boundaries of that division continue to be rewritten, and Tribes have often functioned as the device through which federalists and anti-federalists seek to erase and redraw old lines. We discuss one example—*Brackeen v. Haaland* (2022)—in this chapter, but there are other recent examples, including *Oklahoma v. Castro-Huerta* (2022) and *McGirt v. Oklahoma* (2020).
3 Professor Audra Simpson (2015:115), for example, offers a compelling theory of "nested" sovereignties, but there is as yet very little room in American jurisprudence for such a conception.
4 Professors Kristen Carpenter and Angela Riley (2014) argue Native Nations are actively limiting federal plenary power through the use of international human rights law. As global and regional human rights tribunals have begun to include Indigenous customary laws as a basis for Indigenous rights, outpacing federal recognition of Tribal laws, Native Nations are increasingly looking to international law in their decolonization and self-determination efforts.
5 The Supreme Court decision was released the day that our copyedits for this chapter were due to the publisher, and as of this writing we have not had a meaningful opportunity to review the judgments, except to note the ways in which the majority opinion invokes the problematic concepts discussed here. We also note that Justice Gorsuch's concurring opinion engages some of the history and policy questions raised in this chapter, including important questions about Tribal sovereignty and the scope (and limits) of federal power vis-à-vis that sovereignty (*Haaland v. Brackeen* 2023).

Reference List

Ablavsky, Gregory. 2015. "Beyond the Indian Commerce Clause." *Yale Law Journal* 124:1012–90.

———. 2019a. "Sovereign Metaphors in Indian Law." *Montana Law Review* 80 (Winter):11–40.

———. 2019b. "Species of Sovereignty: Native Nationhood, the United States, and International Law, 1783–1795." *The Journal of American History* 106(3):591–613.

Abrams, Kathryn. Forthcoming. "Toward a Responsive Landscape: The Role of Social Movements in Vulnerability Theory." In *Re-Conceiving Equality and Freedom: Vulnerability, Dependency, and the Responsive State*, edited by Martha Fineman and Laura Spitz. Routledge-Taylor & Francis.

Barker, Jennifer. 2005. "For Whom Sovereignty Matters." Pp. 1–31 in *Sovereignty Matters: Location of Contestation and Possibility in Indigenous Struggles for Self-Determination*, edited by Joanne Barker. University of Nebraska Press.

Blackhawk, Maggie. 2020. "On Power and the Law: McGirt v. Oklahoma." *The Supreme Court Review* 2020:367–421.

Brackeen v. Haaland, 142 S.Ct. 1205 (2022).
Carlson, Kirsten Matoy. 2022. "Bringing Congress and Indians Back into Federal Indian Law: The Restatement of the Law of American Indians." *Washington Law Review* 97(3):725–74.
Carpenter, Kristen A. and Angela R. Riley. 2014. "Indigenous Peoples and the Jurisgenerative Moment in Human Rights." *California Law Review* 102(1): 173–234.
Cherokee Nation v. State of Georgia, 30 U.S. 1 (1831).
Committee on Interior and Insular Affairs, U.S. House. 1978. "H.R. Rep. 95–1386: Establishing Standards for the Placement of Indian Children in Foster or Adoptive Homes, to Prevent the Breakup of Indian Families." (https://narf.org/nill/documents/icwa/print/app1.pdf).
Davis, Seth. 2017. "American Colonialism and Constitutional Redemption." *California Law Review* 105(6):1751–806.
Davis, Seth, Eric Biber, and Elena Kempf. 2022. "Persisting Sovereignties." *University of Pennsylvania Law Review* 170:549–636.
Deloria Jr., Vine. 1979. "Self-Determination and the Concept of Sovereignty." Pp. 22–8 in *Economic Development in American Indian Reservations*, edited by Roxanne Dunbar Ortiz. Albuquerque: University of New Mexico.
———. 1985. *Behind the Trail of Broken Treaties: An Indian Declaration of Independence*. Austin, TX: University of Texas Press.
Fineman, Martha Albertson. 2014. "Vulnerability, Resilience, and LGBT Youth." *Temple Political & Civil Rights Law Review* 23:307–30.
———. 2015. "Equality and Difference—The Restrained State." *Alabama Law Review* 66:626–45.
———. 2017. "Vulnerability and Inevitable Inequality." *Oslo Law Review* 4:133–49.
———. 2020. "Reasoning from the Body: Universal Vulnerability and Social Justice." Pp. 17–34 in *A Jurisprudence of the Body*, edited by Chris Dietz, Mitchell Travis, and Michael Thomson. London, UK: Palgrave Macmillan.
———. 2021. "What Vulnerability Theory Is and Is Not." *Vulnerability and the Human Condition* (blog), July 30 (https://scholarblogs.emory.edu/vulnerability/2021/02/01/is-and-is-not).
Fletcher, Matthew L. M. 2022. "Restatement as Aadizookaan." *Wisconsin Law Review* 2022(2):197–210.
Fletcher, Matthew L. M. and Khalil, Randall F. 2022. "Preemption, Commandeering, and the Indian Child Welfare Act." *Wisconsin Law Review* 2022(5):1199–233.
Haaland v. Brackeen, 21-376, 2023 WL 4002951 (U.S. June 15, 2023).
Harvard Law Review. 1999. "Intergovernmental Compacts in Native American Law: Models for Expanded Usage (Note)." *Harvard Law Review* 112(4):922–39. https://doi.org/10.2307/1342300.
Indian Child Welfare Act 1978, Pub. L. 95–608, 25 U.S.C §§ 1901–63.
Indian Child Welfare Program. 1974. "Hearing before the Subcommittee on Indian Affairs of the Committee on Interior and Insular Affairs." U.S. Senate, 93rd Congress 2.
Johnson v. M'Intosh, 21 U.S. 543 (1823) (www.law.cornell.edu/supremecourt/text/21/543).
Johnson, Susan, Jeanne Kaufmann, John Dossett, and Sarah Hicks. 2009. *Government to Government Models of Cooperation Between States and Tribes*. 2nd ed. Denver, CO: National Conference of State Legislatures.

LaVelle, John P. 2006. "Implicit Divestiture Reconsidered: Outtakes from the Cohen's Handbook Cutting-Room Floor." *Connecticut Law Review* 38(4):731–76.

McGirt V. Oklahoma, 140 S.Ct. 2452 (2020).

Michigan v. Bay Mills Indian Community, 572 U.S. 782, 788 (2014).

Moore, David H. and Michalyn Steele. 2022. "Revitalizing Tribal Sovereignty in Treatymaking." *New York University Law Review* 97:137–91.

Newland, Bryan and Office of the Assistant Secretary—Indian Affairs. 2022. *Federal Indian Boarding School Initiative Investigative Report*. Washington, DC: United States Department of the Interior.

Newton, Nell Jessup, ed. 2012. *Cohen's Handbook of Federal Indian Law § 6.05*. New Providence, NJ: LexisNexis.

NICWA (National Indian Child Welfare Association). n.d. "About ICWA" (www.nicwa.org/about-icwa).

Oklahoma v. Castro-Huerta, 142 S.Ct. 2486 (2022).

Simpson, Audra. 2014. *Mohawk Interruptus*. Durham, NC: Duke University Press.

Singer, Joseph William. 2017. "Indian Title: Unraveling the Racial Context of Property Rights, or How to Stop Engaging in Conquest." *Albany Government Law Review* 10(1):1–48.

Skibine, Alex Tallchief. 2006. "Redefining the Status of Indian Tribes Within 'Our Federalism': Beyond the Dependency Paradigm." *Connecticut Law Review* 38:667–95.

Spitz, Laura. 2021. "Colonialism, Law, and the Social Construction of Humanity on Vancouver Island, 1849–64." Pp. 49–91 in *To Share, Not Surrender: Indigenous and Settler Visions of Treaty Making in the Colonies of Vancouver Island and British Columbia*, edited by Peter Cook, Neil Vallance, John Lutz, Graham Brazier, and Hamar Foster. Vancouver, BC: University of British Columbia Press.

Taylor Saito, Natsu. 2020. *Settler Colonialism, Race, and the Law: Why Structural Racism Persists*. New York: New York University Press.

Tsosie, Rebecca. 1996. "Tribal Environmental Policy in an Era of Self-Determination: The Role of Ethics, Economics, and Traditional Ecological Knowledge." *Vermont Law Review* 21(1):225–334.

United States. v. Kagama, 118 U.S. 375 (1886).

United States v. Sandoval, 231 U.S. 28 (1913).

Williams Jr, Robert A. 1986. "The Algebra of Federal Indian Law: The Hard Trail of Decolonizing and Americanizing the White Man's Indian Jurisprudence." *Wisconsin Law Review* 1986(2):219–99.

———. 2005. *Like a Loaded Weapon: The Rehnquist Court, Indian Rights, and the Legal History of Racism in America*. Minneapolis, MN: University of Minnesota Press.

Worcester v. State of Georgia, 31 U.S. 515 (1832) (www.law.cornell.edu/supremecourt/text/31/515).

INDEX

Note: *Italics* indicates figure and **bold** indicates table on corresponding pages.

For Product Safety Concerns and Information please contact our EU
representative GPSR@taylorandfrancis.com
Taylor & Francis Verlag GmbH, Kaufingerstraße 24, 80331 München, Germany

www.ingramcontent.com/pod-product-compliance
Ingram Content Group UK Ltd.
Pitfield, Milton Keynes, MK11 3LW, UK
UKHW020151200926
475702UK00016B/2648
9781032346632